RAISING FENCES

MICHAEL DATCHER

RIVERHEAD BOOKS
A member of Penguin Putnam Inc.
New York
2001

RAISING
FENCES

A Black Man's Love Story

What follows is a true story. The names of a few characters
have been changed in order to protect their privacy.

Riverhead Books
a member of
Penguin Putnam Inc.
375 Hudson Street
New York, NY 10014

Dee Black's "Second Calling for a Catholic Girl"
is reprinted by permission of the author.

V. Kali's "Raising Children" is reprinted by permission
of the author.

A.K. Toney's "Chronicle Trauma" and "Letter from Father
to Son from Son" are reprinted by permission of the author.

Shakespeare Jr.'s "Daddy's in the Dark, Mama's Asleep,
A Poet Awakes" is used with permission of the author.

Library of Congress Cataloging-in-Publication Data

Datcher, Michael, date.
Raising fences : a black man's love story / Michael Datcher.
p.   cm.
ISBN 1-57322-171-6
1. Afro-American men—Fiction.   I. Title.
PS3554.A8236 R35   2001   00-050991
813'.54—dc21

Printed in the United States of America

10   9   8   7   6   5   4   3   2   1

This book is printed on acid-free paper. ♾

Book design by Michelle McMillian

For Jenoyne, Gladys, Elgin, Cyndi,
and my World Stage family

RAISING FENCES

in the beginning

When I pull the letter from the mailbox, my heart starts jackhammering. I return to my second-floor Leimert Park apartment, leaping two white stairs per stride. Sit down at the heavy wooden desk. Tight-fist the letter opener butcher knife–style to steady my trembling hand:

STATE OF ILLINOIS
CERTIFICATE OF LIVE BIRTH

There I am in Box 3, "Child's Name: Michael Gerald Cole." I've never seen Cole attached to Michael Gerald before. I stare like it's the first time. "Single" is marked in Box 5A, not "twin," "triplet," or "quad." Years of thinking maybe I was a separated-at-birth twin ends there at Box 5A. Born at 5:49 P.M. The box below: "Mother's Full Maiden Name: Mariam Cole. Age: 17." So young, I think. Just a girl. Pregnant at sixteen. But this really isn't about her, it's about Box 7: "Father's Full Name: Legally Withheld." I'm not really sure what I'm expecting to see. I'm hoping for some hint. Some clue. Eye color. Hair color. Height. Initials. Anything. Box 9: "His Age: Unknown." Box 10: "His Birthplace:" blank. Box 11A: "His Usual Occupation:" blank. Box 11B: "Kind of Business or Industry:" blank.

The blanks blur together on the page. I don't know who my father is.

Don't know one thing about him. This truth seeps through the spaces between my rib cage, straitjackets my lungs. I am not going to cry this time. I slide out the top drawer of my black metal file cabinet. Under "Medical," I file the birth certificate, his punk ass, and all the blank spaces in my life. I slam the cabinet shut.

the spinners

I've been obsessed with being a husband and father since I was seven years old. Quiet as it's kept, many young black men have the same obsession. Picket-fence dreams. A played-out metaphor in the white community but one still secretly riding the bench in black neighborhoods nationwide.

When the picket-fence motif was in vogue, only a few of us could get in the game. The swelling ranks of those who couldn't (the Perpetual Second Team) were forced to the sidelines, scowling—and pretending we didn't even want to play.

The bastard children of these Second Teamers stalk the same sidelines. We rarely sit on the bench. Too restless. We can't figure out if we want to beg to play or raise a stiff middle finger. Sometimes we do both. But usually we strike a cool pose. Hide Huxtable-family dreams in the corner: Can't let someone catch us hoping that hard.

We know few people believe in us. We struggle to believe in ourselves. So we pose. We have gotten good. We can pose and cry at the same time—no one sees. We can pose and cry out for help—no one hears. We are the urban ventriloquists.

▪ ▪ ▪ ▪

Of the thirty families that lived in our east-side Long Beach, California, apartment building during the mid-seventies, I never saw a father living in a household. I never even saw one visit.

There were lots of boys in the neighborhood: Ricky, Dante, Pig Pen, Curt Rock. We rarely talked about our missing fathers. Instead, we poured our passion into our skateboards, our marbles, and our mothers. Yet the unspoken sparkled from our eyes whenever any neighborhood men showed us attention. Once in their gaze, we worked to outperform one another, trying our best to keep the manlight from straying.

"Watch this! I can do a back flip off the curb. . . . Heh, betchu a quarter I can make a shot from the free-throw line."

It's likely one of these men laid the seed that sprouted into a back-flipper before them. Neighborhood rumors have a way of falling off grown-up kitchen tables and splattering on ghetto playgrounds.

We flipped, pop-locked, and did the Robot for them, but we were knowing: Men weren't to be trusted. Even when our mothers didn't speak these words, their tired lives whispered the message.

I knew many of these men had kids. Where were they? Why were they watching me spin instead of their own children? No, these men were not to be trusted. How could I accept their advice when their personal lives screamed, "I'm lost toooo"? There was too much fatherhood failure around. The disease seemed to be contagious given the epidemic in our neighborhood. These men could watch me spin, but I couldn't let them get close enough to breathe on me.

The ghetto irony: Many of my generation's young spinners have become the twenty- and thirty-something men who can't be trusted. Making children who will grow up to hate them.

Circumstance, suspect choices, and fear have ways of disfiguring urban hopes with surgical precision. A four-ounce bottle of baby formula becomes much heavier than a forty-ounce bottle of malt liquor. Having five women becomes easier than having one.

camille

I stroll into Hollywood's Club Flame with a slight malt-liquor buzz. Slow my roll so my eyes can adjust to the semidarkness most reggae clubs favor. No air-conditioning. I can feel sweat coming of age beneath my armpits, down my back. The pungent scent of high-grade marijuana flavors the air like designer musk. Invisible men in corners send snippets of Jamaican patois slicing through the dense wall of bass-heavy dance-hall reggae. This island funk is just what I need. It pulsates through my damp chest, lubricating the stiffness that graduate school at UCLA engenders. I'm in baggy black jeans, an oversized black Levi's shirt, and big black stomping boots. Feeling strong and sexy. It's August 1993. The last few weeks before the quarter starts. I need to be rubbed on.

My night vision kicks in. The club is crowded with an international set from the African diaspora. Nigerians, Ethiopians, and West Indians dominate the long bar. Bright colors abound. Accents and dialects I grew accustomed to on Berkeley's campus converge with gymnastic Ebonics of black L.A. folk. I'm in my element.

Despite the steadily increasing numbers, few people are dancing on the boxing ring–sized floor in the middle of the club. Instead, people are checking people. Just beneath the strobe light, a dark-brown sister with her hair pulled back into a ponytail is deep inside the island groove. From time to time she closes her eyes to get deeper. Wearing white short-shorts and a small, bright-red blouse knotted above her belly button, she is moving with the slow winding confidence of a woman accustomed to the gaze of men. With only three or four other couples on the floor, many of the men's casual scanning glances end at her slim waist.

After making my way to the bar to grab a beer, I walk over to the dance floor's edge. I want to watch her dance. I can tell she isn't really interested in the brother on the floor with her. Their bodies aren't communicating. They aren't even making eye contact. She's winding in her own world.

The side winder leaves the boxing ring and returns to two friends near the bar. Guinness in hand, I step to her. Heavily accented loud-bar chatter camouflages my motive for leaning past her cheek, just a warm breath from her ear.

"You're gonna hurt someone dancing like that."

"Hmmph," she says, angling her neck and ear away, eyelids squatting into a defensive stand. "As hard as you were looking, seem like you *wanna* get hurt."

Seeing the choosing-in-progress, her two friends turn away and rest their palms on the bar.

"Where you from, sister?"

"Dominican Republic," she responds, holding gaze to see if I'm duly impressed. Never good at geography, I don't even know where the Dominican Republic is.

"You must've gone to school in the States. I'm not hearing an accent."

"I went to Locke High, then Cal State Dominguez."

"What did you study?"

"Math," she says, her kumquat lips easing into a sly smile. "So don't be saying no shit that don't add up."

Her playful eyes sparkle.

"Is that little dance you do kinda like a Dominican national dance?" I say, winding into a heartfelt version of her hip-heavy groove.

She watches, cards close to vest.

I sneak a glance at her bare thighs. Although the upper part of her five-foot two-inch frame is small-boned, her legs are long and muscular.

"A little Dominican, *mostly me.* I got my own thang."

"You wanna teach that thang to me?"

"If you promise not to sue me when you get hurt," she tosses over her shoulder, leading the way to the ring.

Saucy. Book smart too—and a warm, easy smile to boot. My type.

Up close and personal, her slow wind is even sexier. I'm winding too— and looking her dead in the eye.

She returns my steady stare as our hips, just inches apart, synchronize pelvic circles to the island funk. As the dance floor fills, swaying bodies brush and bump us. I leave her eyes, taking in her long neck, breasts, naked stomach, fixing my stare below her waist. She begins to perform. A slow-motion pelvic orbit. I bring my hand around the small of her sweaty back, guiding her body into mine. Our hips meet in a nervous kiss. We settle into rhythm. Eye contact resumes. We wind close this way for several songs, saying little, but saying a lot.

After dancing together much of the night, I ask for her number. Embarrassed, I lean past her cheek. "Tell me your name again, sister?"

"Camille."

The first year of grad school at UCLA was intense; the second, beginning in a matter of days, doesn't look any easier. The workload is heavy, and there is little financial support in my African-American studies program.

Besides school, I'm working as a Los Angeles news correspondent for Pacific News Service and freelancing for magazines around the country, writing about politics, culture, and music—and working twenty hours a week as a research assistant. Sibling deadlines compete for attention. Stress levels are high. When I call Camille a few days after our Club Flame introduction, I'm looking forward to taking a break.

"Hi. This is Michael, I met you at Club Flame."

"Why is it that guys ask for your number," she coos in what must be her best telephone voice, "then wait a week to call when they want to call you next day?"

I start laughing.

"You know you wanted to call, now didn't you?"

"I'm calling you now."

"You know what I mean. Not a week later."

"It's only been a few days. Why you givin a brother a hard time? What's up with the full-court press?"

We begin to talk. Camille tells me that when she was a child, her parents separated, but she's remained close to her math-teacher father.

"My father's a teacher, and you know how teachers are when they have students who look like them. I didn't mind, though. I've always been good with numbers."

"Daddy's girl?"

"That's right, and proud of it. Do you have a girlfriend?"

"Damnn," I chuckle. "Did Daddy teach you that, too?"

"A man's calling my house and I can't ask if he has a woman?"

"It's not that you're asking; we ain't been on the phone five minutes."

"Well, if you didn't have a woman it wouldn't be a problem, right? You probably got someone . . . or someone got you."

"Nope."

"Hmmph, I bet."

"Why I gotta have a girlfriend?"

"You don't *gotta* have a girlfriend, you just sound like you got one."

Camille insists that I must have a girlfriend, but I don't. Between school and work, I'm not really looking for a lady right now. I tell her that I'm just dating.

"When I'm in a relationship, I like to really be in the relationship, but that's not where my head's at," I say.

There's an awkward pause to match the awkward moment. We haven't been talking five minutes, and my cards are already spread sloppily across the table. Full house, no commitment please. I can tell Camille's a little disappointed. I'm embarrassed. The pace seems too grown. She changes the subject to our dance floor chemistry.

We talk on the phone about once a week. With her Quiet Storm telephone voice and playful, flirting manner, Camille does more than her part to keep the conversations stimulating. Our subject matter often turns to sex. Never overtly between her and me—but we're always the subtext.

"Why is there this sexual double standard?" Camille starts one night on the phone. "When a man enjoys sex he can go out and shake his little pole at any fish biting and it's no problem. But when a woman has a strong sex drive and enjoys expressing that side of herself, she's a ho and everybody has a problem with it."

"Me, myself, I don't have a problem with it."

"Hmmph, I bet you don't."

We laugh and change the subject.

After a month of telephone flirting between busy schedules, Camille and I finally get together. We spend an evening in Santa Monica, eventually taking a late-night stroll along the beach. Camille's got a lot of personality. She wears clear lip gloss that accentuates her sly smile. We talk and laugh about our flirtatious natures. She teases me about the way I dance.

"You get all serious. Looking at me like you'd rather be doing something else."

"That reggae just puts me in a zone, man. Plus, those little short-shorts, working your magic, your Dominican vodun.

"You put a spell on yourself, *okaay,"* she says, turning to face me. "Cause I don't work my spells on the dance floor."

She pivots and starts walking back to the car.

When we arrive at my apartment, we bend and wind and sway with an intensity that leaves my thin, student-budget sheets soaked from our effort.

There are probably a handful of people you're intimate with during your life who really butter your toast. People who touch you in a primal place. When both parties are having their toast buttered, watch out. This is the case with Camille and me. When I talk to her the next evening, we laugh that our dance-floor chemistry was a sign of things to come.

A couple of nights later, writing at my desk, I get a call from Camille.

"Busy?" she asks, her voice melting.

"Could be. Whachu have in mind?"

"I need help on a real tricky logarithm. Just can't seem to work it out."

"Is that right? I thought you had that math thing all sewn up?"

"Well, see, it's one of those word problems, and I figured, *words*... that's your thing, right?"

"Right, right. I'll see what I can do for you."

I make the ten-minute drive up Crenshaw Boulevard, passing liquor stores, barbeque joints, hair shops, and churches. An appropriate mix of opiates for a people concerned with salvation, how they look, and how they're going to get through another day.

As soon as we get inside my place, I swing Camille so she is facing the door, arms raised, legs spread LAPD-style. I press my pelvis hard into her arched 501 blues. All hands, motion, breath, and heat, we hang from the wooden door like a human Christmas stocking caught aflame.

After our first time together, I had tried to figure out what made our intimacy so passionate. When Camille wiggles and writhes free to turn and kiss me, I start to figure it out.

It's the way she looks at me.

Her stare is so intense. Even when she kisses me, she keeps her eyes open. I love her confidence and boldness. She seems to want me as much as I want her. Mid-kiss, I try to unbutton her blouse. She stops me.

Camille wants to undress me. Great.

After she takes my shirt off, she tells me to close my eyes. I can tell she's fumbling through my tape collection in the milk crate against the living-room wall. My dance hall reggae mixed tape begins to play.

"Stand still and keep your eyes closed," she says above the bumping music. Camille steps me out of my jeans. Still in the last stages of my latent Prince period, I rarely wear underwear. When she stands and gyrates her body behind me, it's skin to skin. Spin. Facing me, she reaches up and wraps her arms around my neck and shoulders.

"No peeking."

She brings me down to the carpet on my back. The sound of plastic tearing. She's brought her own condoms. After mounting, she starts her slow orbit. My hands find her concave back. She pleads, "Open your eyes and talk me through this." We lock eyes, wind and talk, and sweat through the night.

▋ ▋ ▋ ▋

After this evening, I start making the ten-minute drive up Crenshaw Boulevard two or three times a week. The more we learn each other's body and mind, the more heated the talk-heavy sex grows. When we are sated, we often lie in bed and share stories about each other's life. Lying naked with someone in the dark facilitates another kind of nakedness.

Three months after our first dance, Camille and I are exchanging "the-wildest-thing-you've-ever-done" sex stories, laughing and getting aroused all over again. Her turn. She grows serious. We're lying naked on our backs. The two white candles on opposite sides of my low-slung bed provide the only light. Camille rotates on her side to face me.

"I had this friend in high school, a really nice guy. He wasn't trying to get in my panties and everything," she starts softly, with a look that makes me uncomfortable.

"We'd talk on the phone and hang out together after school. We were little high school homies. It's hard for girls to have guy friends like that. It was cool. We were going to celebrate my Sweet Sixteen birthday by going out to dinner. I was all excited. I went to the mall and chose my little outfit. My parents were pretty strict, especially my dad. I don't think I even told him about it. It was really one of my first real dates, where the guy actually picks you up. After dinner, he wanted to stop by his place to get something. That made me a little uneasy. You know how you get that little feeling?"

She raises her brow, searching my eyes for understanding. Her voice softens to a cautious whisper.

"But I let it go, I didn't trip. There was no one home when we got inside. He started talking about he had a birthday gift for me and all this other mess. He wanted to have sex. He knew I was a virgin. In a way, I knew where he was going as soon as he said he wanted to make a stop by the house, but I wasn't trippin because I *knew* him. I really knew him. Even though I told him to stop messing around, I knew he wasn't messing around. He penned me down on his bed. I tried to be cool. I kept saying, 'Stop playin, stop playin.' He wasn't trying to hear me. He reached down and pulled out his thang. He tried to push it in. No condom or nothin. He kept trying till he just stuck it in. I started to scream, he put his hand over my mouth and kept saying some stupid mess about 'Let me get this. You're a woman now, you're a woman now.' "

Camille pauses. Her eyes leave me, shift to the blank wall next to my bed.

"When he finished, he got off me and said, 'Come on, let's go,' like he was mad at me. I was devastated. It was like I separated from my body. I couldn't believe what had just happened. He drove me home. I let him kiss me on the cheek. He dropped me off at the curb."

Camille rolls over onto her back again. I'm stunned. You never know the kind of pain people have gone through until you hear their stories. I slide Camille over and rest the side of her face on my chest, stroking her forehead.

"I'm sorry, I mean, I'm really sorry to hear that. I have a sister, you know? That's the kinda thing niggas get killed over. I mean, what happened, what did you do?"

"Nothing," she says, her voice barely audible. "If I would've told my father, my father would've killed him. I'm certain of that. Then what? He's dead, my father's in prison. I was embarrassed and ashamed. I didn't tell anybody at the time."

I just shake my head. There's a long silence.

"I was pregnant. I got an abortion."

I can't say anything. A wave of guilt splashes up my neck, tingling my face. The times I've stood in a circle of men, my weak chuckles cosigning their tales.

"Sometimes you just gotta take the pussy, man."

"She said no, but I know she meant maybe."

Feeling it was wrong but not having the courage to speak out against it. I desperately wanted to be accepted by other men. Allowing me to stand and share in their company meant I was a man, too. Being in their presence affirmed me. That affirmation was far more important than doing what I felt was right.

I glance at Camille, soft-focused by candlelight. My mind is twirling at hyperspeed.

My biological mother and I share a rape story. A perverse thing to have in common. The careless thief left his evidence in my eyes. I find him guilty when I shut them tight.

The father by force. I have spent so much of my young life trying to trade him in. I could get no takers for the rapist—the sticker price too high. My standards were not. All I asked was that a man last. Stay around long enough to allow me to walk with him. To hang with him and his partnas sometimes. To go hear Pharoah Sanders together. Elvin Jones. To scream at the screen during Monday Night Football. To run full court at Venice Beach, hitting jumpers and talking shit. There was so much I wanted to do.

The rapist was resourceful: He slipped the guilt around my biological mother's neck to share the weight. She can't shake it.

The guilt didn't fit me. He passed down the shame instead. I work hard to forget I'm wearing it.

I ignore shame's tight fit, but I can't conquer the urge that accompanies it. The urge to make people like me. The desire to earn a secure place in the lives of others. Seeking outside of myself for a home.

I can tell her rape story with the stoic distance of a network news anchor. Distance, the opiate of the coward. I've never held my pain close. Never dealt with my biological mother giving me up. I've just tried to build a fence between us—blocking her out, securing me in.

I begin to tell Camille the story my mother told me.

"I know this woman," I say, still stroking Camille's forehead. "When she was sixteen, a schoolgirl, she was waiting at a bus stop. A thin, talkative sister. She was at the bus stop and this guy snatched her and pulled her behind a row of bushes. He forced her to the ground and changed her life. She got pregnant."

I can hear Camille's breathing get louder. Head on my chest, I know she can feel my lungs expanding and deflating.

"This was back in the day when being an unmarried, pregnant teenager was nothin nice. The weight of people staring. She had the baby and gave it up for adoption. She must have been in a lot of pain."

I pause to hear my words fill the candle-tinted room.

"Her mother had a friend who wanted another child but because of medical complications couldn't have one. A girlfriend agreement was reached. They decided that this friend would take the baby when the child was born. It was a difficult birth physically and emotionally. The young girl took her child home and it quickly developed an eye infection. The baby was sickly. Troublesome. After five weeks, the young mother called the family friend and said come pick up the baby. When the woman arrived, the girl handed the child and his belongings, stuffed in a brown paper bag, to the woman. She took him home and nursed him to health. That woman was the one who raised me. My mother, Gladys Datcher. Moms."

There is a long silence. Just stroking. Camille raises her head to look me in the eye, then rests again on my chest.

"What happened to your mother?"

"Well, I consider Moms, Gladys, my mother, but Mariam, my birth mother, I think she had a really hard time. I think the rape and giving me up, the combination of those two events rocked her. I mean, as it would anyone."

"Did you ever get a chance to know Mariam?"

"I went to visit her family a few years after Moms told me I was adopted. I had thought about what they might be like, but basically I tried to keep it out of my mind. I was happy where I was at. I went with my brother and sister to Chicago to visit their father for two weeks. While I was there, I spent time with Mariam and Sharon, my biological grandmother."

"Did you stay in touch with them?"

"There were some phone calls during that next year, but I think there was just too much emotion involved. Moms stays in touch with them from time to time. I haven't seen them since that first trip. But one day, I'd like to get to know them better."

Talking about my adoption always heats me. During Midwestern winters, you learn to dress in layers; adoption conversations are like walking into a tiny, hot room in full blizzard gear: I am forced to undress. My swagger straightens and falls to the floor, too. Even with all the love Moms and my family showered upon me, sometimes I still feel like a hand-me-down child.

When I feel shaken, Wednesdays are my relief. After my conversation with Camille, I wait for hump day's sunrise like kindergartners wait for Christmas eve's sunset. The writing workshop I coordinate in my neighborhood gives me a chance to turn some of the hurt into art.

My weekly Leimert Park stroll to the World Stage starts my Wednesday-night ritual. One that I especially need tonight. I'm thinking of reading a poem that I wrote about my adoption drama.

As always, I leave my apartment at 7:00 P.M., walking into the faint echo of African jimbe drums. Leimert Park is a thriving African-American arts enclave pulsing in the heart of South Los Angeles. A magnet for jazz musicians, writers, visual artists, and African drummers. I live on Degnan Boulevard, the main drag.

The West African dance studio, a block up Degnan, starts their warm-up just before seven. The drummers' slow, tribal rhythm signals stretching time for the dancers and serves as birdcall for the rest of this night-owl village. Across the street, my seventy-something neighbor tends to his vibrant flower garden under house lights. These bursts of color in the night are his passion. He looks up from his work just long enough to make eye contact and return my raising chin in the universal blackman wassup sign.

Up my side of the street, two of the neighborhood kids argue about a rule infringement on their latest improvised game. Dusk is gone. Night has settled hard on their playtime.

"Remember I said we had to touch the light pole first."

"Un-unnnh, I didn't hear you say that. I won."

"You didn't win nothin!"

My oncoming presence chills their preteen aggression.

"Wassup littleman?" I say, talking to both.

They raise their chins as I pass.

The few kids on this block of primarily late-middle-age homeowners bring hip-hop energy to this bebop neighborhood. They complete the circle of what I imagine existed in our hoods before I was born. The youth living among the old ones.

Just across 43rd Street, the residential zone ends and a quaint Mediterranean-style village lined with picture-window storefronts begins. The secret sauce from Phillips BarBeeQ shares the air with the jimbe drums. Per usual, Phillips's long line snakes from the Leimert Park contender crowned Heavyweight Barbeque Champ by the L.A. press. Right across the parking lot, rehearsals are about to start at the Crossroads Theater. Its owner, Marla Gibbs of "The Jeffersons" fame, used the wages she earned as a TV maid to bring theater to our doorstep.

Next to Crossroads, shoppers are still inside the Bak-Tu-Jua boutique, trying on the handmade West African–styled clothes, head wraps, and colorful pullover robes that many neighborhood residents wear. The wide sidewalk is crowded with people peeking in and out of the culturally themed gift shops on both sides of the avenue. There is a spirit of real camaraderie. People speak when they pass. *Sister* and *brother* punctuate casual conversation. I love strolling the neighborhood because seeing black kindness warms my spirit.

I cross the wide street and head to the Dance Collective. A large group of mostly men, extending deep into the sidewalk, clusters around the door like extras at an adult-movie set. Some necks and heads strain for better sight lines. Others sling back and forth to the swelling drum rhythms. *Du-Duupt-du-du-du-du-du-Du-Duupt-du-du-du-du-du-Du-Duupt-du-du-du-du-du-Du-Duupt-du-du-du-du-du . . .*

I decide to make a move for the inside. My abdomen tightens, readies to defend my excuse-mes that land on hard stares. I lean and push through, receiving only a few grumbles. Enter into the funky heat of moving bodies in enclosed space. Deafening drum vibrations.

Just inside the door, six drummers' hands are slapping animal skin–covered jimbes, which look like hollowed tree trunks positioned between their legs. Twelve eyes are closed, necks thrown back, heads shaking side to side, hands and dreadlocks flying. A brother in a wheelchair sitting behind the drummers plays a wooden flute that was inaudible from the outside. Another cat keeps time with a cowbell. Everybody is sweating. Two of the drummers already have removed their shirts. Their bare chests glisten.

On the semigloss, golden oak hardwood before us, a thirty-something woman with white fabric skirted around her waist, a white blouse, and a white head wrap thrusts her chest forward, arches her back, throws her head skyward, and windmills her arms in large circles to the drum rhythms.

And again.

The cycle repeats several times to the resounding drums. The twenty or so brightly wrapped women gathered near the back wall watch her intently.

In preparation, some mimic her arm movements, others her heaving chest thrusts. The drummers sweat. Suddenly she stops and shouts, "Okay, I want this now!"

Immediately, twenty chests are thrusting, twenty backs are arching, twenty reflections touching God in the eight-foot-high room-length mirror. The sheer number of women dancing seems to drive the drummers. They play louder. The lead drummer stands, soloing over the collective rhythm. One dancer breaks formation, becoming a spinning Sufi dervish, arms and feet chanting, gyrating toward him.

She is soloing on top of his solo.

Shrieks and shouts of praise from the other dancers. Syncopated clapping begins. Stomping of feet. The dancer and drummer disappear into each other. Only their liquid smiles remain. He plays the break; she snaps her pelvis in acknowledgment. Released, she spins her glowing body back into the group of dancers. Spontaneous applause and calls of *aiyee-ee-ee-ee-ee-ee-aiyee-ee-ee-ee-ee-ee*.

Watching these sisters dance to drumming dismantles the line between spirituality and sensuality.

It's almost 7:30 P.M. I make my way back through the doorway crowd and cross the street to the World Stage. Five or six early birds stand talking in the night air.

"Wassup, y'all?"

"Wassup? Heh, Michael."

I unlock the door. The poets walk into the World Stage Writer's Workshop clutching their lives in tattered notebooks. They stand patiently as I number one to twelve for the open mic list. They place their names in slots: kaleidoscopes through which the complicated patterns of their lives can be viewed.

The room begins to swell quickly with black word slangers. Sophisticated snapping handshakes, flirtatious conversations, and pure charisma make the air frisky. On the counter by the door, I light the candles and Black Love incense. Smoke wafts up toward the slow-spinning ceiling fan twenty-five feet above. The first-timers occupy themselves with the black-and-white photographs lining the wall. Max Roach, Pharoah Sanders, and other jazz greats *live!* at the World Stage.

Akin, poet V. Kali's four-year-old son, walks straight to the stage and settles in behind the drum kit next to the black baby grand. His ritual. A mural-sized John Outterbridge original is the backdrop. Poets sit talking along the white north wall beneath a painting of Miles Davis on fire. Dominating the opposite wall, a pensive John Coltrane seems to observe it all like a root doctor mid-diagnosis.

These nurses and waiters and drug dealers and cashiers and Crips and math teachers and cooks and engineers and titty-bar dancers come to this place, where they are judged only by the quality of their work. The only stones cast are at lazy poetry.

A few minutes after 7:30, Anthony Lyons, the other workshop coordinator, arrives. He takes my seat manning the door. I move through the crowd toward the stage. Motion for Akin to kill the drum solo.

"Good evening. My name is Michael Datcher. On behalf of the staff, welcome to the World Stage Writer's Workshop."

I make my weekly speech about the workshop's three components: the initial hour for works-in-progress, followed by the half-hour featured-reader section for visiting authors, and concluding with the performance-oriented open mic.

"If there are no questions, peace and blessings. The mic is now open for works-in-progress."

A.K. Toney rises out of his seat near the back and rambles toward the stage. Our friend Shonda calls him "an intense ball of black love." He's a beautiful man with the kind of sensitivity that children are drawn to. Five-foot-nine and painfully thin, he walks with the slight stoop of the wounded.

His charcoal face and forehead segue into a microlayer of black hair that covers his scalp. The extra-baggy dark blue jeans sagging off his ass seem to break Newtonian laws with each step. His bony arms jut out of a white T-shirt like two dangling police batons. This twenty-three-year-old man looks like the sixteen-year-old orphan he was and is.

A.K.'s spindly fingers snatch the head of the mic.

"Hotep!"

In unison, the crowd returns this early Egyptian Dynasty greeting, which means peace. He pauses and looks down at the black notebook in his hand.

"I've been working on this piece," he begins, words bouncing from his bottom lip like a basketball dribbled low and fast.

"I recently got out the hospital. I was walking down Broadway near Eighty-ninth with one of my partnas, and this nigga rolled up on us and pulled out his strap. He said something about his seventy-two hundred, his money, to my boy. It was all happening so fast, the shouting, the gun. He just blasted my man in the chest right in front of me. Blood was everywhere. Then he turned to me. I knew this dude, we didn't have no beef. I was like, 'Hold up, man, wait.' He started blasting shots into both of my legs. My legs buckled, and I collapsed right there in the street. Then he just turned around and walked away. Once he turned the corner, I started dragging myself along the ground, crying out, 'Someone help me, please, I been shot. Someone please help me.' This poem, 'Chronicle Trauma,' is about that experience. I need some feedback."

The audience sits still, stunned, as A.K. begins to read.

He's delivering his words with a staccato intensity that is both angry and vulnerable.

Scenario started:
then one day
that night
I was like
b-out
audi early
from work
and then
all of the sudden
I was a nigga
on 89th and
Broadway
a commodity
on the streets
I was in the mix
on the trade
the big part of
a jackmove
Some fool was
enterprising the
gaffle on me
yeah
a nigga demon
was closin in
while I was closin
out at $7,200 a share
fo a half bird
Word! or was it
jus the nigga
I was with?

    A.K. begins to read faster, with more passion. The awkward sounds of people shifting in their seats.

Scenario continues:
Yeah
it was going down
this nigga was going down
Yo blak I wasn't down
with this
but it was too late
so it went like
bom-bom
bom
bom
bom-bom
bom
bom
in a few rounds
from a nine
the other nigga
I was with got
shot five times
me
I
went down
in both legs
yo the other
nigga died
he was dead
yeah
I felt burning
sensations deep
within the wounds
as blood started to
shed
running down

my legs
I scream out
"Yo I've been shot!"
falling down
no walking around
had to move around
pull up
to get up
no I can't plead
hell no I can't beg
with myself or
no one else
but I get the help
as I must
and I have to walk
on these bloody
broken legs
so I yell outloud
"Please, somebody help
please, get help Please!"

The tears begin to chase each other down A.K.'s cheek.

And I make it to
the salvation
to deliver me
to the outside from
my dilemma
as the ambulance arrives
and so does the
one-tyme
hassling me with
a hard time
. . . Brother's got no keeper

> when my nigga's trying
> to put me six feet deeper
> being a trigga from the
> 187 reaper . . .

When A.K. finishes, people are weeping openly. After a long pause, hands slowly raise. This is not a therapy session, it's a writer's workshop.

He gets feedback about simile and metaphor use. Language choice. Alliteration and assonance. It's a strong start, but it can be better.

Usually, I'm very involved in the feedback, but now I'm too moved to speak. When A.K. was in the hospital, I didn't even visit him. I was so caught up in my own drama that I let our other friends do the work of visiting and healing. After I broke free from my schedule, he was already out of the hospital.

He walks from the stage past me. I can't look him in the eye.

A.K.'s openness has made the air more raw, purified by the tears in the room. In that moment, I commit to read the poem about my ill beginnings.

During the open mic, I finally pull the slip of paper with my own name out of the black fedora.

"This piece is called 'Sometimes I Feel Like a Fatherless Child.' "

After the workshop, the poets talk outside 5th Street Dick's Coffee Co., the popular jazz café around the corner. Emotion is still thick in the night air. I'm chilling with A.K. He doesn't bring up my hospital absence. Neither do I. We stand in the humid space between shame and forgiveness.

A brother walks up and introduces himself to A.K.

"I like your poetry, man. I been shot too, and man that . . . that was deep."

They hug. Other brothers join our circle. Stories are exchanged about being carjacked, absentee fathers, wilding in the drug game, black life in L.A. This is not the braggadocio associated with L.A.'s black street soldiers. It's young black men laying down heavy loads.

I am struck by the tenderness of these confessions. They soothe the wounds from my own adoption conversation with Camille. A warm balm for the rapist's son. The listening. The being heard. We're a half block from the corner of Crenshaw and Vernon, disrobing bulletproof-vest lives.

With the writer's workshop, freelance assignments, the researcher job, and grad school, life is hectic. Yet I'm still finding a way to spend time with Camille. Usually intimate time.

"You-can't-leave-this-alone-can-you?"

She likes to rhythmically repeat this breathless mantra, evil-eyeing me face-to-face during hot sex. I start to suspect she's right.

Three or four days a week, I study or write until 10:00 P.M. Call Camille. Eventually pick her up and bring her to my place. We sweat and talk into the night. I get up at 6:00 A.M. Work on my freelance articles. Wake Camille up. Drop her at home on my way to UCLA by 10:00 A.M. Return from campus or work by 6:00 P.M. Eat dinner, then back to writing until about 10:00 P.M. Call Camille. I'm running myself ragged.

This intimacy with Camille is both satisfying and frustrating. Despite all the heat, I'm not feeling her as potentially "the One." The girl I've been looking for. So many years of waiting has me searching for the perfect match. I've got too much at stake to settle for less. I'm longing for a woman with the rare combination of intense sensuality, heightened spirituality, and a love for books so strong she gets wet reading Fanon.

Camille's a cool sister and she could make a Tibetan monk slip. However, she'd rather watch Ricki Lake than read. I've never even seen her with a book. She also doesn't strike me as especially spiritual—not that I'm moon-walking on water, but her vibe doesn't suggest that God is central to her life. She may think the same thing about me, so I could be wrong too, but I have to honor my instincts.

Sometimes I think I'm asking for too much. Being too demanding. But in my heart, I know what I need to be happy. As long as the core qualities are in place, I can deal with everything else. I'm not looking for a perfect person, I'm looking for a perfect match. A coworker to build my picket fence.

The inexact science of the heart. She must be wondering, What is it? We get along well. Have these great talks.

I have spent a lot of time dreaming about what it's going to feel like to be in love. As a teenager, the more my husband-and-father obsession grew, the more I became fascinated with the idea of love. In junior high, I was intrigued with the love songs on the radio. Shalamar's "For the Lover in You," Switch's "I Call Your Name." I wanted to experience that kind of passion.

I began to ask older adults, usually women, around the neighborhood, teachers I'd grown close to, and members of my family. Looking for answers. I had a little battery of questions mentally prepared.

"When was the first time you fell in love? How did you know? What did it feel like?" Questions I asked through high school and my undergraduate years at Berkeley.

I must have talked to hundreds of people about what it's like to be in love. Of all the different answers I heard, the common thread was the vaguest: You will know when the feeling hits you. I'm not feeling it with Camille.

Despite the heated intimacy and all we've shared, my heart isn't fully in it. I like Camille, but I don't love her. An unlove I feel guilty about. I'm forced to deal with the reality that I'm using her—and she's using me. We've become fuck buddies. The kind of quasi-relationship built on convenience, where the only true commitment is doing the chicken wing whenever schedules permit. A relationship with a built-in sinkhole: It undermines strong black families. Doesn't encourage men to fully commit to women. It's the kind of relationship I'm not proud to be a part of.

One night, in a halting, awkward moment, I encourage Camille to date other men.

"You might find someone who's willing to offer you more than I can. I want to see you be happy."

"What makes you think I'm not happy now?" she says coldly, before changing the subject.

Around Thanksgiving, Camille and I are lounging in my apartment, drinking wine and talking. The conversation turns to condoms. Camille complains, "I hate these condoms. They're so uncomfortable. I want the real thing."

She says she wants to stop using prophylactics since she's on the pill. We both have been tested for sexually transmitted diseases, but I balk at the idea. I like having the double-protection plan. We start to make out. I reach for a condom. Camille playfully takes it away from me. I say, "Ooh, nooo," and reach for the plastic package again. She withholds it by fully extending her arm, then proceeds to lay her body on mine. Before I know it, Camille's riding me hard into submission.

becoming adopted

At age four, I became adopted. It was like discovering I didn't exist.

In my tight-knit family, love was a verb. An action word evidenced by hugs, clever banter, and sacrifice. Love was the first word I saw. Gladys Christine Datcher made sure of that.

Moms was my first hero. She had lots of competition. Early seventies blaxploitation stars were dominating the ghetto-hero landscape. Shaft, Foxy Brown, Christy Love, Superfly. Their movies inspired styles of dress, figures of speech, pimp limps, and courage. Their posters wallpapered bedrooms.

Moms outshined them all.

She had a sixth sense, an amazing ability to foretell events. Moms would get a *feeling* about something, and that *feeling* would become reality. It added to her superhero mystique. She was tall and slim, with smooth caramel skin. Brown hair bouncing beyond her shoulders. Her Alabama childhood nickname, "Beaut," stuck for good reason. Moms was the prettiest girl I knew—and also the smartest. She was an elegant woman with an eloquent tongue. But as she liked to say, "Don't let the smooth taste fool you."

One Saturday I was at my aunt Alberta's house playing hide-and-seek with her son Jeff and other cousins. I was bitten by the neighbor's Doberman pinscher (I had jumped the fence looking for a hiding space). Aunt Berta called Moms, who was at home.

Moms rushed next door to see if the dog had been vaccinated for rabies. A frantic group of cousins, brothers, and uncles followed like nurses trailing an ER surgeon.

"Excuse me," Moms started quickly but politely when the door opened, "my son was bitten by your dog. I'd like to know whether the dog has had his shots or not?"

"What was your son doing in my backyard? My dog just had a litter, so you're lucky something worse didn't happen."

I remember the shock of the brassy blonde's comment on my family gathered at the door. Heads were swinging to face each other.

"Lady, I can understand your dog's actions because she just had pups and was clearly trying to protect them. But I cannot understand your careless attitude regarding a dog that bit my four-year-old child."

The woman's shaggy-haired boyfriend appeared in the doorway as silent backup. He placed his hand on her shoulder.

"Come on, honey, let's go back inside."

She yanked away, spun around, and slapped him hard on the face. He turned cherry-Kool-Aid red. She spun back to Moms.

"He shouldn't have been in my damn yard. Now that's all I have to say about it. If you have something else to say, you can meet me in the back alley."

"Let's go!" Moms said, throwing off her jacket.

The woman slammed her door.

Moms rushed off for the alley. We transformed from medical staff to Ali's prefight entourage.

When we got to the alley, the woman was just exiting her back gate. She walked into the middle of the alley and struck a martial arts stand, right in front of Moms.

"Bitch, I know karate."

My mother snapped, "You don't even know me. You don't call me a bitch, bitch! And I don't care what you know . . ." Like a tense rattlesnake strike, Moms's hand shot out and slapped the woman's face. A surprised *ooouuuhhhhh* from ringside. The woman crumpled into herself. Tears skittled down her ruby cheeks. Moms, both fists clenched at sides, eyeballs electric, held ground like Cleopatra Jones. The kung fu master covered her face. Her boyfriend rushed out the back gate to retrieve her.

"Oouhh, Aunt Beaut, you got her good. You said, *Whhhapppp;* Beaut, you a mess; see you done gone and sent that woman inside to call the White Knights."

She shrugged off the lyrical backslaps as if kicking ass was a routine responsibility of the action hero. In that moment, Moms *is* the sho/nuff-superbadmama that don't take no stuff.

She grabbed me by the hand and headed toward the car.

"Let's take you to the hospital, baby."

Moms's entourage clustered behind her. Her pull is the energy of the unexpected. With Moms, anything can happen. She was and is so honest and straightforward. She almost seemed compelled to stand up for herself and our family, regardless of the odds. Regardless of the danger. As a child, I saw her go face-to-face with disrespectful store clerks, out-of-line social workers, and neighborhood men who were known to be hazardous to your health.

Even in my youth, I could see that many people were controlled by fear. That's what made Moms's fearlessness so attractive to children and adults. She was a real-life example of someone standing up for her rights and living to tell about it. Her courage was the standard that my young life embraced. Through elementary school recess, on playgrounds, in our neighborhood, if someone was treated wrongly or cheated, I was quick to speak up. "That's not fair!" was my screaming entrée into many school-age conflicts.

My interventions were so common that when playtime disputes occurred, the other kids would turn to me and say, "Let's let Mikey decide." I had built a reputation for being honest. I couldn't be swayed by Blow-Pops, Snickers bars, or friendship. I was proud to be thought of as fair. A defender of justice. I was trying to be like my mother.

∎ ∎ ∎

Our small Fort Wayne, Indiana, house was a magnet for activity and conversation. Moms was the favorite auntie/sister, so family was thick and storytelling constant. By the age of four, I had fallen in love with language on my mother's knee. Her bony leg was my first library chair; reading full lips was my introduction to literature. In a family of story-tellers, there was always a compelling narrative around. I'd eavesdrop until Moms would say, "Boy, quit looking in grown folks' mouths. Go play."

My sister is her mother's daughter. Nose in a book and the vocab to prove it. A vocabulary filled with kind words, until you cross her. When Cyndi is angry, the adjectives and nouns seem to shoot from her irises, not her mouth. I didn't hear her eyes screaming often. She was too busy look-ing for ways to make her little brother feel loved. She is six years older, so I wasn't competition, I was a favorite live-action toy. Someone to play and make believe with. Early training for the film and television actress she would become. Cyndi would frequently give me a big hug and say, "I love you." I believed her.

My brother, Elgin, who is eight years older than me, was an artist. His sketches, which hung on our walls, had won awards. I was amazed by his ability to turn a blank page into a piece of art. An introspective child, he wasn't a big talker, but when he spoke he did so with deep conviction. I loved being in his presence.

Even at four, I had the sense that our family was special. People were always over at our house. Everyone seemed so proud to be a part of the clan. I was proud, too. One day, while I was playing with a few of my cousins, somebody started talking about where babies come from. Then Nita said, "But Mikey, you didn't come from Aint Beaut's tummy."

"Yes I did."

"No you didn't."

"Unhunh."

"No you didn't."

"I did. Imma go tell Mama."

Close to tears, I ran to my mother, who was sitting in the kitchen with a couple of grown-ups.

"Mama, Nita said I didn't come from your tummy!"

Without missing a beat, she drew me close between her legs.

"Nita is right, you didn't come from my stomach. I made Elgin and Cyndi in my stomach, but you were made in my heart."

I ran back to my cousins, telling them loudly that I came from Moms's heart. But inside, I wished I had come from her stomach like my brother and sister. I didn't want to be different.

The issue came up again when I was five.

"Mama, what's adopted?"

"That's when a mother goes to the hospital and picks out the prettiest baby there. I picked you out because you were the prettiest baby and I felt instant love for you. I knew that God had left you there for me. And I brought you home."

Moms explained later that I came from a girl named Mariam's stomach.

When Moms finished hugging me, she looked me in the eyes. "Is my baby okay?"

I remember smiling. A curtain for the questions that were rehearsing backstage in my mind.

Why didn't Mariam keep me? What was wrong with me? Is Elgin still my big brother? Does he know I'm adopted? Does Cyndi? Does everyone in the family know I didn't come from Moms's tummy?

I had the best mother in the world. I wanted to come from her stomach like Elgin and Cyndi. I smiled. It was my first performance.

I figured the family knew I was different. Maybe if I acted like I didn't know, different would go away.

In the days that followed, I found myself examining the faces of my relatives: Moms, Elgin, Cyndi, and my close cousins like William. I come from a high yella family. Redbones. I had enough yella to fit in, no problem. But now, through my new lenses, I could see the subtle differences. How my nose spread and seemed bigger than Cyndi's. When Elgin and I brushed our teeth in the bathroom mirror, his face seemed wider, different from mine. I really wasn't one of them. I wasn't me. I didn't exist.

In my own mind, my place in the family became precarious. I felt a need to prove myself. It became very important for the members of my family to like me.

Before the revelation of my birth, I lived mostly in my own world. I just wanted to play. When I became adopted, things became different. Frequently, I felt I was performing. I had to be the perfect little boy. Friendly, well behaved, fun to be around, smart. I had to make sure I wouldn't be given away again.

forget me not

In the weeks following the initial condomless session with Camille, sometimes we use condoms, sometimes we don't. A common program among young African-Americans. Urban Russian roulette. Playing with lives not yet ours to raise. Leaving childhood destinies to the whim of indefatigable vaginal swimmers.

I begin to feel the need to pull a lecture off the shelf.

"Camille, you know my convictions about not wanting to bring any kids into the world out of wedlock," I tell her one night, lying in bed.

"What are you trying to say?"

"You know what I'm saying. We need to be more careful."

"Let me tell you something, ain't nobody trying to have yo baby. Stop flattering yourself. I like you. You fuck me good. Since you can't leave me alone, I know I'm doing something right, too. I know we're just *kickin it,* so stop trippin. As far as babies are concerned, when my friend was going through hard times, I took care of her baby. For almost two years, I was doing what I had to do to make sure she had food and Pampers and all the other things she needed. She was calling me Mama, okay? I've been there. I know what it takes to raise a child. It's a lot of responsibility, and I'm not ready to give up my life yet. I've been on the pill for five goddamn years. Ain't nobody up in here gonna get pregnant, so stop trippin."

I can't stop trippin. I never should have agreed to have sex without a condom, even if she'd been on the pill since birth. I'm jeopardizing my dream.

I begin to remind Camille to take her birth control pills. They are now my only line of defense. When she comes by my apartment, she makes a point of taking them out in front of me. But one day, I ask, "Are you pregnant, Camille?"

I just have a *feeling*.

She laughs.

"Of course not. How can I be pregnant when I've been on the pill for years?"

Driving back to her apartment, we get into an argument. It's not just my concern about her getting pregnant. It's the nature of our relationship. Although we're not "going steady," in many ways we're behaving like we are. Camille would never admit it, but I can tell that her feelings are growing deeper. I don't want to hurt her. I suggest we stop having sex and really try to be just friends.

"Now you *know*," she says with much attitude.

"What?"

"We might last a couple of weeks, but eventually if we're alone in the same room for enough time, it's gonna be on. You know it and I know it. Why don't you stop trippin and let's just enjoy what we have? I'm a grown woman. I know what I'm doing. I don't need you to be looking out for my best interests. I can look out for myself."

"Camille, I just think we need to chill so we can walk away friends."

"What if I don't want to be your damn friend?"

A few days later, I call her. Although I was up-front about not looking for a steady lady, I can't help feeling bad. I genuinely like her. Over the phone, we decide to call a truce and make an attempt at being just friends.

While talking the next day, I ask Camille when her period is due.

"Any day."

The days go by; her cycle ain't cycling.

"Camille, are you pregnant?" I demand on the phone.

"I told you I can't be pregnant, Michael. I've just been under a lot of stress, especially from your ass. Stress can throw off my cycle."

"We need to go to the clinic and check this out."

"I'm not going to the clinic. I know my body. I know I'm not pregnant. You're getting on my nerves with all this. I'm getting tired of it, Michael."

"How many days late is it?"

"About a week."

"Oh, hellll no. Make an appointment. We're gonna get a pregnancy test."

About five or six days before Christmas, I pick Camille up and take her to the clinic.

Camille's in the back with the clinician. I'm in the waiting room, nervous as a husky pig on an Alabama farm. I keep thinking about my life. Not a complete circle to be found. I want my children's lives to be different. God, I don't want to have a child out of wedlock with a woman I don't love.

Maybe she was never taking those birth control pills. Maybe she was trying to set me up all along. But that doesn't seem like the kind of person she is. She seems like a straight-up sister. Maybe she's not even pregnant. She keeps saying she's not. Maybe she'll walk out here still saying, "Stop trippin." I'll be happy to hear that now.

I know if she is pregnant, it's just as much my fault as it is hers.

Camille finally comes out from behind the door.

"Well?"

"I don't know yet. They're gonna call my name when the results are ready."

We sit in silence. Camille doesn't look very concerned, which pisses me off. Why should I be the only one sweating?

They finally call her. She leaves and comes back.

"I don't know how it happened."

"Camille, what the hell is this?"

"Can-we-go-to-the-car?" she snaps.

We both walk out to the parking lot. I'm steaming. Really more mad at myself, but since Camille's here, I vent on her.

"Camille, what is this?"

"I've only forgotten a couple of pills since I've known you, and I've al-ways taken two the next day to make—"

"A coupla pills? A coupla pills? Why am I hearing about a coupla fuckin pills in the clinic parking lot? Why didn't you tell me you missed days?"

"Because you were trippin so hard. I was tired of hearing your mouth."

"Well, this is why I'm trippin, Camille. You're pregnant. How many times have we talked about this? You know how I feel about bringing black babies into the world out of wedlock."

"Why's it always about what you feel, Michael? You don't even know how I feel. Stop thinking about yourself all the time. You think I wanna have a baby by some nigga who ain't got nothin? How you gonna support a baby? You can barely take care of your own yellow ass. Listen, I'm tired of talking about it. Take me home. I've got things to think about."

visiting mariam

Moms asked me if I wanted to visit the woman whose tummy I came from.

My brother and sister were going to be visiting their father, Elgin Sr., in Chicago that summer of 1974. Since my biological mother still lived there, I would tag along, then eventually head to her house.

Before our trip, Elgin took me with him and the older neighborhood boys to play tackle football. Tall and charismatic, with a galactic afro, Elgin usually would be one of the two captains who chose teams. All the players lined up horizontally across the field. Elgin and the other captain flipped a coin to see who would have the initial pick. Although the neighborhood was filled with amazing athletes, Elgin chose me first.

"I'll take my little brother."

Beaming, I jumped out of line and ran to my brother's side. Snickers from the unchosen followed me. I bounced up and down like my ankles were Pogo sticks. For a young football fanatic like me, it was hard to contain such joy.

We received the kickoff and huddled for our first possession. Elgin was the quarterback.

"Mikey, I want you to run ten yards and turn around. I'm gonna throw you the ball, so don't drop it. When they come to tackle you, just fall to the ground. Everybody else go long."

When the ball was hiked, I ran as fast as I could and turned around. No one tried to cover because I was so small. The ball came spiraling toward me, stabbing my bird chest. I wrapped my arms around it and fell to the ground.

When we got back to the huddle, Elgin was beaming, too.

"Awright, since they're not covering my little brother, we're gonna run the same play until they stop it. They're bigger, but we're smarter. Mikey, don't drop the ball."

We ran the same play almost all the way down the field. I didn't score the touchdown, but I was the leading receiver on the drive. They finally had to put someone on me.

We won that game and many, many more. Elgin taught me there is always a way to win; I just have to figure out how. It isn't who has the most talented players, it's who has the best plan—and execution.

The winning was addictive and habit-forming. It was a feeling I loved. One that would drive me throughout my life.

After I spent a few days at Elgin Sr.'s house, clothes were packed, hair was combed, face Vaselined, and I was given a ride to my past. I remember turning the corner and seeing a group of people clustered curbside in front of a Southside Chicago three-story house. My welcoming party. There must have been fifteen people staring hard. It would have been rude if their collective smile had not been so bright. I opened the car door, nervous. I immediately began to check their faces. I looked at the shapes of their eyes, searching for matching pairs. I scanned their noses for size and curve. I took in their characteristics like tree-ripe cherries into a paper bag. I hungered to know their stories. Their histories. Their favorite toys. I stared.

Floating, I began to glide toward the frail, light-skinned young woman watching me. Her eyes steaming like my breath in winter. Boiling water threatened to explode down her face. I slid to a stop in front of her. My eyes searched for familiarity. I never had seen myself in someone else. I felt grounded by the blood between us. We stood there, embracing from a distance.

I remember she was trembling. Lips vibrating like her fragile fingers dangling by her side. Arms paralyzed by the absence of a hug she must have dreamed of. We had switched roles. I became the adult responsible for the first step.

"Hi, Aunt Mariam."

The words sprang from my mouth, bounced on the excited air. The blast landed through the very center of her face. Skin and eyes fell like Macy's thick plate glass. My hug, a leap into "I'm sorry." I pressed the side of my head into the tummy I came from. Her water broke again.

I knew she was hurt because I didn't call her a name that children call their mothers, but "Aunt Mariam" was the only phrase that seemed natural. I already had a Moms.

The family swooped to the rescue. Backslaps and ain't-he-cutes filled the space between distance and regret. My arms still wrapped around Mariam's heaving torso, I rode her sobs like a giant water slide's bumps and dips. The family intervened and escorted us into the home I would have grown up in.

The old Southside house was like nothing I'd ever been in before. Big and tall, with arched doorways. There was security, safety in that house. The grace of ownership burrowed through that family soil. The trees that fell in sacrifice for the hardwood floors shined throughout the house. Running was forbidden, but this time it was mandatory. Sharon, my biological grandmother, probably relaxed her children-in-the-house rule because of my reentrance into their lives.

The two kids who lived across the street were open to me. The boy's name began with a B, his sister's a T. They were somehow guarded and friendly. Old faces, childlike hearts.

Tee was skinny, brown, and pretty. Her eyes clung to me like only an eight-year-old girl's can. Bee was a grown black man in a ten-year-old body. He was brown and serious. When we would make up games, even at the height of adventure, his eyes would never smile. When Bee told me the story of what those eyes had seen, Tee was there, sharing the pain that now defined their young lives.

Their mother and father had been arguing in the house. They had argued before. Lots of times. Their father raised the shotgun blowing pieces of their mother on the kitchen wall. Seconds later, he fell by her side. Now Bee and Tee were alone. No matter how many cousins, uncles, and aunties you have, when Mommy and Daddy die, you're on your own.

When Bee told me the story, the passion of our triangle heightened. They brought me into a world where the oxygen was thinner; breathing took more effort when I was around them. It was a breathless friendship. No secrets. The pain they invited me into was intoxicating. No one ever had told me such things. It was like having grown-ups as friends, except that they enjoyed having fun, too. The way they looked at each other was so intense. I wanted someone to look at me that way.

We would run through Grandma Sharon's house, sliding across the smooth floors in our socks. We could play hide-and-seek for hours because there were so many rooms. The top floor had the best hiding spots since it was dark and spooky. Whoever was It would be too scared to look hard up there.

Mariam wobbled around me like a newborn baby chick with a shell on her head. Trying to find a way to see me without being seen, to connect with me without being vulnerable. I could feel her hiding. I don't ever recall us being alone, talking. She had secrets. Unlike Bee and Tee, she wouldn't share. Those secrets kept us just out of reach. The distance made me uncomfortable. I never really knew what to say to her. I just knew not to say "Aunt Mariam."

I never said her name again. I wasn't sure which title to use in addressing her, so I didn't use any. I wasn't raised to call grown-ups by their first names. It made for a series of awkward *shes* and *hers* and *yous*. I wasn't fluent in the language of adoption.

In place of communication, Mariam and I did things.

At the time, Chicago had a huge amusement park called Old Chicago. It was a kid's paradise. Roller coasters with loops, fast spinning rides, giant Ferris wheels, cotton candy, stuffed animals, old-fashioned costumes, games everywhere. All this was inside the biggest bubble-shaped building in the whole world.

Mariam took me to Old Chicago with a guy I think was her boyfriend. When we got inside, I couldn't stop looking up. The roof seemed as high as the sky. It had to be the biggest playhouse anyone had ever built. We rode the roller coasters and bumper cars and everything that spun fast. Mariam kept money in my pocket. I made sure to spend it like the fives and tens were burning holes in the lining. Cotton candy, candy apples, popcorn. I tried to win a stuffed animal. No luck, but Mariam's boyfriend won her a white polar bear the same height as me, only fatter. I had seen bears that big at carnivals, but I thought you had to know somebody to win one. Wasn't true. I saw Mariam's boyfriend win it fair and square.

Mariam didn't play many games. She just watched me and smiled. I smiled back. We didn't say much to each other, but we were having a great time. I remember sitting on top of the Ferris wheel alone because Mariam didn't want to go on. The ride was over. Every couple of minutes, the huge wheel would lurch forward so someone else below could get off. I was as high as the roller coaster.

I could see Mariam way down, waving up at me. I thought, if I lived with Mariam, I could be here all the time. There was no Old Chicago at home, and Mama definitely wasn't stuffing five- and ten-dollar bills in my pocket. I knew just enough about the world to understand that money was very important and Mama didn't have much. I knew the house Sharon and Mariam lived in cost a lot of cash. It was the biggest house I'd ever been in. Mariam had money—and she was willing to spend it on me. I sat on top of the world, thinking what my young life could be like.

A couple of days before I was to leave, I was sitting in Sharon's room watching "The Green Hornet." A big, strong policeman, with a gun and everything, walked into the doorway and called my name. He had the kind of voice that commanded obedience. He told me to sit down on the edge of the bed. Then he sat down next to me.

"I'm your Uncle Gerald," he said forcefully.

He was looking me in the eye. I could tell he was trying not to cry.

"I'm your mother's twin brother. Do you understand what I'm saying?" I nodded yes.

"We never should've given you away. I don't care what anyone says, you will always be a Cole, no matter where you live and who you live with. You will always be a part of this family. Do you understand me?"

I nodded yes.

"Awright."

He stood up and left.

I was dazzled. Uncle Gerald was so big and tough. And sitting on the bed right next to me. I started wondering, would I grow up to be like him? Tough with muscles. Maybe I would be a policeman and get to carry a gun too.

My new world was expanding. Possibilities presented themselves like years of unopened gifts peeking from beneath a bed. My brief stay with Mariam and the rest of the Coles had been the greatest adventure of my life. I was playing in my own history. Discovering heroes in the life I didn't live. It was like unearthing my handwriting in a diary I had not been there to write. Yet this adventure couldn't lead me to the X that I sought— the one marking an answer to why I was given away. No one ever tried to explain the circumstances. As if the situation didn't warrant some clarification. As if I had been away at summer camp for the previous seven years and not living with a different family, bearing a different last name. No one said, "I'm sorry." Sorry for giving me away. Sorry for not trying to come get me. Sorry for thinking I wouldn't come back to haunt them.

On the morning of the day I was to leave, the Cole family gathered downstairs. I was upstairs, squeezing out my last few minutes of adventure. They summoned me. When I came into the living room, a smaller version of my welcoming party was there to greet me. Sharon, Mariam, Uncle Gerald, and other relatives sat bunched together on the couch. Others were standing. No one was speaking.

"Michael, we want you to know that you've brought so much joy and light to this house. . . . Have you had fun here with us?" Sharon said.

"Yeah," I said, caution edging the roundness of my voice.

"God works in mysterious ways. He's got his own way of doing what He needs to do. Sometimes God just up and does something that only He understands. Now God has brought you back in our life, and we want you to know that if you want to stay here and live with us, that would make the whole family very happy."

A chorus of smiling "thasright"s and "unnhunh"s harmonized from the family. They were asking me to return. They were saying I was okay now.

I remember just sitting there, my eyes wide open. The events of the prior two weeks sped by like a film projector rewinding. They all were looking at me, looking like me, waiting.

"I like you all a lot, and I had a lotta fun, but you're not my family. I wanna go home."

Mariam's face broke first. The others fell in succession. Shards of disappointment crowded the room. There was no more space for speech. I rose from the ottoman I had been sitting on, and returned upstairs to sulk. I hated the silence in that living room because I knew I had caused it. I hated the way I made Mariam drop her eyes. But mostly, I hated being adopted. It made people mad at me. Made them not like me anymore. It wasn't my fault they gave me away.

the campaign

Newborn fear cleaves to me.

It's nurtured by the mild shock treatment of pregnant Camille flashing in my mind. The suddenness of these electric visions is jarring. They make the present stand and witness itself. These visions flash in the middle of graduate seminars, on the basketball court, onstage reading a poem, in my sleep.

Pacing the living room late one night, I decide to call A.K.

"Cat, could you meet me in the park?"

"What's goin on?"

"Just wanna rap for a second."

"I'm there."

Pain is needy; it longs to be understood. Reaching out to A.K. is falling into the net of shared experience. Kindred suffering. His father was murdered by the other woman. Gone before A.K. could crawl through the shame to touch him. Know him. We share this unknowing. It's why we both can be so uncertain about who we are. Constantly seeking confirmation in the eyes of men. A.K. understands.

I had Moms, who was more man than many. A.K.'s mother died when he was fifteeen. He was and is a black sheep orphan in a family of yellow

people. We share the writing of the fatherless. A.K.'s story is in a poem to
his unborn son.

Son, I do not know who I am.
We (I) only have same middle and last name of seed that entered egg.
Father, so be it, I add my voice to yours.
I want to know who killed our only image of manhood, then my blood
shed too.
Our father comes in tears, for they too r the people that share this one body.

Son, always teach by action and not words alone.
Do not pay karma's price, spirit is expensive.
Son, my name is Aaron, a word so sacred it means prophet.
I am trying to heal us.
There is no ritual in our life to create.
I am lost in hunger going everywhichway at once.
Son, I am what PO' E.T. is
An extraterrestrial, a stranger bearing gifts at anytime.

The flowers lie to me while I lay in their beauty copying
Their soft ways without knowing.
Son, I am not a girl.
Our Father was suave, but we do not even own a picture of him.
Son, whenever I rise always recognize me.
This comfort of attention is killing me softly.
I say and give this to u.

There is gossip and rumors in my soul I am not telling u.
Story has it, Jan Kenneth Toney
Our Father was a mailman in Detroit Motor City.
He met Patricia Ann Thompson on the bus
They fell in-love, got married, I was born.

Secondly, Your Uncle Artis and I live under the same roof
And sometime I do not even know him, my own brother.

They say our father cheated on our Mother
I guess that's why the other woman shot him in chest, back, then head.
Holy Trinity.
Last thing I remember . . .
Father in casket and asking, "Why is daddy sleeping?"

I knew he (I) was never going to wake up
He was never there . . .

After speaking with A.K. about the stress I've been feeling over
Camille's pregnancy, I stroll from the park up Degnan, luxuriating in the
calm of late night. Solitude in motion. These walks push back reality far
enough so I can see huge pine trees running the grassy median. Their open-
armed branches reach out to one another, forming a canopy that shadows
Degnan on hot summer days. Planted in the early 1930s, they have stood
witness to racially restrictive housing codes and Malcolm X festivals. These
pine trees date the neighborhood like a botanical census. I walk beneath
their night cover, craving the stability of thick bark.

As I walk up to my apartment, I see Wayne sitting on the steps. My
thirty-something upstairs neighbor rises to greet me. An enthusiasm for
life electrifies his walk, carves his smile. Five-foot-eight, he has the mus-
cled pudginess of a fat kid who got tired of being fat.

The boy wonder still survives in his eyes.

"Miiike . . . what's happenin, man? See ya out here doing your little late-
night walk?" he South Central drawls, speaking with the rising accents
of questions.

It's a personal dialect that keeps the listener on his toes because sooner
or later one of the probing questions he asks will not be rhetorical. We snap
and hug.

"So, how's your situation going?"

My lips are forced into a smile by his quick candor.

"It's awright, man. I'm about to go upstairs and call her now."

"Is she still saying things like 'I missed that last appointment cause Mama got sick'?"

I smile.

"Yeah, man. I'm tellin you, she wants this baby."

He shakes his bald brown head in remembrance.

"Yeeeahhman, she wants this baby. You been calling her a lot? Going to spend time with her, see how she's feelin? Asking her if she need anything? And I'm sure she's still asking for *that*? Yeah, you can smile if you wanna, but I hope you haven't weakened on that one Miiike? That's one you definitely don't wanna slip up on. She gonna give it to you good. Make you consider what you could be having with her. A sexy woman and a baby. A family. Not perfect, but not bad. She knows you're adopted and wanted to do the family thing, right? She's thinking, 'Let's work it out together, let's do it.' She's thinking, 'Why can't it be me?' Yeahman, she can see somethin in this. You said she was what, twenty-seven, right? Yeahhhh-man, she can see yall starting those first Lamaze classes together. You rubbin her fat stomach. Kneeling between her thiiighs, coaching her. She wants you, Mike. She wants you in her life. She wants you to be there with her and yall's baby."

Again, I'm caught off-guard. He's conjuring a vision I don't want to acknowledge.

"Well, you never say never, but she knows the deal, man. She understands my situation. We've been talking. It'll be awright."

"How long yall been talking though? You said she was what, approaching three months? Look at it, Miiike. Look at how it's playing out."

"She's just scared, man. And for good reason. That abortion ain't no joke. It's been nerve-racking on both of us, but when it comes down to it, all things considered, she'll follow through. We have an appointment Tuesday."

"Tuesdaaay. Goodgood, Miiike. . . . I'm not trying to scare with you, but it's a lotta days before Tuesday, Miiike?"

I smile because it's the first defense mechanism that kicks in. We've had an appointment before. It didn't happen.

"You just don't know my powers of persuasion," I offer weakly.

"What you doin calling me so late?"

"I've always paged you late, Camille."

"*Hmmmph,* that was when you was tryin to get into somethin."

I have learned to let these lava rocks roll by without chasing them. She doesn't see why we can't get together once in a while. Catch up. It's a sensitive issue.

"How's your sister doing?"

"She doin fine."

"Tell her I said hi."

"I will."

"How you been feelin Camille?"

"How you think I'm feeling, Michael? I'm pregnant. Don't you know what happens to women when they get pregnant? They get sick. I *been* sick. That's how I *been* feelin, Michael."

She's in rare form. I'm cool. Dispassionate. Can't get her mad and have her do something crazy at the last minute.

"Camille, what can I do to help?"

"What can you do to help?" she almost shouts. "You know what you can do. Lord, don't make me go there. You know what I need you to do."

"Is the doctor prescribing anything for your nausea?"

"Now Michael, think. How am I gonna take prescription medicine when I'm carrying a little baby in my stomach?"

Every time she refers to her pregnancy as carrying a little baby in her stomach, my body jolts. I find safety in believing a fetus is not a baby. If they were the same, they'd share the same name. I need to believe this.

"I heard there's an herbal tea that helps with nausea. Maybe I can call around and see what I can find out."

"Yeah, you do that."

"Oh, what time do you want me to pick you up on Tuesday?"

"How am I supposed to know right now, and today is only Wednesday? Anything could happen by then."

"Right, but we know the appointment is at three o'clock, Camille. We should just schedule the time for me to pick you up so we can plan for it. We don't want nothin jumpin up in the way. It's gotta be the first priority. So, what time do you want me to pick you up?"

"Why you always pressuring me? I get tired of this. You're always talking about this damn abortion. That's all you think about. Which is the same as thinking about yourself—which we both know you good at. I told you I'm sick. If I wake up sick Tuesday morning and stay sick all day, like I am many days, when 2:30 P.M. rolls around, do you think I should get up out of a sick bed and go get an abortion? Is that what you think I should do, Michael? Is that how much you care about my needs?"

"C'mon, Camille, you know it's not like that."

"It-is-like-that-and-you-know-it-is, Michael. You tryin so hard to get me down to the clinic so you can protect your little dream. Well, I have dreams, too."

"I'm not saying I'm the only one who has plans for their life, Camille. I—"

"It's not what you're sayin, it's what your actions are sayin. You don't even know if I wanted an abortion. You didn't really want to know what I was feelin, what I really wanted for my life. You just wanted an answer that wouldn't crumble your little world. Your world. That's all you think about. Now think about this—I don't wanna abortion. I been doing it for you. But you know what? Lately, I been thinkin bout me. This is my body."

"I know it's your body, Camille. I keep telling you it's your body, your decision, but my body is wrapped up in this, too. My life is wrapped up in this. All I'm saying is, the decisions you're making are affecting me, too, a fact that should be taken into consideration. That's how I feel."

"How-can-I-not-know-how-you-*feel*? That's all you talk about. Like the way you feel is more important than the way other people feel."

"I just think the best thing for everybody is that we go ahead and follow through."

Follow through. I sound like a snake. Easing in. It feels slithery. What if Mariam had decided to follow through with her fetus?

"No, Michael, the best thing for you. The best thing for me and the best thing for you are not the same thing. I'm not sure if I'm going Tuesday. I need more time."

"Camille, you're almost three months pregnant. There is no more time. Either we do it now or it's not gonna happen. We've got to do this now."

I feel my cool warming, losing its ability to function in this heat. I can tell I'm screaming, but it doesn't sound loud to me. I discern the volume by the warmth of my face. By how the spittle erupts into my field of view. I scream into the phone's mouthpiece—the earpiece is twisted away from my ear, out to where it's not needed. I don't need to listen to her, she needs to listen to me. I have a lot at stake. I can't bring a black baby up in here. I have to get her to understand. I'm screaming unintelligible snippets of words too fast and slurred for her. I feel my mouth moving quick. I look down, see the spit flying like damp confetti. I have to get her to understand. I'm having an out-of-body experience. Looking at someone else's hands, wet with a telling mixture of tears and sweat. Listening to someone else's hoarse voice.

Just as suddenly as I started, I stop myself mid-tirade, struggling to catch my breath. Mid-pejorative. Stop. No words. Only heavy breathing: The former prelude to our shared pleasure has become the rhythmic distress signal of our shared pain.

My life seems so loud. My screams. My heartbeat. My breathing. I just want things to be quiet again. I need some peace. We stay on the phone—breathing—for minutes. Silence filled with air. Images race through my mind. Fragments of my dream materialize before and after breaths. Individual fatherhood episodes reminding me that Camille's got to have this abortion. I have to make her understand.

Click.

welcome to california

Summer 1977. We had just moved to Los Angeles from Indiana. Returning from Gaffey Street pool, I was walking down the street with my twelve-year-old cousin, Jeff, and two of his young buddies. Our shorts still dripping wet. We were making the best of our long journey home by slapping the backs of one another's necks and popping towels. In the chasing and dodging, we ran upon three abandoned newspaper machines in an empty dirt lot, off the main street.

The metal machines, with front-loading, hatchbacklike glass doors, lay on their sides, tangled and smashed. The Rubik's cube–sized coin boxes had been pried open. We shook the machines, listening for money. The clinking of coins in one of them had us wild-eyed with boyish treasure-hunt fever. We circled. Keyed and kicked and rolled the machine with the jingling echo. When the first coin bounced out, we grew more excited and began shaking the newspaper dispenser.

The first police car's frame bounced the way police cars bounced over speed dips on "Adam-12." I froze in an open-mouthed popcorn stare. My face told my friends what my mouth could not. A cops-and-robbers show with no sound (the sirens were off for the surprise attack) was playing itself out before me. By the time I actually heard someone yelling "Ruunnn!"

all four squad cars were racing toward us. I took off, looking over my shoulder.

A good treasure hunter should always have an escape plan. I didn't. I stopped in my tracks, facing a three-story drop to a parking lot below. I turned back around to see a police car coming to a hook-sliding, dust-kicking stop about thirty feet from me. The door flew open. A white man leaped out, clutching a gun in both hands, arms stretched out forward and stiff—just like on TV. His momentum carried him a few steps toward me. He had to squat down to line up the bridge of my nose.

"Freeze!"

No one ever had pointed a real gun at my face before. He was so close. I was shaking violently. My forearms, feet, chin, and knees were stuttering so hard that he yelled "Freeze!" again.

After I was handcuffed, an officer put me in the back of his squad car. A few moments later, the door opened and my cousin Jeff slid in beside me. Our two friends were in another car. I showed Jeff how I could slip my wrists in and out of the handcuffs. The officer who pointed the pistol at me sat shotgun; another officer got behind the wheel, holding a clipboard.

"Okay, who's gonna talk for you two?" the clipboard cop said. My cousin volunteered me.

"We were swimming and we found the machines on that field," I began, talking a mile a minute. "We heard the change so we were trying to get the rest out. It was stuck in there, so we had to shake it and still we only got a little bit over a dollar. That's all we got, a dollar and some change. Yep, that's all we got, huh Jeff?"

"Unnhunh."

That was it. No more questions. They just put the car in gear and we headed out of the lot. As we were driving down the street, the policeman riding shotgun turned to his partner and began a joke with "What do you call five niggers . . ." I glanced quickly at Jeff. He looked as hurt as I felt. The cop's partner ignored him, but the comedian plowed on. I remember feeling ashamed that he would say those words right in our presence. I knew he was disrespecting us. My mama preached the importance of giving and demanding respect. I would not demand respect that time. I was much too scared. His gun in my face had shaken me. He finished his joke, started another, then another. All the way to the police station, he told niggerjokes. Every once in awhile, he'd turn and look at us in the backseat. I couldn't meet his eyes. Couldn't have him see my fear. I didn't want to be a policeman like my uncle Gerald anymore.

The coupling of my shame and fear gave birth to premature hate. Not full-term, but alive and kicking. I despised that cop. He'd hurt me. It was a new kind of pain. He made being black sound dirty and wrong. Most of the people I knew were black, and they seemed cool. He'd kept telling those jokes to be mean. I hated him for that. To know hate so young leaves scar tissue on the heart. Keloids the soul.

After we spent a couple of hours in the holding tank, a cop led us out to Moms and Aunt Berta in the lobby. To my surprise, Moms seemed happy to see me.

"Are you okay, baby?" she said, wrapping both arms around me.

"I'm fine."

"They didn't hurt my baby, did they?"

"No, Mama, I'm fine."

In the weeks that passed, I was too embarrassed to tell Moms what the cop did to us. Plus, I thought she might go to the precinct, cause a scene, and get tossed in jail. I decided not to think about niggerjokes, and I didn't—except when I saw a police car. I knew what all policemen were thinking behind those dark glasses.

After a few months of living together, Moms and Aunt Berta had a major disagreement. Moms came home and told us that she'd found a place in Long Beach. Sounded great to me. I thought maybe the whole city was built right along a long beach. We might even have a view of the water.

Nice names, like nice smiles, can be deceptive.

Although we moved onto the second floor of the building, I couldn't see the ocean from 913 Alamitos Avenue. Neither could anyone else. The two-story apartment complex was shaped like twin Ls lying on their sides, head to toe, creating a rectangular courtyard. The waist-level black metal banisters that ran along the second story provided the best sight lines to the stage below. Mothers would lean forward, hands wide-clutching the black railing, watching us children rehearsing our lives.

When Moms leaned, I was sure to straighten out my tongue. In the house, she preached the importance of speaking correctly. No slang, no niggas. Enunciation was expected. She wanted to hear the g in words ending with g. I obliged in her presence—but flipped Ebonic as soon as she left. I loved the way black people talked. It was full of style and rhythm. Speaking correctly was corny. Dry.

The mothers from the apartments on the first level piped theme music into the courtyard from 102.3 KJLH and 1580 KDAY. Soul and funk filtered through their screen doors, providing a soundtrack to the ghetto narrative. These mothers rarely left their living-room seats; they were content to watch their young understudies through raggedy curtains.

The courtyard was made of concrete except for an antique keyhole-shaped garden area (without the garden or grass or anything green) that ran through the middle. You could taste its fine dust on your tongue (it made you spit a lot) and find its thin film on your coffee table. The keyhole was impromptu boxing ring, marbles pit, and, on some weekend nights, repository for oozing blood.

At the south end of the complex was a dilapidated wooden fence that connected both Ls and contained a gate that led to an alley. The alley was our football field and rock-throwing range. The wooden telephone pole across the alley was chipped, evidence of our marksmanship. "ESL" was spray-painted on the phone pole and on most of the alley garages.

The East Side Longos was the Mexican gang that shared graffiti space and turf with the Crips, who held sway over the neighborhood. The Crips were the ghetto stars of the east side. Their autographs—K-Dog, RayRay, C-Loc—were scrawled in blue spray paint on the sides of houses, liquor store walls, and our wooden gate. They made blocky dark sunglasses, hard-creased 501 blues, white T-shirts, and black house shoes urban chic.

"Wassup, cuzz?" was the greeting of choice and necessity by neighborhood males preteen to Baby Boom. We weren't all gangstas, but we knew what neighborhood we lived in. Blue flags flying from the backs of sagging Levi's saw to that. Wearing red would get you hurt.

Ricky was my best friend in our building. Always had my back. He was born with a condition that robbed him of all body hair. His smooth face was a caramel candy apple, except for matching peeled bananas where his eyebrows should have been. Two tones of brooding intensity. Ricky's smile was as scarce as July rain, a drought caused by too many childhood stares, too many pretty girls caught in the glare of his hairless brows.

The other kids (and mothers) thought Ricky was mean. At thirteen, he was big for his age, and muscular. He lived in a blue knit beanie. It covered what we all assumed was a bald head. No one was asking.

Ricky was the toughest boy in the neighborhood, but he wasn't a bully. He had kicked just enough butt in public to announce he wasn't a kid to mess with. That reputation, along with muscles, two-tone face, and blue beanie, stilled conversations when he walked on the scene. A sensitive black boy in a lot of pain could be dangerous.

One day, as we often did at Ricky's suggestion, Ricky and I were in the alley, throwing rocks at our favorite telephone pole. Ricky's arm was stronger, more accurate. His rock would smash near the pole's top, splintering wood with the sweet thud of a Louisville Slugger on a sloppy curveball. I was drawn to Ricky's strength. I liked how he carried himself as if he were a grown man and demanded respect from everyone who interacted with him. Practicing our aim side by side, we didn't say much. Barely made eye contact. He'd disappear inside himself, a solemn marksman. I'd just take my turns and wait for him to come back.

"This lady at church asked me what I was gonna be when I grow up," Ricky said, firing the rock from his slinging arm.

I stepped up and took my turn without looking at him.

"I told her, 'I dunno,' and walked away." He grunted, rock leaving his hand.

I stepped up, took my turn.

"I'm probably gonna die young, cuzz. That's why a nigga be acting wild sometimes. I wanna get my fun in while I can."

I had never heard anyone say what I had felt so strongly myself. The east side of Long Beach was dangerous; the raw energy of desperation intensified all human interaction. I had seen things. I probably wouldn't see twenty-one.

Anything could happen at any time, and it did. The randomness of the violence gave life a sharp edge at 913 Alamitos. I would practice my little fighting skills in the mirror. Imitating what I saw Muhammad Ali do. Stick the jab and move. Stick and move, stick and move. Right cross–left jab–right cross combination. Ali Shuffle. Stick and move, stick and move until sweaty. I had to make sure that whatever happened, I didn't go out like a punk. Death didn't scare me as much as being embarrassed in the neighborhood. I was going out swinging.

"I hear you, cuzz, I hear you," I said, rock exploding from my hand.

The Homie Shopping Network was the only mall in the neighborhood. Periodically, a brother would knock on the door with a little black-and-white TV. A gold chain. A selection of Timex watches. Two hangers full of slick slacks. To enhance sales and alleviate nerves, the salesmen were always very courteous and professional. Moms bought my first real dirtbike from a young HSN brother. He held the erect red bicycle by the handlebars with one hand, while using the other to display and close like a veteran used-car salesman. Something hot and cool was always for sale at 913.

Seeing the neighborhood's free-enterprise system up close inspired the brainflash I figured would change my life—a Kool-Aid stand at the front entrance. It was a can't-miss plan. People were constantly coming in and out of the complex; it was a hot summer; I had access to Moms's cherry Kool-Aid recipe. My only concern was someone bigger coming over and robbing me of my loot. I decided to ask Ricky to be my partner. Ricky lived upstairs, across the courtyard, kitty-corner to us. He answered the door in his beanie.

"Wassup, cuzz?"

"Wassup?"

"I got somethin I wanna talk to you about. Let's step out to the back."
We walked downstairs, out the gate, into the alley.

"You feel like making some money?"

"Naw, cuzz, I don't wanna make no money," he deadpanned.

"You know how hot it's been, right? I want us to set up a Kool-Aid stand right in front of the building. Fools be through here all day long, cuzz. You know they gotta be thirsty. Instead of going all the way to the store, they get the real thing right here. Homemade. And wait, we can use Moms's recipe."

He did the grunt-chuckle that represented his laugh.

"Nigga, how can you have a recipe for Kool-Aid? It ain't nothin but colored sugar water."

"You know what I mean, not a recipe, but how she makes it. She slips lemon and orange slices in it. Trust me, it'll kill people. But listen, we'll sell it for, like, ten cents. Who wouldn't come out the pocket with ten cents for some ice-cold Kool-Aid? Nigga, how many cups of Kool-Aid could we sell on a hot-ass day? This is nonstop money, man. You down?"

"I'm down."

"Awright, let's shake on it."

We went halves on the sugar, Kool-Aid, paper cups, lemons, ice, and oranges. Ricky's moms let us use her big pitcher as a server.

We set up a little table with our sign hanging from the front:

Homemade
CHERRY KOOL-AID
10 Cents

Ricky and I stood in front of our building like hotel doormen. All afternoon. We shooed away our friends if they weren't coming to buy. This was business. We were going for the grown-up clients, anyway. They had more cash.

As we anticipated, many of the people who were in and out stopped to buy drinks and talk to us. What we didn't anticipate were the complaints about too much sugar, too small cups, and the requests for free refills. We just figured these complainers didn't know a good thing when they had it. They were getting high-quality, cherry Kool-Aid right at their doorstep—for a dime.

We also didn't anticipate the sun switching sides. We loved summer because it was hot, and nothing was more fun than playing in the sun. But we weren't playing. We were standing, selling Kool-Aid on the steaming sidewalk. The sun flipped funny-style from friend to enemy.

Near sunset, Ricky and I counted up our change. We had made a little more than seven dollars. Not exactly the fortune I was expecting. It was way too much time away from playing to make $3.50 apiece. We decided there on the spot, the Kool-Aid business wasn't for us. We'd try something else.

Ricky and I agreed to create Money Gang. The idea: to make a gang of money. Our Kool-Aid experience taught us we needed to get help. If we had to do all the work ourselves, there wouldn't be any time to play. We went over to our friend Dante's house, down the alley. Dante was thirteen, the same age as Ricky. I was ten.

Dante could fix anything, but working on bikes was his favorite. He was big-boned and stocky, with a square brown face shaded by a civil-rights afro. Quiet except when he got mad. Dante was also broke and quickly agreed to be down with Money Gang.

Dante said he would disassemble, sand, paint, and reassemble the stolen bikes we planned to bring to him.

Along with Dante, Ricky wanted to include Pig Pen because they had been friends before I moved into 913 Alamitos. I didn't like Pig Pen. He was a liar and shit starter. He called imaginary fouls when we played basketball, and cheated at marbles. I agreed only because I knew Ricky could keep him in check.

At fourteen, Pig Pen was the oldest kid in our building's crew, but he was the same size as me, the youngest. He was in the early stages of short-man's disease. When we knocked, Pig Pen, as always, spoke through a cracked door like he was in a detective movie.

"Hold up, I'll be out in a minute."

To our knowledge, no one in the complex had ever seen inside Pig Pen's apartment, let alone been inside. If he was ashamed of his crib, when he knew how poor we were, he must've been very poor. This belief was supported by his consistently dirty gear and polychromatic teeth.

Pig Pen jumped at the chance to join Money Gang. The four of us, Dante, Ricky, Pig Pen, and I, went behind the alley and began to plot our strategy.

Ricky had an old lawn mower. We decided to walk around and cut grass door to door. This would be our main source of income. As we traveled the neighborhoods, we'd check for unchained bikes. On a different day, we'd scoop up these bikes and bring them to Dante's house.

It was a scary plan. Moms hadn't raised me to steal. She would be mad and heartbroken if she found out. It was gonna be hard to keep it from her. She was a superattentive mother—and an amateur sleuth.

The next morning Pig Pen, Ricky, and I met at Ricky's crib. After buying a can of gas and trash bags, we returned to crank up the lawn mower. We were in business.

Our neighborhood was a mixture of apartments and small, single-story homes. We walked up and down the sidewalks, pushing our mower and carrying our rake and broom. We stopped at every house we came to. Pig Pen argued that since he was the oldest, he should do the talking. After a heated discussion (settled by Ricky), I became our designated negotiator.

A typical conversation would go, "Ma'am, we're going around the neighborhood cutting grass to make money for the summer. We can do your back and front yard for only fifteen dollars. After we cut it, we'll rake up all the grass, sweep your sidewalk, and put everything in a bag for you."

"Well, baby, that's mighty sweet of you, but I'm on a fixed budget. I can't afford fifteen dollars just to get my grass cut. I've got too many other places for my money to go. About the best I can do is ten dollars, and it hurt to do that."

"Ma'am, we usually don't go below fifteen cause that means for all the work we're doing, we wouldn't even be making five dollars apiece in all this heat. But we can see you need your grass cut, and nobody's gonna do a better job than us. We gonna see what we can do for you."

For dramatic effect, I would turn and motion for the other guys to follow me to the sidewalk to talk. We'd circle, interlocking arms over shoulders, football huddle–style, and talk for about a minute. Then we'd break.

"Ma'am, we decided we will go waay down to twelve dollars, just cause you sweet."

They'd usually be tickled enough by our little routine to accept our final offer. The funny thing was that no one ever accepted our first offer. In neighborhoods where the dollar is skinny, trying to get the hook up is a way of life. Negotiating is a necessity.

Next to shooting jokes and slapping necks, my favorite part of cutting grass was listening to the stories about why they couldn't pay that fifteen dollars. I loved the crafting of body movement, gestures, and smiles into their monetary defense. I loved to be in the moment, responding with my still-developing style of verbal jousting. Trying to learn new things with each negotiation.

As the negotiator, I felt personally responsible for doing a good job on every yard. I was well-prepared, since Moms was the Taskmaster of Clean. I had home training spilling from my Toughskins pockets.

We did good work. Residents often offered us something to drink after we finished. Grandmas especially tried to keep us around to talk about school or the importance of hard work. We could tell they saw hope in us. We glowed in those moments. Even Ricky.

That first day out, we made $102. On the way home, we kept stopping to count and recount. Just before we got back to 913, we divided our shares. Thirty-four dollars. It was the first time I'd ever had my own money. Mine. Not some money Mama had given me. Money I earned. When we stepped into the building, we made sure all the kids heard about our cashmonay. We went and bought candy and sodas and chips and pigged out, talking about all the people we met.

When we finished, we broke to the alley. Someone had left a queen-sized mattress outside of a large trash dumpster. We pulled it over next to the garage. The mattress became a landing pad for our acrobatic leaps off the garage roof. Many of the neighborhood kids soon joined in.

Each time Ricky jumped off, he'd clutch the sides of his blue beanie with both hands. He was more concerned about his hat disengaging mid-flight than flying. He wasn't really having fun.

When he landed again, I stepped to him and spoke from my heart.

"Cuzz, we're your partnas. Ain't nobody trippin off your head. Take that beanie off and let's try some wild jumps."

Ricky hesitated, then reached up and pulled the blue covering from his scalp. The bald yellow dome was a full three shades lighter than his face. A shade lighter than his hairless brow. His eyes darted to check the other boys' reactions. They were smart enough to pretend that absolutely nothing was out of the ordinary. Ricky and I climbed, racing up to the garage top, and back-flipped down. Up again, front flipped down. Up again, swan dived down. He was smiling and laughing. Pure energy. We flew the skies until sunset. It was the happiest I'd ever seen him. Ricky was free.

I never saw Ricky without his beanie again. His escape had been short-lived. His smile got caught, too.

By Money Gang's third day out, many of the other kids had heard us boasting and smacking. They wanted to be down. Our little empire began to grow. We didn't let just anyone in. They had to have a special skill. Be able to bring something to the pot. One little boy's thing was going right to Alpha Beta's candy aisle, dropping a big bag of candy down his pants, buying some gum, and walking straight out. He was known for that. He didn't need us to steal candy. I guess he just wanted to be in a group. A few times a week he would appear with his stash. He'd usually steal bags of Hershey's bars and Snickers. I'd allocate a certain number of bars to each member. Write down the names and amounts to keep a running total.

We then sold the candy for half the store price. Whatever our members sold at summer school or at the Rec, they kept half the profit and brought the balance to Ricky—the bank officer.

Two bike-riding boys filled a hole in our initial strategy. As we cut grass, we had planned to case bikes, circle around, and snatch them. The hole: Once we started talking to people, there was no way we could go back and steal their stuff. It wouldn't have felt right. We could steal bikes only from people whose eyes we hadn't met.

The bicyclists told us that kids in El Dorado Estates just left their dirt bikes in their front yards. One of the bikes they were riding was lifted from that white neighborhood. They said they rode crosstown on one bike, with one boy standing on the horse nuts attached to the back tire. When they saw a bike lying unattended, the passenger would jump off to retrieve it. Both boys pedaled home.

They were in.

We told two second-graders we'd give them a dollar for each day they dug in the alley's dumpsters for aluminum cans.

Another boy had a pit bull puppy. He said if we could steal a male puppy, he'd raise and mate them. We could sell the puppies.

In.

Members would show up for our late-afternoon alley meetings with their loot. Like clockwork. We'd go around the circle and talk about our business day. I'd count all the money and hand it to Ricky. Right there on the spot, everyone got an equal share. There was no kitty. No organizational reinvestment plan. We made it, then we spent it. We'd take a day off, hop on our bikes, and explore. The movies, ice cream shops, pizza parlors, swimming pools. Everywhere. Riding as long as our little money would roll us.

The summer of 1978 found me outdoors as much as possible. Spinning.

Inside, it was a different world. I was the same person in a different key.

I was the youngest, the baby. My straight As spelled hope on the irises of my mother. I imagined that the second job she worked was for meeting the extra need I represented. The economics of adoption. She brought me into a home of tough love, hugs, and laughter. My self-created part in the bargain was not to disappoint her.

Moms liked the idea that I was putting my home training to work.

"How's your grass-cutting business going?"

"Fine, Mama. We're going back out tomorrow. I get to do all the negotiating."

"What have you been doing with your money?"

"Buying stuff," I said, my guard rising, feeling the lecture about to fall from the shelf.

"I know a boy smart as you has been saving some of his money."

"I'm gonna start saving some tomorrow."

"Why are you going to wait until tomorrow? Why didn't you begin saving the first day you started?"

"I didn't think about it."

"Why you think you've got that head on your shoulders?"

I pause.

"Baby, as hard as money is to earn, it's twice as hard to keep. If you're as smart as I think you are, you'll start saving some of that money. You want me to hold it for you?"

"No, I can save it myself."

"If you don't have anything to put it in, I've got one of those big Sparkletts water bottles that I got from Alberta. Why don't you put it in your room? That way you can see your money grow right through the glass."

"Okay, Imma do that."

"Imma do that? Boy, listen to how you sound."

"Okaay, Mama, I'm going to do that."

Moms was serious about her mommy job. Working her day gig so much, she may have felt a need to pass down a little unsolicited Mommy Knowledge whenever we talked. Her proverb: There's a right way and a wrong way to do everything. She owned the right way. I inherited her lessons daily. Moms allowed me to argue my wrong way as long as I didn't raise my voice. We debated often. I could never win. She was palming an ace with "I paid the cost to be the boss" written across the top. Trumped, I just took my home training like I knew who was in charge.

Money Gang had been watching urban commerce in action up close. Now we wanted to be down. We wanted to be cool like Friday-night men in the neighborhood. Men who could pull a wad of folded money from a pocket, no sleight of hand.

I loved when these men said, "Look, here go the little leader." They would laugh, and grab the back of my head. I could tell they thought our crew was tight. I lived for that. I wanted their respect and emotional embrace.

Friday-night men seized center stage at dusk. They were different in the night air. More serious. They sought one another's company in front of our building. Some trying to siphon off a little narcotics business before it reached inside. Others just hanging, drinking Olde English malt liquor.

The twisting of those forty-ounce caps signaled my curfew. Nightfall forced me out of their peripheral vision. Away from their clever braggadocio. Away from their nuts held with brio. They told stories of the mommies in my building. The women they stopped by to see when kids were asleep, and left before kids awoke. Called them their women. Women known only after dusk. These men weren't around when Pampers were needed. When the phone was about to be disconnected. These men clocked in on Friday nights.

They extended their territory from our apartment building onto Alamitos Avenue. I would watch them from my bedroom window, which faced the street. It was a mezzanine seat to the action below. High enough to give perspective, close enough to see the players' street-lit faces.

I was mesmerized by the way they communicated. When they were together, under the sway of brown paper bags and one another, everything was exaggerated. Their voices rose, as if the imaginary microphones hanging from my window could pick them up. They wanted people to hear what they were running down. They stood in crescent moons competing for the floor. Charismatic verbal phrasing and sinister stares were prereqs. Maintaining center stage in such competition brought out the best game in all of them. They shot jokes and put a twist on old lies to make them sound new. They squeezed their scrotums for balance and security. Any weak efforts to grab the floor were quickly squelched. These corner men cut one another with sharpened adjectives. They bled but disguised the wounds with *shhhittt* and *fuck you.* They fought and apologized with these words, too.

Often their knives left the realm of the metaphorical. Real blood flowed. Spontaneous neighborhood crisis teams struggled to keep the guns in the trunks. At times, they too were pulled. Luckily, I never witnessed a shooting; pistols were only props waved wildly behind shit talking. I never had to see a death scene.

These strange friendships among grown men were intoxicating for their danger. Anything could happen at any time, as it had before. Friday night was theirs.

One day, Money Gang was in the alley, waiting for Ricky to return to divide the day's proceeds. When he appeared through the wooden back gate, he was with his brother Brian.

Brian was sixteen and the coolest older boy in the neighborhood. It seemed like he was already a man. He carried himself and spoke with the confidence that made other people want to be in his sunlight. The solar power of young black youth.

Brian had what pretty girls called good hair. He kept it in a glistening Afro Sheen ponytail, hanging between his shoulderblades. His smooth pimp-limp walk was the model for all the younger boys. He led with his dipping left shoulder, swinging forward his stiff right leg; soon as it planted, here came that sly left leg, bent, swooshing up just inches off the ground, hesitating slightly before landing with the weight of the body leaning left on top of it. Brian pimp-limped in front of Ricky right into the middle of our half moon.

"I'm gonna start running this game for yall. You fools could be making a lot more money if yall knew what yall was doin. Now, here's how it's gonna go down. The first thing we need to do is find a clubhouse. We can't be out here in the alley, business all in the street anshit. We need a place to chill and handle our paper."

Mad, I turned to Ricky for help, but he wouldn't return my glance. We'd built Money Gang from the ground up. Now he was letting his brother come in and just snatch it? I was mad at Ricky, but I grudgingly understood. I idolized Brian, too.

"Yall follow me over here."

Pimp-limpin down the alley, Brian led us to a small storage garage that was built like an A-frame house. It was behind the crib that was right next door to our building. We walked to the shack's front door, and Brian pulled out a key. The cramped space was the size of a small bedroom. It looked bigger because you could see up into the wooden crossbeams of the A-frame roof. Brian didn't tell us how he hooked up the clubhouse, but once all the guys squeezed inside, the transfer of power was complete. He had everybody's attention, including mine.

After Brian took over, Money Gang wasn't as fun anymore. A lot of the appeal for me had been in thinking up the ideas and working with the group to see them realized. After the coup, Brian became the idea man. We all fell in line.

About a week into his tenure, Brian decided that it was time to expand the business. He wanted to break into the garage of the old couple that owned the clubhouse. The oxygen in the room caught on fire. Young heads were swiveling, checking the eyes of their partners. Not a real father among the eight of us. We were trying to figure out manhood off the tops of our heads. Freestyling dangerous decisions with the abandon of compulsive gamblers. Searching for guidance in a sixteen-year-old ghetto star, shining without a cause. Charisma and the pure adoration of young black boys pushed him forward into nowhere. We followed him there.

"I'm down," Ricky said, looking at us but speaking to his brother.

"I'm down."

"Me too."

A chorus of echoing place markers, marking the line in the dirt they were agreeing to do. I was down, too.

It wasn't until after I left and lay on my bed that the words made their full orbit.

"I'm down."

This wasn't lifting old lawn mowers out of yards, this was robbing somebody's house. Brian said the garage had been fixed up into a furnished sitting room. This was breaking and entering. If the police had a name for it, I knew it was serious. I kept thinking, What if Moms finds out? It would kill her. Her baby in jail—for real this time. I had always tried to make her proud. But this was different. Moms didn't really understand the neighborhood. She didn't understand that a boy had to get his respect. I couldn't be a punk in front of the homies. How would that look? I was a winner. Naw, she didn't understand none of that. I said I was down, I'm was gonna be down—and not get caught.

I was trying to beat nightfall early that evening, rushing home along the alley from Dante's place. I saw the boy just before he fell. He was running and stumbling through the narrow, overgrown lot across the alley. The police officer, running and swinging just behind him, smashed his baton into the teenager's head. As soon as the baton struck skull, the boy's black body lurched forward, his head snapped back, and a curious smile appeared on his face. I had seen boxers manufacture that same smile just after being rocked by a punch. As the three other huffing officers caught up to his scalp, the boy's you-can't-hurt-me grin disappeared into the dirt.

Everyone knows if you run from the police, make sure they don't catch you. He knew the deal. He covered his head with his interlocked palms and curled up roly-poly–style. The four cops were beating him with an athletic frenzy that was spellbinding. I watched like I was in the front row. Saw history and future coalesce.

I was only twenty yards away. I'm sure at least one of the officers saw me but it didn't matter. This was the east side of Long Beach. The police were notorious for kicking black asses; maybe they thought I'd help spread the word.

When the athletes tired of beating, one of them put his knee in the victim's lower neck, forcing face to dirt, tore his hands from his head, and handcuffed wrists behind back. Nigger Position completed, the boy became invisible. The cops stood around catching their breaths, talking shit to one another. Their jocular manner was familiar.

The fear I had of the police was fierce. It lingered during my playtime and into my bedtime. Made me tremble in their presence. It gave them a control over me that affected my self-respect. I was giving in to fear. Everybody felt fear, but only punks gave in to it.

I went home and lay in bed for a long time, thinking about the beating. Maybe it was a sign from God that I shouldn't go through with the robbery.

On the morning of the burglary, we all gathered at Ricky and Brian's crib. Their mother wasn't home. Brian's plan: "Me, Ricky, and Mike will move on the garage; the rest of yall play lookout near the yard and down the alley."

Brian, lock cutters in jacket, led us from the building, through the alley, toward our neighbor's garage. Strolling, he directed the lookouts to their places. The three of us walked directly to the door. Brian quickly snapped the lock and opened the wide garage door just high enough so I could slide in first. Initially, the darkness disoriented me. My eyes adjusted.

There was an antique-looking velvety couch in the middle of the room. Skinny antique lamps on both sides. Old chests and crates were stacked on top of one another against the walls. They were joined by two tall wooden file cabinets standing side by side. Most of the concrete floor was covered with large rugs. Ricky crouched in next, followed by his brother. Brian stood up, his eyes blinking in adjustment. He maneuvered toward the front of the garage, near the door that led to the house. There were two metal bowls shaped like derbys sitting upside down. He grabbed both the bowls to his chest, then turned and pointed to the two swords hanging on the wall to our right. Ricky climbed up onto one of the boxes, and handed the swords down to me. When Ricky hopped off the box, Brian led us out of the garage. One of the lookouts was pressed back into the bushes, eyes jumping when he saw us emerge. Brian motioned for him to wait. Once we passed, he tossed back over his dipping shoulder, "Tell the other homies to go somewhere."

Brian, Ricky, and I went straight back to their apartment. The two metal bowls that Brian set heavily on the kitchen table were filled with one-dollar coins. Brian began to snatch them out by the handful. Ricky and I dug into the other jackpot. Some of the coins were old, with dates from the 1930s and forties. We started to count. Stacking the dollar coins in rows of ten, we had almost forty rows.

Looking at Ricky and me, Brian said, "Since we did all the work, we should get all the money, but we ain't gonna be that way. We'll let the homies divide a hundred dollars, and we'll keep the rest for ourselves. I'll take a little piece extra cause it was my idea."

I didn't think it was fair. Up to that point, everyone in the gang got the same amount of money. That's what made it fun. We were on the same team. I didn't like the way Brian was doing things, but I was afraid to challenge him. He made me feel like the little eleven-year-old I really was.

Still, I was excited to be hanging out with one of the coolest older boys in the whole neighborhood. His brother was my best friend. We had just stolen all this money, and it was so easy. I had advanced to the next level of the game, doing serious stuff like the Friday-night men. I knew that as word got around, I was going to get much respect. I felt baaad. Yet I couldn't shake the nervousness. It was a struggle to sit there with Ricky and Brian and remain composed. I tried to keep my shaking hands from being noticed. I had crossed a line. A wide, busy street. I could go to jail if someone found out or dropped a dime. Worse, Moms could find out.

"Where have you been this morning, baby?"

"Playing basketball with Ricky," I said, happy I didn't have to lie. To chill, Ricky and I had gone balling after the burglary. Moms was sitting at the kitchen table, doing a crossword puzzle. That was her workaholic way to relax. Work the mind.

"Sit down, baby, and help me work this puzzle."

I was glad we had something to extend our attention to. I wouldn't have to deal with her direct gaze. I felt I looked different. I did. I looked at myself different. If Moms could tell, she didn't let on. We just lobbed suggestions back and forth, counting letters to fit in boxes. Moms loved words. She was the only person I knew who could get all the words right in the newspaper crosswords. One of many talents. I admired her so much. I couldn't let her find out about the burglary.

The next day, I was walking down the alley, straining to read the box scores and batting averages in the *Long Beach Press-Telegram*. I was a die-hard California Angels fan because everybody else in the complex loved the Dodgers. I liked to listen to the games on the radio in my bedroom with the lights out. Lying on my bed, imagining I was Big Don Baylor at the plate.

I was so engrossed in the box scores, I didn't see the police car parked along the alley until I was five yards from the trunk. My heart immediately started to race.

"Man, calm down," I whispered to myself.

Two police officers were sitting in the squad car. Just as I was passing the window on the driver's side, the cop turned and looked me dead in the eye.

"You live around here?"

His tone was short and demanding.

"Yeah, I live right in that building over there," I said, lowering my sports page.

"This house next door was broken into yesterday. Did you see anybody around the garage?"

"Un-unh."

"Did you see anyone carrying some swords?"

"Swords, like swords for fighting? Un-unh, nope. But I've been playing football around the corner almost all day, so I don't really know."

I could tell he didn't even suspect I was involved. He started his car.

"Okay, you're finished. Go home."

As I was about to walk in front of the squad car to get to our building, the vehicle lurched forward. I jumped back out of the way. I waited a few seconds to let it pass. The car stayed put. I walked up several steps and started for my building again. The car flexed forward. I reflexed back. I knew something was wrong. I glanced through the windshield, looking for answers, but I couldn't see the driver's expression. I was too scared to try to cross again. My body froze up; my mind became a maelstrom. What if someone had dropped a dime? Maybe the cops did know. They probably wanted me to run in the other direction, through the dirt lot, so they could beat me down. They were going to beat me down. I had to try to get past that car. I took off diagonally toward our building. The car sprang forward, almost hitting me, forcing me back.

"What are you doing to him? Why don't you let him cross?" Moms said, coming out of our back gate.

The police car slowly pulled off past me.

"Come here, baby."

As soon as she embraced me, I started crying and shaking uncontrollably. Mama held me tighter. The intensity of my sobbing made her cry.

"It's gonna be all right, baby. Ssshhh, baby, ssshhh."

I wanted to stop; I didn't like crying in front of anybody, even Moms, but it had been too much. Crossing the line into that garage; my fear of Mama finding out; the police.

"Come on, baby, let's go inside. Ssshhh, it's okay, baby. Ssshhh, it's okay."

beneath zebras

The telephone sweats in my palm like a slippery relay baton about to be dropped. Camille has pulled her hand away too soon; there will be no exchange.

Her congested breathing has become a dial tone. A dulling, digital reminder that I couldn't reach her, couldn't make her understand. I put the receiver down. Right elbow on my desk, my forehead resting in the valley of my palm. Down here there is a dark clarity. Night vision allows me to see all the mistakes I have made.

I leave my desk and walk to the bedroom. I can't get in my bed tonight. I grab a pillow, pull the black-and-white zebra-print blanket off the top, and drag it into the living room. I don't care enough to take off my boots and clothes. I curl up in fetal position on the floor, feeling sorry for myself.

When I wake up early the next morning, I immediately notice the difference. I can't quite place my finger on what has happened, but I know the apartment feels different. It doesn't feel like my candlelit refuge anymore. The candles offer no solace. They are just red wax poured in a tall glass with a flickering wick. I occupy the space like a shadow of a wavering flame. I'm missing.

There is a sick pleasure to giving in: The comfort of not having to fight.

I need to get to my desk, write, then go to school. Just move through to keep my mind occupied. But I can't even get off the floor. I can't escape from under my blanket. Can't shake my circumstance, so I fly into fantasy.

I become the point guard for the California Golden Bears. It's the last moments of the second overtime in the National Championship game against Stanford. We're down by one. Stanford's whole team seems to surge toward me; I see the fear in their eyes. I plant my feet and pull up for the fall-away jumper: 00:01. Three Cardinal players, with their arms and fingers extended, reach for the ball raised above my head. My 45-degree airborne body is tilted just far enough. I flick my right wrist: 00:00. *Bahnnnnnnnnn.* The back-spinning, high-arching ball floats through the air. *Swwisssssssh.* I'm knocked down by hysterical teammates jumping all over me. The Cal Band rushes onto the floor, playing "Hail California." I lie on my back under a sea of Berkeley blue and gold.

I escape on my back for hours. Breakaway layups, no-look passes, baseline jumpers with a hand in my face, behind-the-back dribbles, fall-away three-pointers, drawing charges, ball-hawking chest-to-chest defense, screaming halftime locker-room speeches, pressure free throws in the last minute, postgame press conferences, thanking my teammates, player-of-the-year awards, getting drafted, going pro, buying Moms a house. I doze off and wake up in the NBA. Doze off, bounce back to high school games. I was always a clutch performer then. When the game was on the line, Coach always called my number. In track, the big races brought out my fastest times. I'm always a winner in my past-time paradise. It's the present that disables me.

In the late afternoon, I crawl from beneath zebras, musty from sleeping on the floor in yesterday's clothes. I stand still, heavy, in the hollow living room. What now? The Achilles' heel of fantasy: Once you return to reality, nothing has changed. I decide to get something to drink. I splash some water on my face, run a brush over my hair, and head out the door.

It's hard to manufacture the hard stroll de rigueur for urban foot travel. In the land where appearing to be baaad is the norm, anything less makes you a target. I've been using this body armor so long that it usually falls right into place when I walk the streets. Not today. My spirit is down. As I start walking West up Stocker toward Crenshaw, I have to struggle to tilt my head back. My furrowed gaze feels forced. My dipping stroll seems awkward. Luckily, not too many people are out on the street. Unlike the feel of safely walking up Degnan into the village of artists, walking toward Crenshaw reintroduces the Number One Law of the Hood: Watch your back, cause anything can happen.

The tall palm trees and 1940s Spanish-villa stucco apartments I pass can be beautiful backdrops one moment, and the next, a yellow-police-taped scene of the crime—even in broad daylight.

When I reach the corner of Crenshaw and Stocker, I have to pull my shield on tighter. The L.A. streets are buzzing. On the northeast corner, I come to a packed minimall housing a neon-advertised $1 Chinese food joint, a nail shop, and the requisite liquor store. The northwest corner is held down by the black-owned Founder's Bank. The southeast corner, on which I stand, waiting for the light to turn green, is anchored by a gas station that sells forty-ounces, and single Newport cigarettes for a quarter. The northwest corner holds my destination: the Liquor Bank. An appropriate name for the place where so much black money rests.

The huge liquor mart is the size of a grocery store. When I first moved to the neighborhood, fresh from college sociology, I was struck by the wide popularity of this "bank." Every Friday and Saturday night, there isn't a single Crenshaw Strip business that has more customers. The wide picture windows are cluttered with fluorescent signs usually reserved for tomatoes and Wonder Bread. At the Liquor Bank, they read:

E&J Brandy
$12.99
1/2 Gallon Bottle!

Olde English 800
Tall Can
99 Cents!

College helped me understand the negative impact of liquor stores on black communities. They medicate whole neighborhoods. Painkillers without prescriptions. Cheaper, too. Now, I have moved from cultural critic to patient. I need to be numbed.

I buy their largest bottle of Seagram's gin for the long haul, and a forty-ounce of St. Ides for immediate results. I can't wait to get home.

Slouched gap-legged in my white Queen Anne chair, I feel a certain power as I clutch the thick bottle of malt liquor. Although it's Camille's body, I'm in control now. I want to get blasted, and that's exactly what I'm doing. St. Ides is an acquired taste. The more you drink, the more you acquire a taste for the numbness.

I sit in my chair for hours. When the malt liquor is finished, I sip on straight gin from a tall glass. No ice. I sit and sip and wait for nightfall to enter through my living-room window. It's better company for depression. Finally, night begins to creep in, slow and cautious, joining me. We sit together, forgetting, in the darkness.

I spend the whole weekend locked in my apartment, chained to the bottle of Seagram's. The telephone ringer is turned off, curtains closed. Don't want anyone to hear or see me in this state. I have an image to maintain: community activist and artist putting himself through school. In a neighborhood challenged by so much male dysfunction, I recognize the symbolism of my young black life. I see hope in the eyes of elders when we speak. I can't let them see that I can't handle my problems. I can't let them see my weakness.

By Monday morning, the cheap, dirt-green carpet has me by the back. I don't even try to get up to write, but I know I need to go to school. Since grad seminars meet only once a week, missing class in a ten-week quarter can be devastating. Two quarters away from my master's, I have to at least show up. I haven't showered since Camille flipped on me. Even though I love steaming hot showers, dragging myself into the bathroom is the last thing I want to do. I don't feel like doing anything. I want to stay funky and nasty, but I know if I go to school like this, people will ask me what's wrong.

Standing before the bathroom mirror, I face the reality of my situation. It's hard to look into the eyes peering back at me. My eyes are telling a story difficult to muffle in public. I look empty. My eyeballs seem to have retreated into their sockets, running from the world they see. Days of not shaving has left my face hairy, bumpy, and irritated. Like many black men, my facial hair is curly, so it grows out then curls back into my skin, creating hair bumps. I run my hand across my cheek. It feels like fleshy Braille. I stand in the mirror, touching my face, looking into the eyes of a man who has given in. A man I do not respect.

I get in my 1980 Datsun 200 SX and head north on Crenshaw Boulevard to the Santa Monica Freeway. The farther I drive west, the lighter-skinned the people become in the cars alongside of me. By the time I reach the San Diego Freeway, not only have the people gotten more European-looking, but so have the cars. It's a different world on the west side.

UCLA is tucked away in the middle of some of L.A.'s most exclusive neighborhoods: Bel Air, Brentwood, and Beverly Hills. Turning onto Westwood Boulevard into campus, past the parking/security kiosk, is like entering a gated community of the rich and famous — or at least the kids of the rich and famous.

I park the car and head to class. Linguist and cultural anthropologist Dr. Marcylena Morgan is one of my favorite professors. The black English class, which looks at linguistic retentions from West African languages, is always interesting. Usually I'm heavily involved in the class discussion, but today I'm just showing up. Trying to look as normal as possible. I wonder if anyone can smell the Seagram's from my pores. I avoid all eye contact with the nine other graduate students, and especially with Professor Morgan. I'm embarrassed. I make it through class and awkwardly hurry out after her closing comments.

On the way home, I make a stop at the Liquor Bank.

Back inside my apartment, I resume my program. In the daytime sitting in my chair, sipping Seagram's, hitting three-pointers at the buzzer. At night lying on the floor semiconscious beneath zebras. I stay on this treadmill until Wednesday afternoon. At around 4:00 P.M., a sense of dread starts to emerge through the numbness.

I can handle faking my way through three hours of a graduate seminar, but standing on a stage in front of people I love and respect is another matter. They will know something is wrong. I'll appear weak. At the workshop, the poets come from a space of honesty and truth. In their poems, people have tearfully shared everything from incest to domestic abuse to murder. I have shared my own pain about my adoption. But even in my most vulnerable times onstage, I always had an emotional buffer: the past. I would wait until I overcame the problem before sharing it, so I didn't have to stand in front of the microphone raw. I didn't want to be that vulnerable. If I wrote about issues I had already overcome, I was guaranteed a sense of victory. I could present myself as heroic. A winner. I thought if they saw my weakness, people wouldn't like me. I needed their affirmation.

I sip on Seagram's right into the darkness. It's 7:00 P.M., time to get ready. Time to face my friends. I make my way to the bathroom and take a cold shower. I gargle with Listerine, trying to drown the taste of gin and self-pity. Pull on my baggy blue jeans and oversized blue Levi's shirt.

Walking up the sidewalk toward the village, I try to rehearse what I'm going to say when someone asks what's wrong. Few answers come. The lies I create don't sound believable. The gin makes focusing hard. I cup my hands over my mouth and blow. My breath smells like I've been drinking gin and Listerine tonic. They're going to know. My heart begins to beat faster.

Calm down, Michael.

Up ahead I can see the early birds clustered around the World Stage door. I reach inside myself and pull up the mask.

"How yall doin?" I say toward the ground, not wanting my liquid breath to blow my cover. I set out the sign-up sheet, light the candles and incense, and adjust the mic, making as little eye contact as possible. The room fills quickly. I bounce onstage, feeling so phony it makes my empty stomach churn. The World Stage has a "No Bullshit" rule meant to keep the space sacred and to discourage corny poetry. Now I'm bullshitting, breaking the rule I made up.

After the workshop, Peter J. Harris, a friend and poet, pulls me outside. His concern is folded in his brow.

"Brother, you awright?"

His probing eyes are knowing.

"Yeah, man, I just got a lot on my mind."

Sequoia walks up next to me, silent, and starts rubbing circles into my back.

"Sure seem like it. You smell like you need to talk."

I smile, deflecting his love.

"Naw, man, I should be awright, just going through a little something. I'll get through it."

"I just wanna be on the record with this here. If you need somebody to talk to, Michael, I'm here."

"I hear yall, and thanks, but I'm gonna be straight, really."

I quickly lock up the Stage and bounce before anybody else can get to me.

When Camille starts to leave messages on my answering machine, I know she's reached her second trimester. It's official now. My dream is dead. A woman I do not love is having my baby.

"Michael, I'm just calling to see how you doin. Call me; Michael, I know you're mad, but we should talk. Call me; Michael, I think we should really talk. Call me."

Her digital voice stirred with the alcohol brings out a rage in me that's animalistic, brutal. It retches itself up from the pit of my stomach. Hatred.

One day in early April, I'm sitting on my chair, drunk. On a reflex, I pick up my ringing phone. It's Camille.

"Have you been getting my messages?"

I don't speak. I can't speak. I can only wish.

"Michael?"

I wish she were dead—or at least dying, like I am.

"Michael, you know we have to talk."

It's just a matter of money.

"You have to stop just thinking about yourself. We have a baby to think about."

I hang up the phone and sit in the dark. I listen to my mind spinning out of control. Scaring myself. As angry as I've been at past girlfriends during heated arguments, I've never hit or slapped or pushed or shoved or choked any of them. Never hit any woman. Never. And now, here I am, thinking about trying to have someone killed? I know I could never follow through, but just the thought has me literally shaking.

Camille calls again the next day. I'm drunk.

"Michael, I know you're mad, but we really have to work this thing out for the baby's sake."

I pause.

"I'm coming over now," I mumble, voice barely audible. I hang up the phone.

I make my way to the car and head north up Crenshaw toward Pico. My world has unraveled. I'm about to have a baby with a woman I don't love. All I can do is shake my head. I blow in front of Camille's apartment and keep the car running. I'm going to be just like every other nigga. A stereotype, making black babies out of wedlock. I hate myself. The apartment door opens.

Camille stands at the top of the concrete steps, hands on hips, wearing a midriff top—looking pregnant. I haven't seen her since we were at the clinic three months before. Seeing her belly sends an unexpected shock of reality rushing through me. She begins to wobble down the stairs. My dream is really dead.

She stops five feet from the car and bends over at the waist to look in through the passenger window. She smiles.

"How you doin, Michael?"

I just look at her.

"I think I'll talk to you later. I'll call you tomorrow."

She turns around and wobbles back up the stairs. I sit there and watch her go through the door. I speed away. I need to be numb.

When the phone rings the next morning, I know it's Camille. We agree to meet at noon. For the first time in months, I decide not to drink my breakfast. When Camille bends to look through the passenger window, she says, "How you doin?"

"Cool."

She looks me in the eye. Pauses. She opens the door and slides in next to me.

"Where do you wanna talk at?"

"There's a little park right around the corner."

We drive to the park in silence. We get out and sit on a wooden bench. A few mommies are watching their kids swing, and play in the sandbox. I'm watching Camille light up watching the kids. She looks beautiful and healthy. She's excited to be having a baby. My baby. She turns to face me.

"Michael, I know this is not the way you wanted things to happen. And whether you believe it or not, it's not the way I wanted things either. I wanted to be married when I had my baby. So we're both a little disappointed about how things went down. But that's life, Michael. That's life. We have to move on and make the best of it. We're gonna bring a beautiful baby into the world together. We have to stop thinking about ourselves and start thinking about what's best for our child. We have to let go of all this anger and drama."

I sit there, listening and nodding. Camille sounds like my mother telling me things I already know. She's saying it's time to be a man and handle my responsibilities. She's right.

We drive back to her building. I keep the engine running. We both sit for a few moments, looking straight ahead. Camille leans over and kisses me on the cheek. I keep my eyes on the road before me. She opens the door and gets out. I pull off, crying hard for all three of us.

tongue knot

Just before my sixth-grade year, we received the confirmation that I had been accepted into Newcomb School's magnet program. Ms. Scott, my fifth-grade teacher at Abraham Lincoln Elementary, had lobbied hard for me. She was the best teacher I ever had. Pretty, too. While she was illustrating correct toe-toucher technique during Presidential Fitness Week, a lone breast came into view for a full second. The first tittie I ever saw.

Ms. Scott was always taking me and another student named Sophia somewhere. To basketball games, the circus, and science lectures, where guys in white coats made liquids explode. I knew she wanted us to feel special. She believed in us. I think I liked her so much because she reminded me of my mother. Ms. Scott called our house to inform us about Newcomb, and she got all choked up when Moms put me on the phone. She would have been my teacher in the sixth grade too, but she felt Newcomb was a good opportunity. She pushed me away, forward.

Newcomb School was in El Dorado Estates, the exclusive Long Beach neighborhood where Money Gang colleagues did dirt. I was excited about checking it out.

After the thirty-minute ride, the yellow bus turned past a sign that said EL DORADO ESTATES. As the bus twisted through the winding tree-lined streets, I sensed an odd familiarity about the houses we passed. It hit me:

The homes looked like houses on TV. They were big and brand new. They had large, grassy front yards with basketballs, Big Wheels, bats, and bikes just lying out there. It didn't even seem like a real neighborhood. No graffiti. No alleys.

When we rolled to a stop in front of the school, a current of noisy excitement ripped through the bus. That's when I realized it wasn't just me who was excited by the whole scene. The bus was filled with mostly black kids who'd never seen an environment like this. We were the best and brightest of the ghetto elementary schools across the city. This was our chance for a better education.

Newcomb was the cleanest and grassiest school we'd ever seen. The adults made us calm down before they let us get off the bus.

When we finally exited, they made us stand single file. All the white boys and girls walking from their Brady Bunch homes were gawking at us. It felt weird. It was as if they'd never seen black people before. They were pointing and making strange faces. We were a line of little monkeys on loan from the zoo. In black neighborhoods you just don't stare at people. A young brother screamed, "Whachu looking at?" That stopped the staring right away.

The white kids fascinated us. They talked different. They acted different. They even smelled different—especially when it rained. I think we fascinated them, too, because they immediately embraced us and wanted to play.

A couple of weeks into the semester, one of the little white boys invited me to play at his house after school. He lived right across the street. I said yeah.

By that time, I had grown accustomed to seeing the TV-house exteriors, but I wasn't ready for the interiors. I don't know what I was expecting to see in those huge homes. I guess a larger version of my east-side apartment.

Walking and talking, we approached his wooden front door, preoccupied with each other. I stepped into the sunken living room, down into my own poverty. I remember standing on the thick, padded carpet, looking around, thinking, My family is really poor. It wasn't just the carpet or the long, cream leather sofa or the thirty-foot arched ceilings with square wooden crisscrossing beams or the floor-model color TV entertaining the sofa. It was a feeling of stability, comfort, and safety that touched me. I wanted that feeling for my life.

We walked into the kitchen, where his mother was preparing something. She was wearing an apron. He introduced me. His mother got us a drink from the refrigerator and talked a few moments about school. I could barely pay attention; I was trying to figure out why Moms didn't wear an apron. Its absence confirmed our poverty. I felt I was acting weird. I wondered if they noticed. I started to feel uneasy. I wanted to go play. I wanted to drink my juice real fast and leave, but I was afraid they might think I didn't have juice at home. I followed my friend's lead. He finished, I quickly followed, and we began walking down a hallway, toward the back of the house.

"And this is my dad."

His words caught me by surprise. We were approaching a sliding glass door that led to the backyard, our play destination.

He had veered to the right. In a La-Z-Boy–type recliner, in a little library with bookcases lining the walls, sat his father. My parental introductions had always begun and ended with the mama because the mamas were the daddies too.

Not in this house. They had real fathers here.

He wore glasses and was smoking a pipe, just like on TV. Reading a folded and redoubled *L.A. Times* with one hand like it was a good hardback. He lowered the paper and said hello. I literally could not speak. It was too unexpected and too much. Immobile, I just stared. My face felt warm with shame. I was feeling incomplete.

"Son, what's your friend's name?"

"Mike."

"It's nice meeting you, Mike," he said, smiling, and continued to read, rescuing me. My friend grabbed my arm and dragged me out to play. He never could have imagined the intense jealousy I felt tumbling into that backyard. He had a father, a real father. I wanted a father, too. He wouldn't even have to smoke a pipe or smile, as long as he called me *son*.

Newcomb and its exclusive El Dorado Estates setting expanded my world. It exposed me to how white people lived. How they were educating their children. The teachers were friendly but very demanding. High achievement was expected. We didn't have interschool sports teams. Instead, there was an extremely popular intramural sports program. Almost everyone competed. There was football, basketball, baseball, track, volleyball, and paddle tennis. We divided the sports into seasons, created a playoff system, and crowned a champion (with trophies and MVP awards) for each sport. Even the teachers were involved (the All-Star games were played against them). This sports system brought an intense closeness to the campus. It was the first time I had been in a place where most of the boys and girls liked school.

The summer after I started getting bused to Newcomb, Moms moved us to a bigger place farther east. I knew I was going to miss my friends, but I was glad we moved. I didn't want to be reminded of the home we'd robbed.

Our new apartment was a townhouse behind a home. Near East 15th and California, our place was right across the street from Long Beach Poly High School. Poly was a perennial national sports powerhouse (it also had an oft-praised magnet program called PACE that attracted some of the city's smartest students). The football, basketball, baseball, and track teams were consistently dominant. Most budding Long Beach athletes would dream of one day wearing the Jackrabbit green and gold. For a sports junkie like me, it was like moving next to the Lakers' Fabulous Forum.

In some ways, Poly was better than the Forum. The Forum didn't have the Poly Pop Warner football cheerleaders. Poly hosted a Pop Warner league where kids aged eight to thirteen got a chance to play serious tackle football.

Home games for the teams (with names like Poly Mustangs) were played at Poly's football stadium. Since people knew that many of the past and current stars of Poly came up playing Pop Warner, the games were well attended. Fans wanted to be able to say, "I saw Chris Lewis play as an eight-year-old quarterback." And of course, the parents came out in full numbers to support their kids.

All this activity made being a Pop Warner cheerleader a highly desired occupation for young girls. As the boys practiced and prepared for the season, the girls would rehearse on the dirt track that surrounded the field. A ten-foot chain-link fence separated the gridiron, the track, and the cheerleaders from the Long Beach streets. Neighborhood boys would line up along the sidewalk and watch the girls do their routines.

These butt-shaking performances were personalized by each member and were waaay too grown. They were pseudo-raps fronting as cheers, spoken over funky beats they collectively stomped out in the dirt—with a lot of personality—in supershort skirts.

The only thing more exciting to my twelve-year-old eyes than watching my little tailback buddies bust through the line and break outside for long touchdown runs was watching these thirteen-year-old girls stomping and kicking up dirt, doing their sassy moves on the track.

"Mah name is Nikki. (Other girls: Yeahh.)/I'm so-so fine. (Yeahh.)/If you don't know. (Yeahh.)/I blow yo mind./(Other girls: Her name is Nikki.) Nikki: Yeahh./(She's so-so fine.) Yeahh./(If you don't know.) Yeahh. (She blow yo mind.) Yeahh. (Now shake yo thang.)"

After practice, some of the boys around the fence would talk to the cheerleaders with such charisma that the girls would give the boys their phone numbers or let the boys walk them home. I was impressed.

In addition to their passion for sports, Long Beach brothers had a passion for macking. Being able to get girls to like you by being a clever talker got you a lot of respect. As much as I wanted to talk to the girls, I couldn't. I'd get too nervous and chicken out. After a few days, I finally asked one of the older boys how he was able to come up with such cool stuff all the time.

"Practice, cuzz. I juss practice what to say in the bathroom till I git it down, you know, make it sound smooth. You juss gotta practice, cuzz. When you at home, juss think about whachu wanna say when you step up to em. Then when you see em in the street, don't look nervous, juss step up and spit yo game," he spat.

From that day, I began to secretly practice my little mack lines behind closed doors.

"Excuse me . . . you cheer like you know what you doin. You mind if I walk with you a little bit?"

I repeated these twenty words in our tiny bathroom mirror with my head cocked to the left. Head cocked to the right. Hand slumped in my pocket. Both hands behind my back. One hand behind my back. This was something I needed to get right.

The California Recreation Center, a park known as the Rec, was across the street from Poly. Soon after we moved to the neighborhood, the Rec became home, part two. There was a game room with Ping-Pong, bumper pool, and carom-board pool. A full-length outdoor basketball court with lights was perpendicular to a full-length court inside the gym.

The Rec was the most competitive place I had ever seen. The men who played there took their sports very seriously, and their attitude filtered down to the kids. Small crowds would cluster around the Ping-Pong table to see two teenagers firing a white ball and verbal taunts back and forth across the net. Bumper pool was the same way. So was dominoes. The basketball games were even more intense.

The gym attracted college basketball players from all over Southern California, as well as Poly's star players. Ballers were drawn by the Rec's reputation as a place to test your skills against the best in the area. The sidelines would be packed with people waiting to play, basketball fans who'd heard about the gym, and kids like me who fantasized about future running and gunning. These sidelines crackled with jokes and sports-commentator lines stolen from Lakers announcer Chick Hearn. Ballers on defense who got faked by a sweet move heard screams of "Popcorn machine!" Ballers turning the ball over while trying to make a fancy pass heard, "The mustard's off the hot dog!" I loved all of it.

What I didn't know about the neighborhood until later was that it was right in the middle of Insane Crip Hood. Like in our old neighborhood, "Wassup, cuzz" was the greeting of choice and necessity, so initially I didn't really notice any difference. But as the weeks began to pass and school started for my seventh-grade year, it became very clear that I had moved up into a tougher league.

Most of the teenagers and young men in the neighborhood draped themselves in sagging blue jeans and blue shirts, accessorized with blue baseball caps (or beanies) and blue shoestrings. Bona fide gangstas wore their ironed, folded, and creased blue rags dangling from their back pockets. The wildest ones wrapped them around their heads. Poly's central location explained the sheer numbers claiming the Insane set. After school, the teenage Crips who went to Poly gathered to chill throughout the neighborhood. The veteran Crips (OGs) kept a lower profile, but their presence was felt.

Gang culture had a powerful impact on the neighborhood. It fascinated me. I liked to just sit in the cut and observe. Even the brothers who weren't gang-banging had to embrace a gangstalike hardness just to walk the streets. Any softness was immediately marked and recorded as weakness. The cross hairs on the back of your neck came next. Exploiting targets was the easiest, fastest, and safest way to build a rep. Targets were in demand.

One day, heading to the Rec, I was waiting to cross the street when a brother in his early twenties rode up next to me on a ten-speed. A young teenaged brother wearing a blue beanie, pedaling a dirt bike, pulled up to him and said, "Wassup, cuzz?" The guy hesitated, and said, "Wassup?" The Crip reached over and grabbed the back of the ten-speed's seat.

"Raise up, nigga!"

The guy on the ten-speed punched his hand away and took off up the street through traffic. The Crip immediately followed in hot pursuit.

The Crip caught up to him quickly, tried to knock him off the bike. The ten-speed wobbled, then pulled away. I crossed the street, shaken. It was broad daylight. Something clicked in my mind. I understood in that moment why so many of the scowling men strolled the neighborhood with their fists balled: If you stay ready, you don't have to get ready. I started strolling with my fists balled too. I already had my scowl down.

I took off my scowl each morning when I got off the bus at Newcomb. The lily-white school gave me a chance to just relax and be a student. It was at Newcomb that I began to fall in love with reading.

I already had a love of language from being around so many charismatic, gift-of-gab black folk. Books gave me a chance to deal with language on the page. There was a popular detective series called Encyclopedia Brown. The protagonist was a young boy who solved mysteries in his hometown. The book would drop clues so the reader got a chance to solve the mystery as well. I devoured those Encyclopedia Brown books. Our librarian saw my interest. She'd let me know when each new book in the series arrived. Unfortunately, I wasn't the only one who had a passion for Encyclopedia. It got to the point where boys were madly running to the library at morning break (the first free moment after the library opened). If someone got the jump on me and I missed out, I would be near tears.

No one in my neighborhood could have imagined this sensitivity. I was a quick study. As soon as I stepped off the bus, I stepped into my neighborhood shield. There was no way I was going to become a target. I was hard.

My double life was stressful. Spending most of my day in plush El Dorado Estates meant that usually I had my shield down. I could be just a human being. I wasn't walking through campus with tight fists, eyeballing fools. Over time, the less aggressive environment began to change me. I could feel myself getting softer. I began to feel vulnerable. I used to talk to my best friend, Donnie, about it. Like me, Donnie was bused from a rough Long Beach neighborhood to Newcomb. We began to spend more time at Newcomb's after-school sports program, playing basketball and talking to girls.

When I did come straight home after school, I'd go over to play basketball on the Rec's outside courts. One day toward the end of my seventh-grade year, I was on the court when I recognized a kid walking through the park. It was Bobby, one of the few white kids I knew from fifth grade at Lincoln Elementary. I hadn't seen him since I'd started getting bused to Newcomb. He had the same blond hair and gangly athletic build, except he was taller. One of those cool white boys who was comfortable around black people. He knew how to chill and be himself.

Just as I was walking off the court to call him over, two teenage Crips in matching blue sweatshirts and beanies rolled up to him. They were riding dirt bikes. As one passed by, he threw a wild roundhouse that hit Bobby right in his nose. Blood splattered. He went down. Like a tag-team veteran, the other Crip immediately leapt off his bike and started kicking Bobby in the head. The other boys I was playing with rushed to the fence next to me, oooohing and urging.

"Drill that white boy."

Another kick to the face.

Their presence choked the cry for help hot in my throat. A kick to the back, a kick to the stomach. I was afraid to speak. Afraid to cross that racial line. A kick to the face. Bobby started screaming.

"Pleasssse, why are you doing this to me? Pleasssse."

A kick to the mouth. Blood splattered.

"Oooohhh, they're jackin his ass up."

"Pleassse, stop. What did I do, what did I do?"

Kick to the mouth.

Bobby curled up into a ball with his hands over his head and stopped screaming. I thought, Oh my God they're gonna kill him right in front of us. I still wouldn't go and help. The Crips' viciousness and the cheering cosigners had me terrified. Punked. I always had stood up for people, but this time there would be no screams of "That's not fair!" I couldn't open my mouth. Couldn't make myself leave the court to help. I thought they might turn on me.

A kick to the head.

"Heh! Get off him."

A brother in his thirties, both fists raised, ran up to the boys.

"Get off him."

The cat was serious. The Crips said something to him, then sped away on their bikes, laughing. He helped Bobby to his feet. It seemed like his whole face was a bleeding wound. His formerly blond hair was a red matted mess. The man grabbed him by the arm and walked him out of the park.

The ball players were going crazy.

"Didchu see that? That fool got worked, cuzz."

They provided spontaneous instant replays all over the court: swinging, kicking, laughing. I leaned back against the fence, staring blankly at them. I knew that kid. I liked him. He was cool. I had just stood by and let him get jumped. What kind of friend was I?

I was devastated by Bobby's beating and my response to it. I didn't go back to the park for weeks. I would stay late at Newcomb, catch the last bus home, and chill in the house, watching TV or reading. At a very early age, I had to deal with very complicated issues. Did my being black mean I couldn't help a white friend? What if the boy had been one of my new white friends at Newcomb? Would I have stood by and let him get beaten, too? I didn't know the answers. All I knew was that I felt vulnerable and weak. I was ashamed of myself.

As the end of my second year at Newcomb approached, I drew inward. In the past, my neighborhood was hostile, but not toward me, so the hostility was exciting in the way danger can be exciting. But getting off the school bus each late afternoon, I began to recognize my neighborhood as hostile toward me. By my last month of seventh grade, danger had lost its appeal.

Coming home to the neighborhood then became an act. As opposed to being hard, I began to act hard. The gentle side of my personality threatened to make me a target. I was getting older and bigger. Gangstas in the neighborhood paid more attention to me when I walked the streets home.

You grow up fast in the hood because you're chased out of childhood. The scabs from sore lives split open, spilling pus all over the streets you have to walk. You're constantly stepping into black pain. The urban oxymoron: The ghetto slows you down and speeds you up at the same time.

I'm not sure if my stuttering was brought on by the neighborhood stress, but it began in earnest as seventh grade was ending.

After school one day, I walked over to the Rec's outside courts to play ball. The courts were crowded with young players trying to get their skills tight so that when they got older they could play inside the gym. Other junior high school players filled the sidelines, shooting jokes, waiting for their games to come up. I walked over to the court with the shortest wait.

The routine for getting a game involved finding out who was last on the invisible waiting list and claiming the spot after that person. I stepped up behind the basket into the crowd of familiar faces.

"Wh-wh-wh-wh-who's got last?"

As the heads turned, I felt the blood rushing to my face. The laughter and jokes deepened the color.

"Damn, nigga, wh-wh-wh-whachu say?"

More laughter. I tried to play it off by laughing, too. Humor was a short-lived coping mechanism because it wasn't funny.

The stuttering would just pop up. I already spoke at a fast clip. As I would be rolling along in casual conversation, I'd trip over a word with a hard consonant sound: ba-ba-ba-ba-ba-building, pa-pa-pa-pa-pa-pencil, ti-ti-ti-ti-ticket, ca-ca-ca-ca-ca-carpet, Da-da-da-da-da-Darnell. When it would happen, the person I was speaking to would drop his eyes. Embarrassed for me. Sometimes I would look down, feeling my lips tapping each other, trying to get the words out. I also began to slur words. Basketball became bahetbahl. Playoffs became puhyoffs. Exercise became essercise. It was as if I were losing control over my ability to coordinate my lips, tongue, and breathing. Like someone was shooting me small doses of Novocain in my sleep. Saliva built up in my mouth when I spoke. Spittle would fly on people. My lips felt big and sloppy.

By the beginning of my eighth-grade year, the condition had worsened. Before the onset of the stuttering, I would sit in the front of the class, loving the competition of trying to answer the teacher's questions before anyone else. I was also conscious to be articulate because Moms had informed me about the connection between speaking ability and perceived intelligence. It was an even stronger connection when black people were speaking among white people.

The teacher would pose a question, and I would hesitate to raise my hand. I would rehearse what I was going to say several times before I spoke. These silent rehearsals just made me more anxious. When I finally did raise my hand (if the question wasn't answered by that time), I spoke with a nervous quickness, running my words together. I would feel my face redden as classmates shot glances at me. I sounded dumb. I knew that's what they were thinking. One of those bused-in black kids. He can't even talk right.

Outside of class, if I really concentrated, I could make myself slow down and enunciate clearly, but as soon as I got excited about a topic, I would start speaking fast again, then the stutter: ba-ba-ba-ba-ba-beautiful. That look people gave me, a swirl of shame and pity, would devastate me. I thought that maybe if I practiced speaking aloud to myself, it would help.

When I assumed no one was looking, I would begin an imaginary conversation with myself, trying to enunciate and say certain words without stuttering. I'd do it walking to the bus stop in the morning, from the bus stop in the evening, at home in my room. I didn't want people to think I was crazy, so I exercised caution. When I would walk past someone, I would allow the conversation to continue in my head. I began to notice that my mental speaking voice didn't stutter. It was only when I opened my mouth that the words began to trip and fall.

The stuttering began to affect my life dramatically. The anxiety of not knowing if I would be able to communicate when it was necessary unnerved me. I always had been articulate. I always had used my speaking skills to get people to like me. If I couldn't speak well, how would I get people to accept me?

When I really concentrated, sometimes I could hide the stuttering. At other times, my mouth seemed to be detached from my face. It was always the worst when I was in class.

Teachers began to call on me more because I stopped raising my hand voluntarily. When it was time for me to speak, I could feel my heart pounding, the tingly pricks of anxiety live-wiring my body. When words got stuck, my face would tense and contort like the face of a bodybuilder trying to bench-press more than he should.

I felt ugly and deformed during those times. The students around me strained to listen and understand. When the words would finally start to come, they'd gush out, spittle wetting their rushing entrance into the awkward air. A hot silence always followed, creating a space no speaker wanted to enter into immediately—not even a teacher.

During my last year at Newcomb, a black English teacher named Ms. Jones was hired. She was the first black teacher I had seen at the school. A veteran, the middle-aged woman liked to verbally joust with students. She was smart and feisty. She challenged students to test her.

Though I didn't talk much in class, I did well. The school was having a speech contest to celebrate the founder of the school's birthday. After class one day, Ms. Jones pulled me aside.

"Have you thought about entering the speech contest?"

The question itself scared me.

"No, I haven't."

"You write well; I think you could do a good job. To my knowledge, no black students are entering the contest, and I think it's important that we're represented. Don't you?"

I knew she could tell I stuttered. Was this some sort of test? She sat there, looking at me, waiting for a response.

"I'll be here to assist you if you need any help; we'll make sure you'll have them on their feet, clapping."

We spent the next couple of weeks working on the speech. I would bring my drafts to Ms. Jones, and she would tell me what she thought would make it stronger. I'd take her suggestions and keep practicing, repeating the speech aloud over and over again in my bathroom mirror. On the day of the contest, I couldn't think about anything else. I knew that meeting this challenge could give me the confidence to slay the anxiety crouching near whenever I opened my mouth.

The five orators sat on the balloon-rimmed stage in front of the entire school population. Mrs. Newcomb, the septuagenarian widow, was sitting next to our principal, who was sitting next to us. I wanted to go first. I felt that if I dove in, things would go smoothly.

The first speaker's name was called. As she read her speech, I remember focusing on the words. How normal they sounded. I began to wonder whether my words would come out right. What if I were to stutter in front of the whole school? In front of all my friends and teachers? I wasn't second. I had to sit through the whole third speech, too. My confidence was flagging. I just wanted to get it over with. I had my speech in my lap. I sat there, reading, listening to the words form crisply in my mind. I wasn't fourth. God, I was going to have to go last. It was getting difficult to hold my nervousness in check. Each time I would start practicing in my mind, I'd become distracted by images of me at the podium with no words coming out.

"Next we have Michael Datcher."

My heart started thumping soon as I heard *Michael*. I stood up, smiling. I could feel the phony expression shaking like the speech in my hand. I put the speech down. It was too low for me to see. I looked up quickly. The people in the audience, sitting in neat rows of white chairs across the sprawling soccer field, were waiting for me to start. I could hear them rustling. I picked up the shaking speech in both hands. My face began to warm.

I opened my mouth. I was short of breath. No words were coming out. I felt my face strain. I bowed toward the mic as if it would bless me. Consonants and vowels exploded. A barrage of wh-wh-wh-wh-wh-wh-ka-ka-ka-ka-ka-mm-mm-mm-mm-mm. A bouncing, indecipherable tangle of slurred notes. My face was on fire. I knew the audience couldn't possibly understand anything I was saying, but I pushed on. If I stopped, I'd have to look up from the paper into the audience's gaze. Watch their eyes drop like horizontal rows of translucent dominoes falling on the manicured lawn.

Instead, I kept going: ba-ba-ba-ba-ba-du-du-du-du-du-ta-ta-ta-ta-ta-ta-pi-pi-pi-pi-ca-ca-ca-ca-ca. I started speaking faster, to get through this ordeal. Pressing more. Stuttering harder. Amplified over junior high school loudspeakers, the halting speech sounded like Max Headroom making fun of Stepin Fetchit. But it was me on the PA system, embarrassing myself. It was my mayday, mayday, voice flying over neat platoons of people, sitting in front of me: tu-tu-tu-tu-tu-ah-ah-ah-ah-tu-tu-tu-tu-

tu. Tightly clutching the vibrating speech, I became a stuttering nose dive, spiraling down through the last page.

"Th-th-th-thank you."

I pivoted, my hand reaching for the chair behind me like a blind man feeling his way. Speech in lap, I couldn't make myself look up. I turned the page over so the words would stop staring back at me.

daddy

This is my baby. I've got to take care of my child. This is flesh of my flesh.

I sit on my chair, repeating this truth aloud to myself. Over and over and over again. Flesh of my flesh. I need to feel my lips meet to shape these words. I need to hear them coming out of my mouth. Over and over and over again. Flesh of my flesh. It becomes a game in which I convince myself of what I already know. The game's only rule: I can't win. I can only make decisions that remind me of the rule.

Decision number one: I need to get a job with benefits. Freelancing allows me the freedom to maintain my bohemian lifestyle. I love working for myself. Not having to answer to anyone about what clothes to wear, what time to come in. In a plot twist, impending fatherhood strangles the boheme.

After I finish UCLA in June 1994, I have an artist's residency commitment to fulfill in Ohio. I know once I return, I'll have to start sending out résumés. I'm still feeling resentful toward Camille. Although I know we created this dilemma together, my heart points a finger at her. I blame Camille for this child I do not want. I blame her for this guilt. For this lost dream.

We talk on the phone, but I don't see my baby's mama much. Each time I'm in her presence, I feel like I got got.

When I get back from Ohio, it's early July. I call Camille.

"It's Michael."

"You think I don't know your voice? How was the trip?"

"It was cool. How you feelin?"

"Very pregnant. All the weight's been making my back sore. It's all your fault, too. I hope you feel bad."

"You need anything?"

"What I need you won't give me. Keeping that good thang all to yourself—or, should I say, just keeping it from me?"

I let that one go.

"I've been going to the Lamaze classes; they've been helping. Since you back, you wanna start going with me?"

Silence.

"Fuck you, Michael," she says calmly, and hangs up the phone.

I'm not ready to have that kind of intimacy with Camille. I couldn't handle sitting there, rubbing her belly. My spirit is still not right.

In between sending out résumés, I'm freelancing full-time, writing about politics, culture, and music for *Vibe,* Pacific News Service, and publications around the country. Stacking chips so I can take care of my baby. She's due in August. I don't have much more time to get my head together.

I've been waiting for this call so long that when the phone rings, I know it's Camille.

"You've gotta baby girl, Michael. You're a daddy," she says with a mixture of anger and triumph. On the day I always imagined would be the happiest of my life, I'm completely devastated.

"What's her . . . ?"

The shame of having to ask my own daughter's name.

"Nicole Ann Datcher, born August 30, 1994, eleven-fifteen P.M. Eight pounds, four ounces, looking beautiful like her mommy—with your yellow-ass complexion."

"When can I come and see her?"

"I'll let you know. I gotta go." *Click.*

I thought I had prepared myself, but I'm not even close. I learn that you never get prepared for your dream's flatline. I have fathered a baby by a woman I do not love.

I keep thinking back to when Moms told me I was adopted. The zeal I had for my fantasy family. I wanted something different. Special. I wanted to be in love, married to my soul mate. Wanted to get the news of the pregnancy with her. Embrace. Make love. Wanted to be up in every Lamaze class, helping her breathe, rubbing the belly that held our future. Wanted to be in that delivery room every minute of labor, holding her hand. Wanted to watch new life come into the world. Hold fresh life in my arms, fresh hope in my hands. God, I wanted so much. I needed so much.

I wasn't even in the delivery room. I wasn't there for my daughter when she entered the world. I can't say I was among the first to see her. God, what kind of father am I gonna be? If I wasn't there for her at the violence of birth, will I be there for her at other times of trouble? Will I be there when she needs me? I've been a father for two days and already I'm missing in action. Already a stereotype. The very thing I hate, the very thing I rail against, I'm on the road to becoming. I need to be numb. I leave the house, heading for the Liquor Bank.

sex, lies, and videotape

The summer before I started high school, Moms got us as far out of the hood as her paycheck would take us: Cerritos. The racially mixed neighborhood thirty minutes from Long Beach was so suburban that it was hard for me to believe we could afford to rent the crib. No El Dorado Estates home, but it was a corner house with nice-sized front and back yards. The avocado-green exterior didn't do justice to the interior. The living room had twenty-five-foot arched ceilings. There was a huge carpeted kitchen (matching avocado green), and a small den with a sliding glass door that led out to the backyard.

The neighborhood was about 50 percent white, 20 percent Asian (mostly Filipino), 15 percent black, and a 15 percent mixture of folks from around the world. Basketball backboards and hoops hung from most of the garages. They were among the first things I noticed as we drove the U-Haul through the neighborhood. What luck. Moving to a suburb with basketball lovers.

As we were unpacking the truck, a high school girl came up to welcome us. She wasn't especially fine, but she seemed genuinely nice—and she was wearing tight cutoff blue jeans and a pink halter top.

"I'm Tiffany," she said, reaching out to shake my hand. "I saw your truck when you first pulled up. I wanted to stop by and welcome you to our neighborhood. It's a nice, quiet place. It's really super."

She sounded like the white girls at Newcomb.

"Thanks. I'm Michael. Where you stay at?"

"I live nearby."

"Seems like we're neighbors, huh?"

"Yes, that's right. We sure are."

"I need to help my folks get this truck unloaded, but why don't you come back later and we'll talk some more?"

"I think I'll do just that."

She reached out and shook my hand again, then walked down the street.

Not a bad start to a new neighborhood.

Later that evening, the doorbell rang. Through the screen, I could tell it was a woman, probably another neighbor. When I got to the door and heard her say "Hi," I knew it was Tiffany.

"Who's at the door, Michael?" Moms yelled from the kitchen.

"It's Tiffany, the neighbor we met today."

I opened the door and invited her in. She looked very different. Her hair was curled under into a Kim Fields bob. She was wearing a pink dress made from material that stretched. It rode up when she walked. She had on foundation, which covered the blemishes I'd noticed earlier. She was wearing red lipstick—and was smiling real hard. I could tell that she was enjoying my excited reaction to her. As we stood there talking awkwardly, I kept glancing at her breasts. She wasn't wearing a bra. Her nipples seemed like jelly beans glued inside her dress. I was all shook up. I thought, If Moms sees her, she'll make her feel uncomfortable or ask her to leave.

"Lets go to my room and talk."

When we got to my little bedroom, I closed the door. I was trying to be cool but was having a difficult time. I had never had a girl in my bedroom before. Definitely not a girl with jelly bean nipples. Although most of my friends at Newcomb had been having sex since the sixth grade, I was still a virgin. They would sit around and tell stories, often verified by other homies who were there—or by the girls themselves. I would toss in my stories, but they were always lies. The guys began to catch on when someone confronted me and asked what the color of come was.

"Yellow."

I argued my position vehemently.

"Sometimes it does come out yellow."

Word began to spread.

"Datcher's scared of pussy."

They were wrong. I was terrified of pussy.

I didn't want to have sex, then have word get out that I didn't know what I was doing. One of my biggest fears has always been getting embarrassed in public. My Newcomb homies would have teased me first period to seventh.

We were sitting side by side on my twin bed with our thighs almost touching. I could feel my dick harden in my jeans. I could tell she knew I was nervous. She seemed to be enjoying it.

"Did the unpacking go well?"

"Yeah, it was cool. Everything is pretty much straight."

She seemed so different now. She was talking softer and sitting so close.

"Do you know what school you're going to?"

"It looks like the one on Del Amo."

"What grade are you going to be in?"

I was a little ashamed to tell her, considering how grown she was making me feel.

"Ninth."

"Wow, I thought you were older. You carry yourself with a lot of maturity. You must be, like, fourteen, right?"

"Yeah. How old are you?"

"I'll be seventeen next month. You mind if I take my shoes off? I just bought these, and they're a little tight."

"Knock yourself out."

Tiffany used the toes on one foot to peel the shoe off the other, then reversed the process. She lay back on the bed and looked at me. I hesitated and looked back at her for a few moments. It's hard trying to appear cool and deciphering clues at the same time. I knew Tiffany's lying back was a pretty big hint. She wanted me to do something. I figured I had to at least try. I leaned over on top and french-kissed her. She placed my hands over her breasts. Yess. I had to see them. I pulled one of her shoulder straps down. Her left breast sprung free. The thick, dark-brown nipple obstructed my view.

"Bite it."

Her flesh collapsed between my teeth.

"Har-der."

The deepness of Tiffany's voice startled me; the urgency of Mama's voice snapped my head up. She was calling me from the front room. My pupils became silver dollars.

I could feel Tiffany staring at me. She saw the panic in my eyes. I tried to recover with a smile, but it was too late. I wasn't cool and mature. I was a pre–ninth-grader.

"I think I should be going now."

"O-ka-kay, if you think you should. It is getting ka-kinda late."

"Yes it is."

Tiffany's breast and smile disappeared. I walked her to the front door. We said good-bye.

"Michael, can I talk to you for a second?" Moms said, summoning me into the kitchen.

She was standing among boxes at the sink, unwrapping dishes from newspaper and washing them. She turned to face me, toweling her hands dry.

"Baby, when you have female company over to the house, you entertain them in the living room. You don't bring them back to your bedroom. I know you were just talking, but it doesn't look right and it reflects poorly on that young girl. You just don't do that sort of thing, okay?"

"Okay."

The next day, I took a walk through my neighborhood, hoping to run into Tiffany. On the way back, I saw her outside her house, a two-story white-and-gray home with a huge RV parked in the driveway. When I walked up, Tiffany was talking to a pretty white girl with blond hair running down her back. She, too, was struggling to keep her acne on the downlow with a liberal application of foundation. She was wearing a Black Sabbath T-shirt and tight white shorts.

Tiffany again was in cutoff jean shorts and an oversized T-shirt. She introduced the girl as her best friend, who lived around the corner.

Two junior high school–aged boys came rambling out of Tiffany's front door. One black, the other white. It was Tiffany's little brother and the little brother of her best friend. As we talked, the two boys ran around the yard chasing each other. The young white boy ran behind his sister and pulled her T-shirt up. She wasn't wearing a bra. Her large pale breasts just hung there for a second, until she snatched her T-shirt back down. Her little brother, clearly aroused, ran off laughing with his little black horny partner. Tiffany seemed to be looking at her friend's titties as hard as I was.

The friend excused herself to go to the bathroom. As if on cue, Tiffany grabbed my hand and led me through the house's wooden side gate. The chimney was a ten-foot walk-in. She stopped, leaned her back into the right-angled corner, and propped her leg up, pulling me into her body. We started grinding and kissing and groping. She wasn't wearing any underwear. Hands shaking, I pushed a nervous middle finger inside of her. Her body engulfed it, pelvis pumping. She closed her eyes and spread her arms back, holding on to the chimney bricks behind her. She left me. I just stood there, listening to her heavy breath, watching her ride my finger, wetness oozing down into my palm. Suddenly, Tiffany's eyes flashed open.

"Get outta here!"

I shot a look behind me. Her little brother had his big head poked over the gate, his eyes electric. He didn't budge. Tiffany began to pump her pelvis harder.

"Get out of here," she said slower, less convincingly.

I glared at him. He jumped off the fence. Tiffany's pumping body began to come all over my hand. It was white. I had heard so much about orgasms from all the shit-talking sessions at Newcomb, but I couldn't have imagined the intensity. The force of her double-clutching pelvis, her quick breath, the guttural moans, my opaque palm. I was spellbound by her scrunched face. How every few thrusts of my finger brought a new wrinkle, a slight shift in facial expression. Her uncut pleasure was instantly addictive. It was the most excited I had ever been in my life.

Tiffany and I started hanging almost every day. There was an openness about her I found magnetic. While I was always trying to be cool, I had the sense she was just being herself. That self was smart and very sensual. A week into our making out, Tiffany said, matter-of-factly, "I think I'm a nymphomaniac."

I had heard the white boys at school talk derisively about girls who were "nymphos," but I didn't know exactly what it meant. I was too cool to ask. I gathered they were easy girls, as the white kids called them. Nasty. Tiffany didn't seem embarrassed by her nastiness. She thrived on it. She was the first person who ever told me she masturbated. It wasn't a confession, it was a declaration.

When we weren't talking about sex (all my stories were made up) or listening to Prince, we were kissing and groping. Tiffany never wore panties, which gave groping an added charge.

After a week of heavy petting, I began to get scared. I was too ashamed to tell Tiffany I was a virgin. I had tried to create a sexual history wild as the one she proudly shared with me. Each time the petting was about to cross into intercourse, I'd find an excuse for us to stop. It really aggravated her. I was stuck. I was afraid that if I didn't follow through, she'd kick me to the curb. If I did follow through, she'd see my sexual history was make-believe and I'd end up on the curb anyway.

It was the middle of the week, so when I rang the doorbell and her stepfather answered, I was taken off-guard. Tiffany talked a lot about her stepfather. She didn't seem to like him very much. It was her stepfather's house, her stepfather's RV, her stepfather's money. He was an extremely large, heavyset man. He had an intimidating presence, and he knew it.

"Is Tiffany home?"

"Who are you?"

"I'm Michael, a friend of T-Tiffany's."

"A friend from where?"

"I just moved down the street."

"Tiffany! Some boy's out here to see you. Wait out here."

He went back inside, slamming the door behind him.

Later that day, sitting on Gridley Park's grass, Tiffany told me that the stepfather was trying to get at her.

"He's always looking at me crazy, making little stupid comments. 'Your ass is starting to get nice and round, girl.' Can you believe that? I can tell he wants to do me. Pervert. I didn't tell my mother the grimy details, but I told her he's been making me feel uncomfortable for a long time, making sexual comments. She said she didn't believe me. I don't believe *her*. It's so obvious. She said he was probably just joking with me. Said I should stop walking around the house half naked anyway. I'm her daughter. How can she take his side over mine? She acts like she's scared of him. The weird thing is, sometimes I wonder what would it would be like to just give in and let him have it. His thing must be massive."

"Don't say that!" I blurted out. I was hurt that she would even be thinking about having sex with someone else, let alone her fat stepfather.

She smiled, her lips pantomiming. "Isn't this cute, little Michael is jealous." I kissed her hard. She stopped me.

"Give me your shirt."

I had been playing basketball before I went to see her and I had my gear on. Oversized basketball jersey, baggy shorts, and sneakers. The ground was still wet from the sprinklers. I thought she wanted to lie on top of it so we could really make out. I pulled it off. She looked around. There was a soccer league game in progress about 100 yards from the tree we had been sitting under. She pulled my jersey over her head and pulled down her shorts—and lay back on the grass.

OhmyGod. It was going down. I kneeled in front of Tiffany and positioned myself between her legs. She was lying there, looking at me intensely. I was afraid to make a wrong move under her gaze.

"Come on, Michael," she said in the low, husky voice that materialized when she was especially turned on.

I lowered my shorts enough to free myself. I didn't want to look down and guide it in with my hand. That seemed amateurish. I wanted to find my way there naturally. I began to poke and slip and miss and poke and slip and miss. She was so wet I kept slipping and missing, slipping and missing. A slight panic began to rise in me. Her heavy breathing, a response to my hard dick sliding all over her lubricated thighs, kept me trying. I thrusted hard. She closed her eyes. She began to pump her pelvis. I pumped back. I just kept pumping, and thinking, I'm not a virgin anymore, I'm not a virgin anymore. Suddenly she stopped and opened her eyes. She looked mad.

"What are you doing?"

I hesitated. I didn't know what to say.

"You're not inside me."

My God. I looked down. I wiped the wet soil off my penis and used my hand to guide it inside Tiffany. Right away, I saw why sex was such a big deal. The moist tightness made my mouth immediately drop wide open. After almost ten seconds of fevered thrusting, I began to come. When the sensation started to hit, I remember my eyes detonating, my jaws stretching wide. I thought I was urinating in her. I tried to pull out. Too late.

"Uhhhhhhhhhhhh."

It was over.

"Did-you-already-come?" she snapped in disbelief.

I couldn't even respond.

"Let me up."

She pulled up her shorts and gave me my shirt back.

"I'll talk to you later, Michael."

Tiffany started walking back through the park toward her house.

I stood there, feeling stupid. I was humiliated. My budding manhood was shocked back into its seed. I felt like a failure as a man, and I wasn't even a man yet.

For years I had been hearing older brothers talk about having women screaming their names, rocking their worlds. Being able to please a woman had always been presented as a true test of manhood. What was wrong with me? I couldn't even find the pussy. My first real sexual experience was with some wet soil. I was devirginized by Mother Earth. I stood there, thinking, Something is very wrong with me.

High school became a tool to fix myself, to reclaim the manhood I didn't yet have. Living in Cerritos helped. It was nothing like Long Beach. It was grass, trees, homes, and safety.

I spent the rest of the summer working on my basketball skills. Though football was my first love, I had become better at basketball. In the summer between my seventh- and eighth-grade years, I was shooting around at the Rec. Like many seventh-graders, my outside shot was of the 1950s corny set-shot variety. A pushing of the ball toward the basket. I hadn't developed the coordination to shoot the smooth jumper like Phoenix's Walter Davis, Golden State's World B. Free, or Seattle's Downtown Freddy Brown. I could hit the set shot, but it could be blocked easily and got a zero for smoothness.

The jump shot was an art form of rhythm and precision. Just as the dribbling palm was flicking the ball back to the ground for the last pre-jumper bounce, the knees bent quickly, causing the whole body to coil down into itself. As the bouncing ball returned to the dribbling palm, the body would unfurl upward, and both hands would catch it, raising the ball in one motion overhead and extending it up into the trampoline sky. At the exact apex of the jump, the cocked wrist would flick, leaving it limp as the backspinning leather arched over the earth, snapping down into the net like the round tip of a bullwhip. A sweet jumper demanded physical harmony. My individual body parts didn't seem to know their roles.

Something happened that day at the Rec. I was practicing hitting my set shot from twenty feet. I decided to try some jumpers. When I would retrieve the ball and return to the top of the key, I would coil down on the bounce, spring into the air, and flick my wrist. The release felt so nice, so pretty. All net. I ran the ball down and quickly dribbled back to the top of the key. Coil and raise. All net. Retrieve and back. All net. Again. My heart was pounding. The adrenaline had my whole body tingling. All net. All net. All net. It was a miracle.

I really believed God had just blessed me with a jump shot. A minor miracle to some, but to me, I was walking on water. I was afraid to stop shooting. If I didn't shoot enough times, the process wouldn't be imprinted and I'd wake up the next day, back to a set shot. Coil and raise. All net. All net. All net.

Every morning from 8:00 to 10:00 A.M., I dribbled down to parks around Cerritos to buff my game. I wasn't a great athlete, but my experience of winning with Elgin had taught me that if I had a plan and executed it, I could make myself into a great basketball player.

I tried to imagine all the possible situations I would encounter in a game, then created a drill that would replicate each scenario. Faking a defender by dribbling quickly back and forth between my legs, then flashing to the bucket. Ten times on the left side of the court. Shoot two free throws like the game's on the line. Ten times on the right. Shoot two free throws. Behind-the-back drills. Two free throws. Ten jump shots from the right baseline; ten on the left baseline; dribbling full court and pulling up for the top of the key jumper; ten left-hand lay ups; ten bank shots from the right side—and two game-on-the-line free throws after each drill.

I started high school with a lot to prove. My young ego had been smacked. I had wrapped myself in soft leather all summer. It was time to take off the gauze. Time to show and prove.

I made the freshman basketball team as a starting guard. Our center was a five-foot-eight Mexican/Hawaiian kid with incredible hops named Jimmy Cardenas. Our first contest was at home. We full-court pressed the whole game. We were short but quick. Our opponent played a zone. I played a zone buster. Coil and raise. I hit seven of ten jumpers. Fourteen sweet points in my first high school game—and we won.

Coach Johnson was a tough-nosed man who knew how to bring the best out of each player. He saw right away that I was needy. He was hardest on me, like a father coaching his own boy. He even called me son when he was screaming. I played not to let him down. Coach Johnson felt it. When the game was on the line, he called my number in the huddle. I loved fighting through the pressure, the fear, and coming through for him. I spun on his belief in me.

Our freshman team ended the season as league champs. I was a win-

RAISING FENCES ∥ 109

ner again. It felt great. I decided to run track and cross-country to stay in shape for the following year.

I was being groomed as the varsity team's next point guard. We were Southern California's number-one-ranked 2A team going into the play-offs. Our high-scoring forward (future NBAer Tom Tolbert) and number-one ranking meant press coverage for the team. We were high school celebrities.

Yet my stuttering seemed to go progressively downhill month by month, victory by victory. I was losing control over my open lips. I kept them closed as much as possible. My celebrity status gave me an image to hide behind. I became the "cool black basketball player." A stereotype.

My stuttering had drawn me inward, but I could lie in the cut and not say much because my image told people all they needed to know. Although I was an A student, I rarely spoke in class. Outside of class, I held the philosophy that the less I spoke, the fewer opportunities there would be for me to embarrass myself.

At lunch, I would sit on the tables with other black students, listening to them shoot jokes. Each person would take the stage for as long as their charisma could hold the group's attention. I'd think: That used to be me in the circle, battling for the floor.

I had become an observer. I paid close attention to everyone's speaking style. I watched their mouths. I was constantly looking for anything that could help my speech. I tried breathing slower, breathing faster, talking with a slight New York accent, speaking from my abdomen. Nothing I tried seemed to help. I retreated behind my image and adjusted to being on the periphery.

Stereotypes can't have deep friendships. I spent so much time trying to cover up my stuttering that I always had something to hide. Deception is a lifestyle. I couldn't let people get too close to me: They would discover. I created an image and retreated in the cover of its shadow.

By the beginning of my senior year, I was stuttering in my mind. The physical speech impediment had made its way into my subconscious. When I rehearsed mentally just before I was to start speaking, that silent voice stuttered too. It was a devastating development.

∎ ∎ ∎ ∎

I didn't even know there was a speech therapy office at school. The stutterers weren't talking. The clay-colored door megaphoned its occupation in large black block letters. I looked over my shoulder when I slid in at an angle.

The speech therapist would have me read aloud lists of words that began with hard consonant sounds. Do breathing exercises. Record and play back my voice with a handheld device. I didn't know much about speech therapy, but I was hoping for more concrete treatment. A machine to help coordinate my lips, tongue, and breath. A pill. After the first few treatments, it was clear that no such miracle existed. I stopped wasting my lunch period.

Along with playing basketball, I had a part-time job at Taco Bell. It consisted of folding Burrito Supremes and saying, "Welcome to Taco Bell. May I take your order?" With practice, my tongue could handle that.

One day an attractive, light-skinned black woman with shoulder-length hair came in with her man. They stood a few feet from my register, checking out the menu board above. By the way they were unconsciously touching, I could tell they were either married or longtime lovers. Smiling, she stepped up to my cash register. Her man hovered a couple of feet behind.

"Welcome to Taco Bell. May I take your order?"

"I-I-I-I-I-I-I-I-I . . ."

Her smile twisted into a painting in Rod Serling's "Night Gallery." Veined eyelids strained into a slight flutter. Face muscles taut. Mouth stuck open in a pose of horror. She stopped and tried again.

"I-I-I-I-I-I-I-I . . ."

I smiled and kept eye contact, trying to calm her. She stopped, offered a desperate smile, and prepared to try again. She placed both hands on the counter and squeezed the edge tight. The assistant manager at the next register was staring.

"I-I-I-I-I-I-I-I . . ."

Her long fingers clawed the wood counter.

"I-I-I."

She broke. People are so good at masking their emotions, it's rare to see such raw distress. Hurt and water ran along creases in her pretty caved-in face. Her man quickly stepped up, placed one arm around her shoulder, and ordered for them both. She kept her eyes down, away from mine. He paid, and they stepped away from the register. I had never seen a woman stutter that severely before. Men tend to be struck more intensely and more often. I felt for her.

It became clear that ordering food at Taco Bell was a speaking exercise. I was sure she had practiced in her mirror. When she was lost, how did she ask for directions? Was she able to communicate with her own children? What was her marriage like? I wondered if her silent voice stuttered too.

I knew being so attractive made things worse. Beauty is a magnet for attention. The severe stutterer doesn't want eyes on her lips. The woman couldn't make herself stop crying. She and her companion walked out the door. Their food never made it to the counter.

A few weeks after the incident, our boss wanted to promote me to assistant manager. I declined. Being a manager meant asking other employees to carry out tasks. I stuttered hardest whenever I tried to form questions of any kind. How could employees respect me if every time I had to ask them to do something, my face contorted, my mouth opened—but it took three seconds for the words to come out? It was far too humiliating. Turning down that small promotion made me think about my future. Since I had started high school, I had thought about one day becoming a sports writer. But sports writers ask questions for a living. There was no way I could make a living asking questions.

It depressed me to think that I had to find a job that didn't necessitate verbal communication. I loved people, but I couldn't even talk to them. I was going to end up in front of some computer or on some assembly line. My good grades didn't matter if I couldn't work with others.

In my senior year, I was captain of the basketball team and had developed a solid reputation as a clutch performer. Late in the season, during an important league game, I was having the worst shooting performance of my career. Moms was in the stands for the first time. She was always working so hard that she simply wasn't able make athletic events—except on that one night. I was a nervous wreck. I knew the game would probably be my only chance to show her what I could do.

I tried to do too much too fast. I was turning the ball over and repeatedly missing easy jump shots. Our team was trailing by only one point when we got a steal with less than ten seconds. We called time-out.

Under normal circumstances, it would have been my time to shine, but I was playing horribly. I had made one basket the whole game. I couldn't help but wonder what Moms was thinking: Has he been lying all these years? I was hoping Stacey or Glenn would be able to score for us. A victory would take the sting off my disappointing effort. Coach turned to me in the huddle.

"Datcher, can you make the shot?"

All the eyes in the circle shifted to me. It was a ball player's fantasy. Even at my worst, the coach believed in me.

"Yeahh," I drawled for dramatic effect.

He called my play. We inbounded the ball and reversed it back to me on the right side of the court. The opponent was in a zone defense. Coil and raise. All net. *Bahhhhhhnnnnnn.* The gym exploded. The whole team was jumping up and down. I leapt into Glenn's arms. I turned to see Moms and Cyndi pogoing in the stands. In that moment, I understood the power of someone believing in me.

My joy was brief. Our team got upset in the first round of the playoffs. I was first team All League but no colleges offered me a scholarship. I was good but not great. By mid-February 1985, my athletic career was over.

A few months earlier, at the urging of guidance counselors, I had applied to colleges around the country. I applied only to schools that had good basketball programs: North Carolina, Vanderbilt, UCLA, and Duke, among others. If I couldn't play, I wanted to be in the stands.

When the letter came in the mail, I was confused. I had been accepted to the University of California at Berkeley, but I hadn't knowingly applied to the school. Although I had written the name UCLA on my application, I had accidently inserted Berkeley's school code. Berkeley admitted me, but their basketball team sucked. In fact, I didn't even know where Berkeley was. In the sports world, the team was simply known as California. I had to get a map to learn that the school was near San Francisco.

I knew nothing about the university's academic reputation. Nothing about its activist tradition. It was just some school that hadn't been to the NCAA college playoffs in years. I was a little disappointed. Maybe North Carolina would say yes.

Berkeley was the only school that accepted me. My high school had a wall on which they posted the names of seniors and the universities they'd been accepted to. The wall was in the main office, so it greeted the faculty every day. Each name was felt-tipped onto a piece of a colored construction paper, shaped like a football-sized Nike swoosh. Only twelve names swooshed in a school of 2,000.

A couple of weeks after I received my acceptance letter, students on campus began to congratulate me. Teachers whose classes I had taken years before stopped me in the dim halls to chat and catch up. I began to realize that Berkeley had game. I was with a winner.

Some of the students who approached gave me respect, then added the awkward comment: "Now how'd you get in there?"

All they knew were the jump shots, the black-and-white letterman's jacket, *Datcher* printed across the back. They didn't know that my mother's expectation was always the A. She didn't have a handle on the whole college system, but she knew she wanted her kids to be the best at whatever they did. Both Cyndi and Elgin took college courses and eventually graduated as adults.

My Advanced Placement English teacher had gone to Berkeley. She was a white woman in her late thirties who loved literature and preferred her black skirts short. She favored thin black turtlenecks, which flaunted her bralessness while she walked through the classroom, lecturing on Hemingway, Dostoyevsky, and Poe. Well read and well traveled, she spoke her mind quick and sassy to students and teachers. The AP class system had just been created, and hers was among the first on our campus. Ms. Green relished teaching the school's brightest. People loved her or couldn't stand her. I was a fan.

In late April, Ms. Green said she wanted to speak to me after school.

She seemed to like me, so I could tell she wanted to talk about her connections at Berkeley. Help me navigate the system when I got on campus.

After the bell, I walked to her class. I hovered as the last of her students from the previous class straggled out.

"Michael, here, pull up a chair next to me."

I sat facing her.

"When I saw your name in the office, it reminded me of my time at Berkeley. It's a magical place."

She laughed aloud, but for herself. She was smiling, going back.

"When I was a freshman, I fell in love with this boy. It was a whirlwind. Having campus picnics with wine and roses, talking about world politics and our lives. We were creating our own college experience—which oftentimes took precedence over going to class."

I loved the excitement in her eyes.

"At a school like Berkeley, this is going to be a problem. This, of course, is why I ended up on academic probation at the end of my first year. I actually got kicked out but later was reinstated and did fine from that point on. What I'm getting to, Michael, is that Berkeley is a very challenging university. I think you would be better served by a school that is not quite as difficult. Maybe Cal State Long Beach or one of the less rigorous Cal State schools. I simply don't think Berkeley is the best place for you."

I sat there, stunned. It was so far from what I was expecting to hear. Like walking into Spanish class to find that the teacher is speaking German. She was my Advanced Placement teacher. Her students were supposed to be getting into the top schools. I couldn't understand why she would say such a thing.

Though I worked almost thirty hours a week outside of school, she knew I was an A student. My sports victories and awards were reported over the homeroom loudspeaker, so she was well acquainted with my athletic abilities. I had been hearing that colleges looked for well-rounded students.

My mind was racing. I knew there was no way she would have told a white student with my credentials that he should reject Berkeley's offer. I looked at her sideways. Although I had experienced a great deal of

RAISING FENCES 115

racism in my dealings with white policemen, my disdain had not spread
to other whites. My mother had raised us to treat everyone as a human
being. She preached one love. Ms. Green shook me. She wasn't a cop, she
was my AP English teacher. But like all the cops in my life, she was trying to hurt me. This was some white shit.

What if she was right, though? I wondered, What if I can't hang? She's
smart, and she got kicked out. Maybe she was really just trying to spare
me some grief. Doing me a hard favor. Maybe I should try a Cal State
school.

No. This was just some white shit.

"Thanks."

I got up, walked out of class, and dipped home second-guessing myself.

nicole

The next morning, Camille calls.

"Okay, you can come by today. I hope you can make it at two because I've got things to do. If you can't make it, I'm not sure when you can see her."

"I can be there at two."

"Okay, gotta go." *Click.*

Strangely, what I should wear is the initial thought that pops into my mind. I want to look nice, want to make a good first impression for this baby I don't want.

I slip on my baggy black jeans, black Levi's shirt, black boots. I can't help but think of the irony: I was wearing these very clothes when I met Camille.

When I'm nervous, I pace hard. Motion clears my head and calms my spirit. I start walking back and forth in my living room. From my desk to the kitchen, back to my desk, stroking my goatee along the way.

I always had imagined holding our child in my arms and seeing myself in the delivery room. A relative who looked just like me. No question marks. The experience my own father missed out on.

I pull up in front of Camille's apartment and turn off the car. I sit, looking up at the food-stained concrete stairs. Open the door and drag myself out. Lean against my ride, facing the street for a few minutes. Breathing. Automobiles whiz by, heads turning at my streetside meditation. I'm not ready for this blind date. I consider going home and calling Camille to reschedule.

I move around the car, onto the sidewalk. There is no doorbell on the outside of the building, no security phone to reach residents. I have to wait until someone comes out. It hits me. This is the first time I've ever been to this door. Through all of our heated rendezvous, I beeped and Camille came down to the car. I've never met her mother and aunt, who share the apartment. Or her younger sister, who also lives in the building. Now the list also includes my daughter.

A middle-aged Latina woman exits, giving me a chance to enter. Inside, the building looks like a raggedy hotel. On the first floor is a dimly lit hallway covered with soiled, greenish-brown carpet. There are long rips throughout.

Doors at ten-foot intervals line both sides of the corridor. To my left, a row of foot-long rectangular metal mailboxes hang punch drunk against the wall. Banged-up and bent, most of the gold-tinted aluminum boxes don't have locks. Junk mail overflows from the bin beneath, making a pallet on the floor. Balled and crumbled envelopes lie among candy wrappers and suckerless sucker sticks. I detect the faint smell of exterminator spray.

An old wooden staircase stands directly in front of me. A thick pine railing runs down from the top of the stairs to the bottom. The middle of each cherry-wood step is semicovered with a strip of the same dirty carpet in the hallway.

Up through high school, I viewed steps as vehicles to expend energy. I ran up two at a time, as if the ones in between were trap doors. Moms was always yelling, "Boy, quit running in this house."

I climb the carpeted stairs to Camille's apartment one at a time, using the rail as my crutch. No need to skip in-between steps. They all are trap doors. At the top of the stairs, I pull out the scrap of paper with Camille's apartment number. I can feel my heart begin to beat faster. I walk softly, almost tiptoeing to the middle of the hallway. I stop and face the door. Shove the piece of paper back into my pocket. My hands are trembling, but not as fast as my heart. I raise the small O knocker. The door flies open before I can return my hand to my side and look calm.

"Ahhhgh!" a petite gray-haired woman screams, and slams the door. The peekaboo window behind the knocker opens.

"Ooh-Lord-you-scared-me." Her quick-paced, high-pitched voice screeches through the tiny opening. "I-thought-you-were-my-daughter-she-just-left-a-few-minutes-ago-I-thought-she-forgot-something-ooh-Lord. You-Michael-right?"

"Yes, ma'am."

"Okay-okay-hold-on. Camillllle-Camille-he's-here-right-outside-the door-whooo-he-scared-me-he's-right-outside."

Footsteps. Camille snatches the door open.

"Come in."

I step through the door. The raggedy carpet follows me. There is a love seat against the back wall. Camille's mother sits on it, next to her identical twin sister. They glare at me with an odd mixture of contempt and curiosity. Every few seconds, their eyes dart from me to each other, back to me. They seem to be sending telepathic missives. Comparing notes on the father in this circle of women.

Still standing just inside the entrance, I can hear Camille moving to my right, behind the apartment's only bedroom door. To my left, I can see just inside the kitchen. Heavy traffic has ripped up a section of the vinyl floor in front of the sink, exposing water-damaged wood planks. Above, food-caked plates, forks, spatulas, spoons, and skillets rise out of the washbasin like a post-Thanksgiving meltdown.

"You-might-as-well-sit-down," Camille's mother says, looking at her sister.

I take a seat on the couch against the wall nearest to me. I feel the twins' eyes swallow my bending frame. I didn't even notice the baby crib when I entered because of the blankets and jackets lying in it, over it. There's an open pack of Huggies diapers littered among yellow plastic blowup balls, hair brushes, and a phone book.

The crib is a cluttered storage bin until Nicole can make use of it. Scanning the living room floor is an assault on everything-has-its-place. Everything is everywhere: Coke cans, Taco Bell wrappers, two-liter Pepsi bottles, loose diapers, Whopper remains. They keep a nasty house, Moms's voice says through my eyes.

I become conscious of my nostrils flaring. The air is scented with a potpourri of funk: the fragrance of shitty diapers, unwashed bodies in an unventilated room, kitchen trash in a brown grocery bag, days-old dishes, and despair. The bedroom door opens.

Camille walks out in a baby-blue houserobe, cradling a moving blanket in her arms. She doesn't make eye contact as she walks toward the love seat. Her mother gets up and sits on the arm. Camille sits down. Twin noses also dive into the folds of the blanket. Their harsh faces disassemble into cooing smiles. Camille is smiling, too.

I stand up. Heads jerk. Smiles end. I step over and down to one knee. Camille pulls the blanket back and turns Nicole toward me.

My God. Her eyes.

I lean close. Her brown irises lick my face, suck the frown from my lips. Her tiny feet and hands kick and grab with the abandonment of new life. She's so small. I place my pinkie inside her delicate palm. Nicole clutches and studies.

"Nicole."

Her startled eyes dart to my startled eyes.

"Nicole," I whisper.

She smiles. God. So beautiful. This is my daughter. My baby. My head begins to swivel slowly side to side. I can't believe I almost killed you. Nicole's wide eyes can't judge me. I do it for her. My first task as her father.

"I'm soo sorry, I'm soo sorry, I'm soo sorry."

I begin to mouth the words louder.

"I'm soo sorry, Nicole, I'm soo sorry."

I can feel the heat of Camille's family's gaze. They're tripping off me. I don't care.

"I'm sorry, I'm soo sorry."

Camille tries to hand her to me.

I shake my head no. I'm afraid to hold her fragile body in my arms. "She's too small."

I lean forward and kiss Nicole on the forehead. I feel the tears coming. I need to get out of here.

After asking Camille what type of baby formula she's using, I quickly exit.

In a matter of minutes, my world has shifted. I walk down the dark hallway, hands shoved in my pockets, trying to get a hold of my emotions. When I get inside the car, I have to chill. I'm too shaken to drive. I'm disappointed at myself for bringing this baby into the world out of wedlock, but I'm so glad she's here. I've never seen a baby so beautiful. I've got to get her out of that nasty house. I don't want my child living in those conditions. Got to make more money and help Camille get an apartment. God, she's so beautiful. Nicole Ann Datcher. Imma father.

berkeley

Saturday night.

I was standing in our Griffith Hall elevator, talking shit with Nolan, one of my dormmates.

"Hold the door, please," a voice curved in from down the hall.

A thirty-something black man wearing thick glasses with a reddish brown beard, matching mustache, and sideburns glided in. His five-seven frame allowed me to see his hair thinning on top. He thanked us for holding the elevator. I continued with my profanity-laden, black-top discourse. I found that using harsh-toned expletives helped me mask my stuttering. It gave my speech a hardness that helped cover the soft insecurity my stuttering brought forward.

"Is that cross for decoration," the man started, looking at the gold graduation present hanging around my neck, "or do you really believe in God?"

His deep-voiced directness caught me off-guard.

"Yeah, man, of course I believe in God. What kinda question is that?"

"Okay, well, if you believe in God, how you think God feels hearing you cursin with a cross around your neck?"

"Listen, cat, I don't know how God feels. Ne-neither do you, cause no one knows how God feels but God. Th-this is just the way I talk. God ain't trippin off a few cuss words. Hell, God is busy."

The elevator reached the lobby floor, and we stepped out.

"My name is Arno."

"Michael."

We shook hands.

"This is my friend Nolan."

Nolan nodded. He wasn't trying to get in the conversation.

Arno turned back toward me.

"I'd like to invite you to my church tomorrow. Here's my card. The address is on the back."

"What kind of church is it?"

"It's a nondenominational Christian church. We just believe in the Bible. It's called the Church of Christ."

"Awright, I'll see what I can do. If I decide to roll th-through, maybe I'll bring Nolan along."

Nolan shot me a look.

"Well, service begins at nine. I hope you both can make it. Yall take it easy, now."

When my alarm blasted on at 8:00 A.M. Sunday morning, my head was ringing, too. I got up and dressed anyway. It seemed stupid, but I wanted to show up for this brother I had just met. When grown men showed me attention, the spin cycle could kick in at any time.

The church was only a few blocks from campus. Walking up to the building, I was surprised to see so many young people outside, mingling. Church was a place for old black sisters in white gloves and fly hats. Jesus was their first, last, and current love. Church was where they came to spend time with His other women.

As soon as I walked in and sat in the back pew, I knew these weren't real Jeeesus lovers. The old women didn't even have flowers in their hats. Not even the few black women in attendance. Although the church had a multicultural look, it was what neighborhood folks called a white church.

The aesthetic was white. Everything from the unsoulful singing and off-the-beat clapping to Tom Brown, the white, thirty-ish evangelist. A far cry from the black Baptist churches I had stepped into during my youth. No choir working out tunes that compelled parishioners to rock side to side. No black women wildly running around the worship hall's perimeter screaming in tongues. No white-gloved ushers helping them up when they fell.

In place of tried-and-true soul, the Church of Christ tried hard. There was an elasticity about their friendliness. It gave the distinct impression that something had to be stretched for them to carry on. That's probably why Arno, talking excitedly across the room, stood out among the white believers. He seemed genuine. When he finally recognized me, he walked over. I could tell he was surprised.

"I'm glad you made it. What did you think about the service?"

"It was cool. A little different from what I'm used to, but it was awright."

"You could probably get more out of the service if you had a little more background in the Bible."

"What makes you think I don't know the Bible?"

"I'm sorry, I wasn't trying to say that you didn't know the Bible. Our Church simply believes in having a firm grasp on what the Bible has to say. You may have noticed that when Tom was preaching, he asked the congregation to follow along in their Bibles. I've been studying the Bible for years, and I still feel like I have a lot more to learn. I think we all do. If you like, we could get together and study."

I paused for a second.

"Awright, I guess we can do that."

Arno came by my dorm room all summer, carrying his leather-bound Bible. We'd sit on my bed and go over scriptures with a thoroughness that seemed extreme. Arno took this Bible stuff seriously.

His deep convictions made me want to believe, too. He had such a strong faith. A belief that God was real and could do anything. I was pretty sure there was a God, but I didn't really feel Him. Maybe I didn't believe in Him at all, but my desire to want to believe was strong enough to create the feeling of belief. I wanted the kind of faith Arno had. I wanted to be able to call on Jesus and know He was coming.

I wanted the son of Mary to come straighten out the knot in my tongue. Allow me to speak in my true voice. If Jesus was as powerful as Arno seemed to think, the messiah certainly could allow me to talk without trembling. I needed to test this theory. By the end of summer, I decided to get baptized.

The line to enter 155 Dwinelle, the largest lecture hall in the building, was moving slow because students were already sitting on both sides of the smooth concrete stairs leading down to the wooden stage. Empty seats were scarce. The few available were located at the middle of the auditorium. Unlike the people sitting on the steps, I was still contemplating squeezing, tiptoeing, and sliding past fifteen pairs of knees and Nikes for a center seat.

I immediately recognized him as he walked through the far entrance, engaged in a gesture-filled conversation with an attractive brown-skinned sister. I couldn't make out what he was saying, but it was enough to have his companion riveted. She was standing close, looking up into his mouth like it was someplace she wanted to go.

I exited the auditorium, walked across the lobby, and squeezed through the opposite entrance.

"Excuse me," I said to him, interrupting his conversation. "I was in the Summer Bridge ELL-90 final a coupla weeks ago. I dug how you screamed, 'I busted!' to the whole room when you turned in your test. I wanted to introduce myself. Michael Datcher."

He smiled big.

"Absylom Sims."

His fine friend had taken one of the remaining empty seats near the middle.

"Now, did you really bust an A or was all that hype a false alarm?"

"Well, brother," he said, his face growing serious, "unless the grade card my instructor sent me in the mail is incorrect, which, as you know, is possible, because people are prone to make mistakes, especially under the pressure of deadlines, but if my grade card is indeed correct, I did receive an A in ELL-90. The first of many—or so I expect."

He smiled again.

The formality of his speech surprised me. He carried himself with a confident flair that was familiar, but I wasn't ready for the elegance that followed the opening of his mouth. It made me smile.

"What grade did you receive?"

"I don't know, I didn't send in a grade card. I felt pretty good about it, though. I probably got a B-plus or A-minus. Anyway, I just wanted to introduce myself, brother. I'll let you get back to your friend."

"Man, I just met that sister in the lobby. Come on, let's grab a seat together."

We stepped down toward the front, then excuse-me'd our way to two seats in the auditorium's middle. As soon as we sat down, a six-foot-eight muscular brother long-strode across the stage toward the podium. He was wearing a semiunbuttoned brown silk shirt (showing a swinging gold medallion). The silk was tucked in the waist of leggy brown slacks that were a little too short: His brown ankle-high boots were showing too much brown ankle leather. The overhead lights gleamed off his bald head. His graying goatee and glasses completed an image straight out of an imaginary film called *Shaft the Intellectual*. I looked at Absylom. Absylom looked at me.

"Okay, quiet down, quiet down," his Temptations bass ordered. "My name is Doctor Harry Edwards. If you're not here for Sociology Three, you're in the wrong place. Don't step on people on your way out. Those who are enrolled, don't be alarmed by the masses on the floors and steps around you. It's been that way in this class for twenty years. Let me start by informing you of the class rules. One: If you can't come to my class on time, heh, don't come at all. Two: No dogs in my classroom. Some of you all smell like canines when you get wet, that's enough dog smell for one lecture. Three: No funny cigarettes. Cloud your brain on your own time. Four: If you're caught cheating, not only will you receive an *F* for the course, I will also do everything in my power, employing all my considerable influence, to get you tossed right out of this university. You think I'm joking, test me. Any questions?"

Wooooo. This cat was hard-core. During the whole lecture, I was caught up in his vocabulary. I had never seen a black man command the attention of white people by using his mind. Intermingling academic, multisyllabic language with the phrases and rhythms of black speech, Professor Edwards reminded me of some of the charismatic brothers I use to spin for in Long Beach, except he used bigger words.

Absylom and I came early and sat in the front row of Dr. Edwards's class all semester. Abs developed a dead-on imitation of Edwards that showed how close he was paying attention. It was hard not to.

Edwards lectured without notes during the biweekly hour-and-a-half sessions—and he told stories. About going to college on a football scholarship, literally not being able to read. About going on to Cornell University and writing a 1,200-page dissertation that created the discipline Sociology of Sport. About organizing the famous Olympic protest at the 1968 summer games, where Tommie Smith and John Carlos raised black-gloved fists on the Mexico City victory stand to call attention to discrimation against blacks in America.

Professor Edwards was notorious for challenging his students' intellects. Belittling them in front of the whole class. I finally gathered the courage to ask a question. He acknowledged my front-row hand with the open greeting he reserved for us few black students.

"Yes, young brother?"

I loved how he made us feel we belonged there. I took a deep breath and posed the multipart question. The query was full of Edwardsesque language and stutter-free because I had written it out and rehearsed it the night before.

He threw his head back and laughed when I finished.

"Young brother, that's a pretty intelligent question from someone who looks like you."

The class laughed with him. I was prepared for the cap. I shot back, "Well, I did my best, considering the distracting glare reflecting off your head."

The class roared. He had to laugh too. When he finished, he answered my question.

From that day on, Absylom and I brought questions to class every week. I think Dr. Edwards found us amusing. He not only began to engage us in front-row, highfalutin repartee, but also began to rap after class. Taking us back, journeying through his history of activism, including clips from *Shaft the Intellectual.*

After leaving class, Absylom and I would hang tough at the Golden Bear, a large, sophisticated tutoring center on campus. It served as the de facto chill/mack/study spot for black students.

Absylom was a magnet for attention. He was the second youngest in a very close-knit, musical family of twelve kids. He knew how to get the spotlight and keep it shining in his direction, which quickly became our direction.

We were sitting in the Golden Bear one afternoon when a head-turning sister walked through the front double doors. While others swiveled, Absylom stood up, extended his outstretched palm, and broke into a soulful version of Stevie Wonder's "You and I." What struck me (and made the sister stop in her tracks) was his complete commitment to the song. Absylom stepped up to the girl and kissed her hand.

"Sister, you forced Stevie Wonder from my lips. You are so beautiful."

She lit up like Sirius on a cloudless night. Absylom semipirouetted and returned to his seat to a chorus of *damns.*

Berkeley was intellectually intoxicating. At Telegraph and Bancroft, the mouth of campus, there was usually someone passionate stating her position on world events. Students, university employees, and Berkeley locals provided a constant audience.

One afternoon, I crossed Bancroft into a thirty-ish white guy's harangue about how drugs were bringing down the U.S.A. People were sitting on the steps of the student union, while others were crowding around. The street lecturer was talking loud and accentuating points with an index finger raised high above his head.

"Peee-pole are looking for ways not to deal with their livesss. They're running away from their prob-lemmss, even when they know they can't escape from themselvesss. Peee-pole who do drugs are scared of life. They're cowardsss."

A guy lounging on the steps with about ten other people shouted out a question: "You ever consider that maybe some peee-pole just like the feeling of being highhh?"

The audience laughed and cosigned with *yeahs*.

"Yes, I have considered that possibility. But why must you take some chemically engineered druugg to make you hap-pyy? That's the very problem I'm speaking of. . . ."

"Marijuana is not chemically engineered, it's 100-percent all-natural, wholesome, organic," someone else shouted from the steps.

"It comes up right out of the earth like potatoes and celery and onions, and weed doesn't even make your breath stink."

Laughter.

"Poison ivy comes out of the earth and it's 100-percent natural, toooo. I don't see pee-pole trying to roll that up in those funny little papersss."

More laughter.

That kind of topic exchange was happening all over campus. On the Supreme Court–type steps leading up to Sproul Hall; in the square courtyard of Dwinelle; at the main entrance to Moffit Library.

As I made my way around campus, I was constantly stopping to listen in. I had never been in a place where so many people were excited about ideas. It seemed they had been discussing these subjects all their lives. Everyone was so smart.

Although I'd always been a good student, I walked around Cal in my letterman's jacket feeling like a dumb jock. All the Summer Bridge talk about black students choking under Berkeley's rigorous academic program had me intimidated. I was feeling ill-prepared. Inadequate. I wanted these white students to know I was as smart as they were, even though I didn't believe it myself.

I went to the optometrist just off campus and bought a pair of black-rimmed, circular glasses. I thought that maybe if I looked smarter, people wouldn't challenge me as much. Find out that I got into Cal through affirmative action. That my high GPA couldn't keep the SAT from drop-kicking me. I had to get on these people's level before I was discovered.

I started fixing myself. Enunciating my words the way Moms would make me do when I spoke in her presence. I started to ask myself what I believed about abortion, the Democratic party, Ronald Reagan, and a host of other issues. Berkeley was forcing me to turn up my mind.

I poured myself into my studies, in and out of class. The teach-in never went out of style. Scholars held lectures in living rooms, on patios, at house parties. Many professors favored office hours in cafés. Their presence added to a stimulating mix of young Marxists, acoustic guitar players, painters, French-cigarette smokers, double cappuccino-drinkers and poets. It was knowledge under the sway of passion. The more I learned, the angrier I became. It seemed like much of my precollege education had been filled with half-truths and straight-out lies. Why hadn't any of my government teachers told me that George Washington owned African flesh? I had learned about Thomas Jefferson's brilliant mind and humanism but about not his slaves and concubines. No teacher had explained the CIA's role in undermining governments worldwide whose economic systems didn't provide America with the chance to come in and make money. No teacher had explained that the cowboys were the bad guys, murdering Native Americans, snatching their land. Nobody had told me that no matter how much education I acquired, I'd always be a nigger.

By the middle of spring semester, I was sick of white people. I had been learning so much about white oppression perpetrated against blacks: slavery's almost unbelievable horrors; the Black Codes; lynchings and the burnings of black bodies around the turn of the twentieth century; the racially motivated murders of the twenties, thirties, and forties; separate and unequal schools in the fifties; the FBI-sponsored assassinations of Black Panther party leaders in the sixties and seventies. It hurt so much. I knew such savagery was a commentary on how white Americans felt about my humanity.

It began to dawn on me. The propagandistic history I had been learning about black people wasn't true. We weren't the violent, less civilized race. We weren't the lynchers and baby killers. We weren't the trainers and financiers of Latin American death squads. It was the white people who were debased. And here I was, trying to seek their approval? Wearing corny glasses and speaking like them so they'd embrace me? Trying to become them? Seeking their affirmation for my own humanity? I felt like such a fool.

For the first time in my life, I thought deeply about my relationships with white people. I thought about my English teacher who tried to convince me not to come to Berkeley. The police. All the bright young brothers from my Long Beach neighborhood relegated to using their brains for criminal enterprise. How we couldn't use slang in the house, we had to talk in what Moms called "standard English," which meant white English. I thought about the things my Southern mother would tell me growing up. How I couldn't be as good as the little white boys, I had to be better.

In public, we couldn't be too loud, lest we stand out and seem too ghetto.

My proud mother, born and reared in Alabama during the Bull Conner era, had taught her children to be able to compete in the white world. A practical strategy, but it always positioned white as standard. White people became the high-water mark. The mirror in which to see if we'd arrived yet. Stamp of Approval holders. The place we went to have our significance affirmed. A dangerous choice of location. When you look outside yourself for affirmation, you give extraordinary power to the affirmer. When people have extraordinary power, they tend to abuse it.

The spring of my freshman year, I threw myself into the Divestment movement on campus. Student leaders Aurora and Pedro Noguerro, Mia Barber, and Michael Stoll developed a thoroughly conceived strategy to force the University of California to divest itself financially from South Africa. The country was under Apartheid rule at the time, so there was much money to be made off the backs of underpaid black workers.

When the international community was condemning and boycotting South Africa, America stood strong and wrong by the country's side. Worse, my school registration fees were indirectly supporting a racist government. It was just more white shit. I started sporting my bright yellow T-shirt with a large green map of Africa (South Africa in red) that read across the top: *South Africa Must Be Free!*

We built shantytowns in the football-length grass median in front of the chancellor's office at California Hall. People lived in them during the weeks of demonstrations. Hundreds of us stormed Sproul Hall, the main administration building, and took it over. We stayed into the night, studying, and singing songs of freedom until the police finally came and dragged us all out in an early morning raid.

With some students chaining themselves to the building, we took over California Hall until we got an audience with the chancellor. The international press converged on Berkeley like it was 1968. Absylom and I built a friendship among the red ribbons and justice chants.

The protests created so much havoc that we landed on the front page of the *New York Times* and eventually forced the university to divest. It was the first time I ever had participated in a large, primarily African-American group, led by African-American people, that stood up and challenged a system of obvious injustice. It was extremely empowering. My increased political awareness assuredly contributed to the distance I felt toward the Church of Christ membership. Although I went to church almost every Sunday and the people seemed nice, I couldn't really commit myself to a church full of Caucasians. I would blow in for morning services, then blow out. I was too mad at white people to really feel a strong connection to the parishioners. Yet I was hesitant to leave the Church. My stuttering seemed to be coming under control—and I was concerned that leaving the Church of Christ would jeopardize my salvation.

I decided to stay in the Bay Area and work during the summer after my sophomore year. Absylom's family extended an invitation for me to live with them rent free. I knew that doing so was quite a sacrifice for them because their small, three-bedroom home was already bursting at the seams with three daughters and two sons.

Abyslom's deeply religious family was heavily involved in trying to improve the living conditions of African-Americans in Richmond, a black working-class city twenty minutes from Berkeley.

It was awkward that first week. It's difficult moving into a close family's house and trying to find some way to fit in.

The Sims family had formed a band called the Gems. It was a thumping gospel group with great musicianship. Elizabeth, a music major, was the musical director and co–lead singer with Absylom. Abigail got funky with the bass, and sixteen-year-old Israel was a prodigy on jazz guitar. The oldest sister, Melita, played the drums. In a house full of musicians, people were always practicing. Elizabeth working through her high-pitched classical chops; Israel putting in two hours a day on his ax.

All this music was mixed with a heavy dose of love and laughter. As with most large families, the competitiveness manifested itself with teasing and joke-shooting. It immediately became apparent that if I made a mistake, had a bad-hair day, or my breath was kind of humming, I was going to hear about it.

On many a Friday night that summer, the instruments came out and a jam session would be live and direct from the living room. They'd hand me a tambourine, then they'd fall out once I tried to make my small musical contribution. I didn't mind the teasing. It made me feel like a part of the family. After these sessions, Absylom and I would sit up late into the night, talking about politics and women and our dreams. He was thinking about becoming a lawyer to right some wrong answers black people have been getting from the legal system.

By the time the fall semester began, I had lucked upon a great apartment. One of the Christians graduated and gave me his spot at 2709 Channing, right above College Avenue. In Berkeley's outrageously competitive housing market, a crib with a three-block walk to campus was a godsend.

The last weeks of summer, I had been thinking more and more about my commitment to God—in part because going to church had become an awkward exercise. I had been keeping Jesus in the closet, out of sight from my progressive black friends. The Church was starting to do a great deal of preaching in public places, putting the messiah on street corners and BART trains.

The Church of Christ's growing reputation as a cult made our aggressive outreach even more controversial. The Cult Awareness Network distributed leaflets warning students about us. The Church had its problems, but I didn't think it was a cult. People were simply misunderstanding some of the Christians' intensity about Jesus. Nevertheless, the cult talk made me very uncomfortable with publicly identifying myself with the Church.

The Church was big on campaigns. A goal would be announced to bring a specific number of people to services or baptize a given number of disciples by a certain date. The Church would be in a frenzy trying to meet those goals. Everyone would be excitedly sharing their faith on the bus, at work, in the market, doing public preaching.

A Bible talk leader would take his or her seven-member Bible talk to a street corner or café, and do an entertaining ten-minute Bible-based presentation. Immediately following, the Bible talk members would fan out, working the crowd and inviting people to church.

When school started, this practice grew extremely popular. The first week of class, our Bible talk leader, Todd, decided to do a public preaching right next to the Golden Bear: black territory. I seriously considered not going. Everyone I knew hung there. Since Todd recently had made me an assistant Bible talk leader (an effective ploy to get me more involved), I showed up anyway.

At a quarter to noon, we arrived at Sproul fountain, right next to the Golden Bear. The whole fountain plaza was packed with hundreds of primarily black students searching for familiar faces. I had been working at the facility since my sophomore year, tutoring students in Harry Edwards's Sociology 3 class. I saw my homie Melvin standing across the plaza. He navigated his way through the crowd to greet me. It was our first time seeing each other since the past semester.

"Wassup, Datcher?" he said, sliding me his palm for the snapping black handshake. He eyed the white and Asian posse I was rolling with.

Six-four and lean, Mel's the kind of cat who plays things close to the vest.

"So, Datcher, you gotta little something going on over here?"

"Yeah, man, we're bout to . . . well, Todd, here . . . Todd, this is one of my partnas, Melvin. Melvin, this is Todd, the cat who leads the Bible study I go to."

They shook hands.

"Yeah, Todd's gonna do a little quick preaching here on top of the fountain."

"Is that right?" Mel said, raising an eyebrow.

"Datch, you're not gonna kick a little knowledge from the good book, too?"

"Not today, bruh."

"Awright, Datch, Imma let yall handle yall business."

"Awright, Mel."

Snap.

Todd gathered us into a football huddle. It was about to go down. Lanky and a little goofy, with a great heart, Todd was shaking the huddle with his pregame jitters.

"Okay, here's what we're going to do. We'll sing a song to get people's attention. As you're singing, be sure to clap loud to ensure that people who can't see us can hear us. That'll be the key to gathering—"

"We're gonna sing?" The words stampeded out of my mouth.

All the heads in the huddle swung first to me, then to Todd.

"Yes, brother, we are going to sing," Todd said sternly.

This is it, I thought. I'm about to get outted in front of hundreds of black people. My black nationalist/activist reputation is about to take a major hit. I'm an operative controlled by the Man's cult apparatus.

"Okay, you guys ready? Let's pray and go win some disciples for Christ."

Todd jumped on the two-foot-wide brim that circled the fountain. We arched into a half-moon in front of him.

He started to sing and clap; we joined in from the moon.

Don't you wanna gooo to that lannnd,
Don't you wanna go-ooo to that lannd,
Don't you wanna gooo to that lannnd
Where I'm bounnd, where I'm bounnd?

The people sitting around the fountain twisted their heads toward Todd. So many of the black students on the crowded plaza started looking at me singing, I had to close my eyes to concentrate on the words. My body was stiff and tense. I too was clapping off-beat.

We finished the song and Todd began preaching in his early-Tom-Hanks-in-"Bosom-Buddies" sorta way. After he finished, we fanned out and invited people to our Bible talk. I didn't even think about inviting anyone black. I was searching for white faces like they were the missing on milk cartons.

There was a certain freedom in being outted. I wasn't under the pressure of having to hide my connection to the Church anymore. I knew it was time to make some decisions.

I had serious reservations about the Church of Christ, yet I saw some powerful things happening. The Church was growing rapidly, and people's lives were being changed. Everyone seemed so excited. I was tired of being on the struggling list. More important, I didn't feel confident about where I stood with God.

I had been half-stepping since the beginning, entering the Church to see if God could stop my stuttering. My two years of really just hanging around had shown me at least that God was real—which meant hell was probably real, too.

I called Todd and told him I wasn't sure if I really was a Christian. I asked if I could study the Bible with him. Take me through the lessons again. Really help me see where I stood with God.

Before our first study, I came clean with the things that I'd been involved in. How my first couple of years being around the Church, I was basically still partying and having sex, living like most other college students.

The confession seemed to make my heart softer. We spent two weeks going through the scriptures and praying. The Bible affected me deeply for the first time. I was extremely touched by Jesus' sacrifices and the suffering He went through so that my sins would be forgiven. At night I would go into the hills above campus to reflect on my own life. Maybe God didn't want me to know my biological father so He could be the only father I'd ever know. I liked the idea of being God's son. I knew He wouldn't give me away.

The week after Todd baptized me in the bay, I held a dinner at my apartment. I invited several of the friends whom I had been hanging with my first couple of years at Cal: Melvin, Nolan, and Absylom (who couldn't make it), among others. I made the cats a nice pasta dinner with white sauce. We sat around and talked and laughed.

I stood up.

"I invited yall here tonight cause I wanted to let you brothers know how much I value your friendship. I want to share a very special development in my life. I've recently made a decision to really try to dedicate my life to becoming a stronger Christian."

Heads nodded in understanding.

"My problem is that I'm weak. I'm such a fleshly cat that when I'm around my partnas, yall, I want to do some of the same things you big playas have been known to do. The temptation is . . . I just can't handle it. At least not now. Maybe when I'm stronger. Anyway, I've gathered you here to tell you that for now, I'm not really gonna be hanging out with you cats anymore. I'm gonna work on getting stronger and making myself into a better man of God."

There was a stunned silence in the room. They were hurt, but no one said anything. Instead, they all stood up. One by one, they gave me a hug and bounced out of the crib.

I sat on my couch feeling the strange mixture of joy that comes from making hard decisions and shame for pushing away friends who'd had my back.

Absylom hadn't returned my calls over the weekend. I knew something was up. Monday I decided to swing by the Golden Bear to look for him.

Just after noon, on one of the Bay Area's sunny but cool September days, I walked past Sproul fountain through the throng of backpacks and thick wool sweaters. I could see Absylom standing in the elevated doorway of the Golden Bear. He was talking to some of the brothers. I walked up the wheelchair-access ramp toward him.

"Wassup, Abs?"

"Wassup, M.D.? I'm sorry I missed your dinner. I heard you threw down on the pasta. I'm still trying to get a class. I'll catch you later, man," he said, walking past me.

"I can't get a return phone call, cat?"

He stopped at the bottom of the access ramp.

"Aw, man, you know I've just been busy, M.D. School just started, trying to get my classes. Then I talked to Melle Mel. He told me that we're a bad influence on you, so if that's the way you wanna roll with it, that's the way I'm gonna roll with it."

"Abs, don't trip off this stuff, man. I'm just tryin to get my life right, cat. You've just got to accept a brother tryin to make some changes."

His eyes detonated.

"I'll never accept that damn Church!"

He was yelling at me.

"Got you leaving your friends. Why you gotta leave your friends to follow God? Man, show me that in the Bible. Where's it at, Michael? Pull out your Bible right now and show me that a man's gotta leave his friends to know God!"

My body was pulsating. I had really hurt him, and now he was screaming that hurt on me. People began to come out of the Golden Bear to see what was going on. I could also feel the stares swing up in our direction from the plaza below.

"Absylom, I'm not leaving anybody, I'm just taking some time to get myself together. You gotta accept that, man."

"I don't gotta accept nothin!" he shouted, his high yellow face turning light red. He was breathing hard.

"That damn Church, naw, that damn cult, that cult's got your mind man, got you leaving your own friends. You just can't walk away from people because some Church told you. God wouldn't ordain that. Michael, that's crazy."

He began to cry.

"Nobody told me to do anything, Absylom, I—"

"I don't care what you say, you're in a cult." He turned and started walking toward the fountain, megaphoning, "Michael Datcher's in a cult, Michael Datcher's in a cult."

I wasn't embarrassed by what he was saying, I was paralyzed, wondering what people would think if I ran after him. Shattered by indecision, I just started shouting after him, "Absylommm! . . . Absylommm! . . . Absylommm!"

He kept walking.

"Absylommmmm! . . . Absylommmmm!"

He stopped and spun around about fifty yards from the Golden Bear, right in front of the fountain.

"Absylomm, I love you, cat!"

"I love you, M.D.!" he shouted, then pirouetted into the crowd.

she loves me not

I stand in front of Camille's door, a plastic bag full of Similac baby formula cans hanging from one hand, a family-sized box of Huggies diapers clutched in the opposite arm, waiting. The dark hallway has become familiar. I know the boot-sized hole to my right. I know the thick smell of fried grease, the sound of television *en Español*.

They make me stand in this hallway just to dig at me. It's still payback time. I can hear the movement behind the door. Camille's voice rises sharply, momentarily distinguishing itself from the dull tones of black discontent. I've been coming here almost every day, after work, for a month, and they put me through the same tired routine.

Camille finally snatches the door open. The women sit in the converted jury box, watching me enter. Camille's mother and her twin sister sit side by side on the loveseat, facing me. Camille's sister stands in the doorway leading to the perpetually nasty kitchen. There are no smiles. No one speaks.

I sit on the couch, placing the Similac and diapers down next to my feet. The apartment is funky again, or always. Clothes, food wrappers, and diapers seem like avant-garde furniture.

Camille comes out of the bedroom, cuddling Nicole close to her face. Like most evenings, she is in a light blue house robe, although it's only a few minutes after 8:00 P.M. She hands me a towel. I drape it over the shoulder of my blue sports jacket. Flip my red paisley tie over the other shoulder. Camille places Nicole in my arms without making eye contact.

"Hand him the bottle."

Camille's sister disappears into the kitchen and returns with a warm bottle. Camille sits on the arm of the loveseat next to her mother. I sit on the couch, feeding my daughter in the silent, bitter gaze of the women who will shape her perspective of me.

While she sucks on the nipple, her eyes devour my face. I tell her elaborate stories she cannot understand.

Nicole is serious, like her father. She seems to be looking for answers. She doesn't know I'm also looking for answers in her face. What will I say when she asks me why I tried to abort her? Will her mother and family turn her against me? When I get joint custody, will I be able to make enough money to support her?

Nicole finishes her bottle. I put her over my shoulder and tap lightly on her back, the way Camille taught me. She lets out a series of bass burps. They make me smile. I slide down the couch into a 45-degree angle and lay Nicole on my chest. She eventually falls off to sleep with neither of our questions answered. I watch her until my eyes close.

"Okay, it's time for you to go," Camille says, grabbing Nicole from my arms. I push myself off the couch and make my way to the door. There are no good-byes. I walk slowly down the dark hallway. I'm tired. Since I took the job as the editor in chief of *Image Magazine,* a glossy black-men's start-up, I've been working ten, twelve, sometimes fourteen hours a day. Straight from work to Nicole, unless it's just too late.

I get in my car and drive down Crenshaw. September weekday nights are also tired on the black community's main drag. It's after 10:00 P.M., and Woody's BarBQ is closed, West Angeles Church of God in Christ is quiet. I make a left onto King Boulevard and a right onto Degnan. I park in front of my apartment building. It seems like too much energy to get out of the car and walk upstairs. I recline my seat all the way until it touches the backseat. Lay my head down and close my eyes.

There is a great possibility that Camille and her family will try to turn Nicole against me. I decide to start writing her letters. I'll eventually compile them into a book and present her with the letters on her sixteenth birthday. The title idea comes: *A Song for My Daughter.* No matter what anyone says about me, I want Nicole to have her father's side of the story from the very beginning. I want her to know that her father loves her.

Friday, September 30, 1994
5:22 a.m.

Dear Nicole,

Today you are one month old. Happy Birthday! I've been coming to see you, holding you in my arms until you fall asleep, feeding you, and telling you stories. Although you can't understand these stories yet (though I know you pretend you do), I like telling them to you anyway: my exploits as a baby. See, when I was a baby, babies in general were real babies. Tough. None of this crying stuff. Youhearme? The real Baby G's. Anyway, you seem to like them. You smile and stuff when I really get into them. Then again maybe it's just gas. I didn't come and see you yesterday. Your moms was having a rough day. I think I missed you. It was the first time. Pops is out. Peace.

Daddy

Image Magazine is drilling me. In the position since early August 1994, not two full months, and I'm receiving angry calls from freelance writers and photographers who haven't been paid. The phone calls are distressing because I've spent years supporting myself as a freelancer. I know what it's like to be waiting for a check and that check is not in the mail.

On my half-moon desk, fifteen pink sheets are impaled on a message spike. They are joined there by my attempts to bring my former life to my new suit-and-tie world. Two white safety candles encased in tall clear glass anchor each end of the desk. On the six-foot bookcases against the wall in front of me, editing-related texts share space with *The Essential*

Etheridge Knight, The Bluest Eye, and *Linden Hills.* Coconut-scented incense wafts up from the office's back corner, blessing the Malawi mud cloth hanging behind me.

The messages are disturbing me. At nine, I call over to J. Giles's extension to see if he's in yet.

"J., it's Michael. You have a second?"

"Yes, come by in ten."

I walk through our Studio City offices, past the editorial and production cubicles, where the mock-up for the next issue is laid out on the floor. Through the lobby to the administrative side and knock on the door of J. Giles, *Image's* publisher.

"Come in."

J. is sitting behind a desk the size of a Ford Bronco's front end. At six-two, 260 pounds, he's a big man in a big blue tailored suit, complete with cuff links. J. Giles exudes power. Everything from his mischievous smile to his Mr. T biceps to his carefully folded hands resting on the desk says "I'm in control, here."

"Mr. Datcher, how can I help you this morning?"

"In the last week, I've gotten about fi-fifteen calls from writers and photographers who are trying to track down their money."

"Really? What are their names?"

"You haven't heard anything about this?" I say, knowing that J. micromanages all things having to do with money.

He doesn't like to be challenged. He shoots me a look that is intended to remind me of this.

"Listen . . . Michael, bring me the messages. I'll contact them each personally and ensure that the situation is resolved."

"I'm just looking out for the long-term interests of the magazine. Word travels fast when a magazine isn't paying its writers. We won't be able to secure good talent if the money is funny. And frankly, I'm not gonna feel comfortable having my colleagues write for the magazine if I'm not sure they're gonna get paid. So, is everything cool? Is our money straight?"

"Mr. Datcher, you worry about the editorial side, let me worry about the financial side," he says tersely. "Now, bring me the messages in question, and they will be handled expeditiously. Everything's fine."

A sly grin eases across his face.

"Awright, Mr. Publisher, but all ticking FedEx packages are being forwarded to your office."

I work until about 7:00 P.M., then go directly over to Camille's. The small peephole door opens and shuts. The big door flies inward.

"You can't be poppin up here unannounced," Camille says, eyes blazing.

"You know I come by after work and—"

"Some nights you don't come."

"Camille, what are you talking about? I've been here almost every night after work."

"You need to call me from now on."

"Camille, you don't have a phone."

"Nigga, you knew how to page me when you wanted some pussy, you can page me when you wanna see your daughter. That pager's working just fine."

I clench my teeth to keep from saying anything. Stakes are high, and she's got the best hand.

"Come in."

When I walk in I don't even want to sit down. I'm mad, and the house is nasty. I've got to get my daughter out of here.

I stand in the living room watching Camille through the open bedroom door. The TV is on BET's "Rap City" video show. No one else is home. She brings Nicole over and hands her to me.

"Can I get a towel?"

Camille grunts.

Before Camille returns, Nicole begins to cry. I start walking back and forth with her in the small living room, stepping over cans and wrappers. Camille places the towel over my shoulder. Nicole is crying louder. She's screaming. I sit down on the couch and bring her up to my face. She's crying so hard that she begins to shake. Her little face turns beet red. She's scaring me.

"Nicole . . . Nicole," I whisper into her hysteria. My voice sends her octaves higher.

"Damnn," Camille says, as bewildered as I feel.

"Here, give her to me."

I hand Nicole to Camille, who gets up and starts walking with her, patting our daughter's back. Within a couple of minutes, she stops crying but is still breathing hard.

"What was that about?" I say, still shaken.

"Maybe she doesn't like that body oil you wear."

"It's never been a problem before."

The next evening I come to see Nicole, the same thing happens. This time Camille's mother and aunt are on the couch. Nicole has added an incessant kick to her tantrum repertoire. Her screaming is so violent that Camille's mother, head swiveling, palms both her own ears.

"Camille! Camille! Camille! Come and get this chile, you know my mind can't take this noise."

Camille gives me a hug before I leave.

When I stand in front of Camille's door on the third day since Nicole's fits, I'm the most nervous since my first time seeing her. I've stopped wearing body oils of any kind, changed to Ivory soap, and started using unscented underarm deodorant.

Camille opens the door, leans out, and gives me a peck on the cheek.

I become conscious of her breasts for the first time in many, many months. Her light blue robe is barely overlapping, exposing her sternum and the inner sides of both her swollen breasts.

"How was work?"

"Awright."

I let her take a few steps inside, then I follow. She heads toward the back to get Nicole. No one's home. I'm tired. I sit on the couch.

Camille walks out of the bedroom, bouncing Nicole up and down over her head. Nicole is cooing. Camille stops right in front of me, looking up at Nicole. As she bounces, the robe's belt, which was already loose, loses some of its conviction. The front of her robe goes from overlapping cotton to two sides of an elevator door one finger push from opening. My dick hardens. Her waist is eye level. I know she doesn't have any panties on. She wants to show me.

I'm mad at myself for wanting to see so badly. I feel weak falling for this obvious manipulation. Camille keeps bouncing. The belt is slowly sliding away. I hear Camille's breathing. I know it's not because Nicole is heavy. The elevator door cracks. I'm transfixed by her freshly manicured pubic hair. I can feel her glancing down, watching me remember. I want to hop on my knees, slip my tongue deep through the door until she's forced to grab my head. I want to feel her on my taste buds. She's stopped bouncing, stopped pretending. She's staring at me. We both are remembering.

"Can I get a Pepsi?"

She has to smile.

"Yeah, I probably can find one for you."

When she returns from the kitchen, her robe is retied. Camille hands me the soda and sits down on the opposite loveseat, holding Nicole on her knee. We make small talk. Nicole makes baby talk. I start getting very nervous. God, please don't let her cry.

"Here, hold her for a second while I go to the bathroom."

Just as Camille is handing her off, Nicole's eyes meet mine. Her eyes widen into a look of terror so real, so genuine, so intense that I have to concentrate not to drop her. As I bring her to my chest, Nicole starts to scream and kick and twist and shake and kick and scream like each of my fingers is a red-hot branding iron searing the flesh off her tiny bones.

"Sshhhhh, Nicole. Sshhhh, baby."

The sound of my voice throws her crimson face and body into violent spasms. I have to hold her tighter so I won't drop her. This just makes her shake more intensely. My broken face looks up at Camille's collage of pity and triumph. She reaches down and takes Nicole. Starts walking back and forth, cooing in her face.

"It's okay, Mama's right here. It's okay, little mama, Mommy's right here. Sshhhh, Mommy's right here."

I look at Nicole calming down in Camille's arms. What is wrong with me? My own daughter hates my guts. This is not the way I imagined fatherhood. Maybe I have some evil spirit. Maybe that's the real legacy of my own rapist father. Maybe he left some genetic remnant that Nicole can pick up. I've heard that children are sensitive to that sort of thing. Maybe God is punishing me for trying to abort my own child. God, please, don't do this to me. Please. I don't wanna cry in front of Camille. I ball my fists and shove them beneath my thighs. Clench my teeth. It's not supposed to be like this.

"Camille, what do you think it is?"

"Think about it, Michael, think back," she says, sitting down on the loveseat. "Remember how you were treating me when I was pregnant? All that screaming and cursin you were doing? Babies can hear that, they can feel that. You have to understand that when you got me upset, you got her upset. She was inside me, Michael. Think about it. Nicole remembers your voice. It's probably taken her a couple of months to put it all together, but she remembers your voice, Michael."

"You really think that's it?"

"Unnhunh. I think she's scared of you."

My face breaks into smaller pieces.

"Camille, I don't know what to do, I just don't know. Tell me what to do, Camille."

"Hummph, you should have thought about that when you were screaming at me. I don't know what to tell you. Hopefully, over time she'll get used to you."

"Maybe if we spent more time alone together at my crib, we could bond faster."

"How can you spend time at your place if soon as you touch her she throws a fit, and I'm right here? No, I think you better just keep bringin yo butt round here and hope she can stand you one day."

"No, really, Camille, I think that would help. We need to spend some time alone. She's my daughter, too."

"First you wanna kill her, now you wanna play daddy? You listen to me: This is my baby. You're out of your mind if you think I'm gonna let her go and stay with you."

Payback's hard-core. I let it go.

"I'm gonna break out," I say, standing to leave. She stands and walks toward me, smiling.

"What you need to do is slide that thang right in here. It'll make you feel better."

Her eyes are electric.

I get mad at myself for allowing her to turn me on so easily.

"Your friend down there got me in enough trouble as it is. I'm out like Ornette Coleman."

I walk toward the door.

"You know you miss this."

"See you tomorrow, Camille."

Tomorrow comes and turns into next month and next month and next month, and nothing changes. No matter what toys I bring, silly songs I sing, each time I try to pick Nicole up, she convulses into a tantrum. To make matters worse, in December I find out that Camille reported me to the District Attorney's Bureau of Family Support. She didn't have to do that. I'd given her every indication that I will take care of my child no matter what. She's got us both caught up in a system that could care less about black life.

It's February 1995, and Nicole still hates me. *Image Magazine* is also quickly failing. We are having serious cash-flow problems. Not only are freelancer checks bouncing, but so is staff payroll. Morale is low, and turnover is our motto. I'm trying to save the ship by working even more hours. The late nights give me an excuse not to go see Nicole as much. My heart needs a rest.

One night after work, I drive down Camille's street but I keep on going past her building. I just can't do this anymore. I can't take it. I'm running myself ragged for a child who can't stand me. I drive home and park in front of my building. I need to think.

Maybe it would be better for everyone if I just gracefully exited Nicole's life. That way she wouldn't have to be upset every time I come around. I could keep sending Camille money. Maybe even set up a trust fund. I could keep in touch through Camille or just wait until Nicole's old enough for us to have a relationship where we can talk to each other. Her screaming is driving me out of my mind.

I'm in the car for a long time, thinking about Nicole. The weight I feel is all the heavier because I haven't talked to my brother, sister, or Moms much about the whole situation. They've always been so supportive, but as the baby in the family, I'm still trying to establish myself as a responsible adult in their eyes. I'm embarrassed by my state of affairs, so I'm keeping my family at arm's length. Moms is the only family member who's even seen Nicole. The more I think about my life, the more I shake my head. My own upbringing without a father. Am I really going to abandon my child after all the drama I've experienced being fatherless? Am I really going to give up on my own daughter? Is that the kind of man Moms raised me to be? A brother who dreams about family then deserts his own flesh and blood when the game gets rough? That's not me. I've got to pull myself together. Maybe if I can get joint custody, she'll eventually come around. I've got to believe I can win her over.

The next morning I call my old high school friend Jimmy, or James R. Cardenas, to his lawyer friends. Jimmy's a paralegal. He's already helped me research how to respond to Camille's child-support claim. He agrees to help me with custody issues. I'm going to fight for my daughter.

Monday, February 13, 1995
5:14 a.m.

Dear Nicole,

It seems like it has been so long since I've written you. I can't talk to you now because you are too young to understand. You said your first words on Saturday. Your mother said that you said, "Daddy." I didn't even want to believe it was true. Because whenever I pick you up you cry. I don't get the opportunity to spend time with you at my house because your mother is using you as a weapon, a pawn to try to wield power against me. So I go to your grandmother's house or your aunt's house and feel like the outsider in your life that I am. I'm so good with children. They seem to respond to me. But not you. You just cry when I pick you up. It kills me inside. I pray that as you get older you'll understand and we'll be able to kick it much better. I've been going through a lot, honey. At Image *the magazine is still struggling. It just seems that everything is hard now. I know I haven't even scratched the surface yet. I can't wait until we can really spend some time together getting the opportunity to chat. I'm still working on myself so I can be the man I need to be. So that you can have someone to look to as an example. I'm feeling insecure about our relationship. I don't know if you'll be able to love me. Knowing what your mother is like. Knowing that she'll try to run interference. So now I'm going to go through the court to try to win joint custody. Who knows what will happen with that. I'm just trying to stay afloat. I pray that you will be a woman who is true to herself. Peace, little sister.*

Love,

Pops

disciple

I viewed the fight with Absylom as a step toward Jesus. The Bible called for sacrifice; I laid my best friendship on the altar. I was ready to change my life.

In 1987, I threw myself into the Church of Christ. I went from fringe to center. Wednesday night was house church, Thursday Bible talk, Friday devotional, and Sunday church.

I dove deeper into the Bible's beauty. I loved to sit at Café Milano and read King David's psalms. Longing in his heart for God. The realness of his love. Childlike. Words coloring his thirst the color of sand. His heart was so passionate. So pure. It inspired me. I woke before the sun did, and fell from bed to knee. Every morning. Midday I stopped on campus in a cove along Strawberry Creek. The running water helped to ease the prayers from my lips. At night, I would climb into the rugged hills above Clark Kerr and shout prayers among the owls.

I was seeking the heart of David, but all of my former passions were seeking me. Making me remember the faint musk of parting thighs. The wanderlust of tongues. The exquisite agony of fingernails on my back. These images would constantly dart through my mind. I struggled to fight them off with impromptu prayers. I felt like the wild nigga I used to be and still was—squeezing into a tight-ass suit.

My postadolescent life was steeped in all things sensual, but the Church of Christ demanded celibacy from me. Not just a physical abstinence but a denunciation of desire itself. This demand is what made my transition so difficult. I missed sex, but I missed seduction more. The electricity of the brazen stare. The anticipation of lust becoming spankings. I had to re-program myself. Had to find something else to obsess over. I was hoping it would be Jesus.

I began to share my faith everywhere I went. Walking to class, I would start conversations about Jesus, telling of His influence on my life. In class, I became the messiah's ambassador, taking His message to History 7B, to Psych 160, to Bus Ad 150. Lecture halls became temple courtyards where I reasoned with nonbelievers. Trying to convince them to live that which I struggled to live myself. I figured if I worked hard enough, my heart would come around. That if I fully committed myself to the work of Jesus, He would give me the strength to embrace this new lifestyle.

I was sitting at Café Roma, reading the Book of Acts between classes. It was October 1987. Roma was one block down from the International House, the residence of many of Berkeley's foreign students. Café Roma was the international hangout.

Inside, a line of students was hooking up their caffeine fix. Around the outdoor courtyard's small round tables, French, Italian, and Spanish blended with the rising steam of double cappuccinos and bitter espressos. Slow-burning filterless cigarettes hung from the corners of mouths, squinting eyes guarding against pluming smoke.

I was reading about how Stephen, one of the early disciples, was stoned to death for following Jesus. As a people pleaser, I struggled with having people dislike me for my new Christian beliefs. I was consumed by what others thought. Reading about Stephen's willingness to face even death for his beliefs made me feel like a coward. His courage moved me.

I put my Bible and notepad inside my backpack and slung it over my shoulder. I stood, walked to the center of the courtyard, and jumped on one of the wooden benches. My heart was ricocheting around my rib cage.

"Ex-cuusse me, ex-cuusse me. May I have your attention for a second, please?"

I was shouting so loud that many of the conversations in the area were silenced.

"I'd like to invite all of you to a really wonderful Bible study that I attend right near ca-campus. Twenty-seven oh nine Channing, seven-thirty p.m. There'll be food, drink, and most important, a perspective on Jesus that will make you wanna take a closer look. Thank you for your time."

I stepped clumsily off the bench and out of the café. I was so nervous I forgot to wait to see if someone was interested. I didn't really think anyone would be. Standing up was more about conquering my fear than anything else.

I began to stand up and make announcements everywhere. On the BART train, in class, in other cafés, on campus. I even did a short impromptu sermon while standing on the rim of Sproul fountain. I was trying to stop hiding my faith. Trying to commit.

The more I committed, the more the Bible began to touch my heart. The more I began to be inspired by Jesus and His disciples, the more I began to feel closer to God. I began to believe that He had placed me on the earth to spread love and bring people to a knowledge of Christ.

I began to lead my own Bible talk. The Bible talks were the engines of the Church of Christ. These small groups of four to seven people worked very closely to bring people into the Church. Participants of the Bible talks ate together, sat together in church, and worked at making disciples together.

What made the Bible talks run were the discipling relationships mandated by the Church. Every Church of Christ member had a discipler, someone who was more advanced spiritually, who could help the disciple grow. The disciples were strongly urged to seek advice from their disciplers on everything from whom to date to how to study the Bible to whether to go home or stay at Berkeley for the summer. Disciples were strongly encouraged to imitate their disciplers, as their disciplers imitated Christ. The discipler was also the person to whom you confessed your sins.

I began to learn these things when I entered leadership. After Sunday church, there were strategy and accountability meetings for the Bible talk leaders. It was during these gatherings that we reported how our Bible talks were doing: how many people had attended the weekly sessions; how many had gone to church; how many Bible studies we were conducting; how many people were baptized; who was "struggling" in our Bible talks. These stats were retrieved weekly and passed up the chain of command.

I was taken aback by all of this at my first meeting. Although the Church was having a strong impact on the lives of its members, these meetings seemed to reduce people to numbers. I soon learned that if you couldn't produce, you were yanked from your position. It was during this same time that the Church began to stress the importance of supporting leadership. Members of the Church who did not heed the advice of their Bible talk leaders or the Church leaders (known as evangelists) were labeled "rebellious" and quickly placed on the struggling list.

It all seemed a little strange. When I began to inquire about some of the practices, the response was always the same: "If a corporation is expected to be organized to make profits, Christians should be that much more organized to save souls."

The Church's bad press began to complicate matters further. The TV news show "20/20" did an investigative report on the Church of Christ and labeled it a cult. Students on campus commonly held it as such. They became very resistant to our message, especially the black students. That was hard. I had started focusing on trying to bring strong black students to Christ. I wanted to help them know God in a more complete way. They weren't trying to hear it. The word on campus was "They got brother Datcher, don't let him get you."

My family heard these rumors from several friends and became very agitated. They started saying I was brainwashed. They were concerned for my safety. Familial tensions ran high.

I felt my family misunderstood. I believed that the vast majority of the members, including me, were trying to help people know God.

Although I tried to dismiss it, the "20/20" episode shook me. I had sacrificed so much to join the Church: close friendships, my reputation among black students, good family ties, sex. The Church's many activities also had an effect on my grades. There were not enough hours in a week for church four times, studying the Bible with people, working thirty combined hours

tutoring at the Golden Bear, and working in the weight room while trying to excel at one of the top schools in the country.

What if I was wrong about the Church? What if I really was brainwashed? How do brainwashed people know they're brainwashed?

A major turning point occurred that fall. The leadership began to con-
firm what had been suggested implicitly in the Church's doctrine: Church
of Christ members were going to heaven, while other Christians were not.
The rationale given was that we were the only ones out there making disciples according to the Bible's definition. We were the Kingdom of God
on Earth that the Bible was talking about. We were the remnant who had
a true relationship with Jesus. It was our responsibility to go out to all na-
tions and bring as many people with us. These statements were never
made publicly, but within the leadership meetings they increasingly became the rhetoric. I couldn't buy it.

When a person left the Church of Christ, it was called "falling away."
The logic was that since no other Church appeared to be making disciples
the way Jesus had commanded, to leave the Church of Christ was to leave
Jesus and therefore to leave God. This didn't sound right, but I really
wasn't sure. I didn't know of any other Church where the rank and file
members were so involved in bringing people to Christ. Maybe the Church
was the Kingdom of God. I went on a ten-day water-only fast, asking God
for answers. Nothing seemed clear anymore. I was paralyzed.

I couldn't commit to the Church to the same degree as I had before. Yet
I was afraid to leave because of the possibility that I was leaving God. My
doubts got me yanked out of leadership. I was placed back on the struggling list. A return to the fringe.

By the fall of 1988, I was having a very difficult time. I missed the community of black people I had been a part of in Summer Bridge.

I took an African-American literature course with a teacher named, co-
incidentally, Barbara Christian.

Dr. Christian, a five-foot-four West Indian woman with short natural
hair, had received her Ph.D. from Columbia. She was a black feminist lit-
erary critic who had been influential in the black arts and black studies

movements during the sixties, and was the country's leading expert on Toni Morrison. Dr. Christian had been teaching at Berkeley for twenty years.

Professor Christian was in a dead heat with Harry Edwards as the most charismatic teacher I'd ever had. When she lectured, she walked slowly along the rows and aisles of students, stopping and turning dramatically to make important points. She infused her analyses of Amiri Baraka, June Jordan, James Baldwin, and David Henderson (whom she was married to) with personal anecdotes. The stories behind the stories. The late-night strategy meetings in tiny Harlem apartments. The post–poetry reading rap sessions. The interpersonal intrigue that led to the poems and essays and that chronicled those intense times. Barbara Christian had been there. She took us back with her every Tuesday and Thursday. It was intoxicating.

No one ever had made literature come alive for me the way she did. In all my years of passionate reading, I had been exposed to few black authors. Dr. Christian exposed me to a world of writers who sounded like me. I found Long Beach street-corner vernacular worked into high art. At a time when I desperately needed it, Professor Christian gave me something else to believe in.

I had been celibate for more than two years. It was one of the hardest things I'd ever done. As my questions mounted about the Church, my resolve weakened. I began masturbating obsessively, slipping out to X-rated movies. And then that Christmas break, I had sex with a young white woman whom I had met at a Church retreat. I had never wanted anyone or anything that bad. It had been so long.

When she left my apartment, I was wracked with guilt. She was a woman I had at one time tried to lead to God. Instead, I let her slip to her hands and knees.

I had let God down, and I was very afraid of the consequences. I was sure God had left me. The next day, I didn't leave the house. I was scared I might literally lose my life. Fall down the steps. Be hit by a car. Shot.

I began to live a double life. I remained in the Church of Christ, but my heart was elsewhere. So was my penis. I began to have passionate but guilt-ridden affairs with women at Cal and surrounding universities. They all were white except for two who were Asian. I figured my chances of getting discovered would increase if I got involved with sisters. It's a small black world.

I had made such a public display of my Christianity on campus—debating on street corners, preaching on fountains, constantly sharing my faith—that it was hard for me to back away from the image I'd created.

I still shared my faith on campus, inviting people to church, even though I didn't feel sincere in my heart. In church on Sunday morning with the faint smell of pussy on my goatee. I was still talking an odd mix of Jesus and black nationalism, but living deep inside as many white women as I could slide into. I had become the hypocrite I railed against. I was disgusted with myself.

In the fall semester of 1991, I took June Jordan's class called "Poetry for the People." Jordan, the long-time poet, essayist, and activist, had been hired the year before. She brought a high level of energy and a gift for organizing and inspiring students. She taught us that poetry is a medium for telling the truth. She urged us to tell our stories.

I had so much to tell. I began keeping a journal, documenting all the frustration, fear, and guilt I was feeling. I had almost forgotten what it was like to be honest—even if it was with only myself. I cried my life between parallel lines in cloth-covered notebooks. I began to craft those tears into poems. I would read them to myself over and over.

I was reading poetry voraciously: Langston Hughes, e.e. cummings, Countee Cullen, Michael S. Harper, June Jordan, Robert Hayden, Amiri Baraka. The more I read, the more I wanted to write. Poems about the Gulf War that was taking place. Poems about the white women I was sleeping with. Poems about the free clinic that I was sneaking to for my AIDS tests.

waiting room c
(at the berkeley free clinic)

waiting and wondering
trying
to remember
to refigure
probability ratios
recalled from statistics 2
a numerical buffer
for my mind
it may be too late
for my body
and soul

Poetry had me. I performed during Poetry for the People's major readings on campus with full press coverage. I read at political rallies, in cafés,
on street corners. Poetry became a second religion. Other students in the
class also were being moved. They told their immigrant stories, their mo-
lestation stories, their love stories with such raw emotion that we were
packing 200-seat rooms. Audiences testifying. Students cheering and
crying.

I was so inspired that I raised campus funds to put together an anthology. I wanted to tell black-men stories. I sent out calls for submissions all
over the country. I received hundreds of poems. The result, *My Brother's
Keeper: A National Anthology of Black Men's Poetry,* hit bookstores in February 1992. The anthology featured the full range of black male humanity. Poems by straight and gay brothers. Brothers who worked in
prison-orange jumpsuits, and those who worked in blue blazers. College-
aged and grandfathers.

The media found it valuable. Soon I was on television and radio talk
shows discussing the book. There were newspaper articles and book re-
views. A group of the contributors flew in from around the country for a
reading and to get to know one another. We hung out in my apartment,
drank wine, and talked among ourselves. The gay brothers spoke emotionally about being discriminated against within their own race. How it

broke their hearts that straight black men viewed them as traitors. We talked about the violence that we perpetrated and had been victims of. We discussed the fear we engendered among people who looked like us. I spoke of my own hypocrisy. We got drunk, hugged, and cried.

The Poetry for the People and *My Brother's Keeper* experiences strengthened me. Yet I wasn't quite strong enough to break away from the Church of Christ. Fear is a cord that untwists very slowly. Since joining the Church, my stutter had reduced significantly. I figured God was blessing me because of my commitment. I was afraid that leaving would undo the blessing and retie my tongue. I was also afraid that leaving would send me to hell.

Unlike before, when I had challenged Church doctrine from a position of relative righteousness, my current life was a direct affront to the Bible. I couldn't challenge anyone or anything because my life was suspect. I felt weak and indecisive. I wanted to leave but couldn't. That's when I began to think that maybe I was brainwashed. I couldn't act on what I thought was best for me. I needed help.

There was no one to turn to. In my pursuit of Jesus, I had alienated my close friends, and I wasn't close enough to the new friends I was developing through poetry. And I was too proud to let my family know of my emotional fragility.

In April I was accepted to a graduate program in African-American Studies at UCLA for the coming fall. The Church was in the process of setting me up with the Church of Christ in L.A. I was praying that once I left Berkeley, I'd be strong enough to leave the L.A. Church because I didn't have the same bond with them.

On a Wednesday afternoon, I had just finished making photocopies and faxing paperwork that I needed to send to UCLA by 4:00 P.M. I stopped by the Sufficient Grounds café to grab a cappuccino and relax. The café was crowded with its usual mix of local intellectuals and students studying to the classical radio station they always played. I spotted a free chair near the back. I was going to set my backpack down, then jump in line to get my double cap.

"We interrupt this program for a special news bulletin. The verdicts are in from the Rodney King trial."

A jolt of electricity shot through the café. Some people instinctively rose from their seats and stood in front of the large speaker hanging from the wall. I pivoted where I was and stared at the speaker, too.

"Not guilty."

When I heard the foreman say and then repeat those two words, I snapped. I could tell there was a commotion in the café. People seemed to be screaming at the speaker. My mind slung back to age ten. Watching those cops' batons slam against that boy's skull. The cracking sounds. Watching him fall with a boxer's I'm-not-hurt smile on his lips. I saw Rodney King cowering, his arms trying to protect his head too. I saw the policeman's gun aimed at the bridge of my ten-year-old nose. I felt my body shaking violently. I stumbled out the café and walked over to the computer center on campus. I wrote Kevin Powell, a fellow poet in New York.

April 29, 1992

Dear Kevin,

It's 3:56 p.m., on Wednesday, thirteen minutes after the white judge read the four not guilty verdicts handed to him by the white bailiff, who carried it from the white foreman, leader of the predominantly white jury that just set free four white police officers who beat up yet another brother (on film) and I'm surprised at myself for being so surprised. Something has fallen off the shelf inside of me to disturb the calm that I was allowing myself to enjoy these last few weeks before I leave for graduate school. I really don't know what to do, man. I am so hurt. I am so disappointed. I feel betrayed.

I know there will be riots in the streets of L.A. tonight. I know that people will die tonight. I want them to be white people, Kevin. I want white people to die. I want innocent white people to die, and experience injustice. To experience the land of equality like we experience it. To experience the America the Beautiful like we experience it. To experience the melting pot when the heat is up and they ain't the ones stirrin. I'm sick of this shit, man.

blood

One of the first things Jimmy suggests to improve my chance for getting custody is to stop giving Camille money in the form of cash.

"Mike, you've got to have proof that you've been actively involved in supporting Nicole," he says, talking in the hurried tones of the busy lawyer he will soon become.

"Cash is very difficult to document. Use checks or money orders. And Mike, keep receipts for everything you buy. I mean everything. If you buy a pacifier, keep the receipt. In the court of law, the paper trail is everything."

I have to shake my head. It's February 1995, months away from our ten-year high school reunion. My former center is suggesting defensive strategies in my custodial case.

After doing all he can, Jimmy suggests I get a fee waiver and obtain a lawyer. In May, he sends me to go see Tony Giovanni at his downtown office.

Jet-black hair combed back Pat Riley–style, intense eyes barreling forward, Tony Giovanni sits behind his large desk like a man with lots of things to do in very little time. He rises quickly to shake my hand across the desk.

"Sit down, Mr. Datcher. How can I help you?"

I tell Giovanni that I want to secure joint custody of my daughter. I explain that her mother won't allow me to spend time alone with Nicole. I tell him that though I've been bringing baby formula, diapers, and other items to my daughter, and giving her mother money ever since Nicole's birth, her mother has filed a child-support case against me.

"Okay, first things first," Giovanni responds. "Are you sure it's your baby?"

"Yeah, I'm sure. Mr. Cardenas helped me research the answer to my baby's mother's child-support claim. I brought a copy of it."

I hand him the paperwork, and he scrolls down it briskly.

"Have you filed anything else or done any more paperwork?"

"No."

"Good. Okay, start from how you met Camille and quickly tell me what has happened up to now. The more honest you are with me, the more I'll be able to help you."

I recount the highs and gigantic craters of my relationship with Camille. Giovanni listens intently, nods, occasionally says "Unhunh," and interrupts me to ask questions.

He decides to take my case, which makes me a little nervous. Since Nicole's birth, I've been trying not to upset Camille. She has the best hand and could easily raise the stakes. That's why I've hesitated to get a lawyer. I know it will take things to a whole new level. Camille doesn't have a clue that I've been seeking legal counsel.

Giovanni tells me he wants to amend my answer to the D.A.'s office.

"You do what's best for me," I say cautiously.

In all caps, customary of legal paperwork, he changes my gentle language concerning our relationship to:

MOTHER HAS COMMITTED AFDC FRAUD. CHILD SUP-
PORT AT ALL MATERIAL TIMES. THERE HAS BEEN NO
DETERMINATION OF PARENTAGE. THERE CAN BE NO
CHILD SUPPORT ORDERS. D.A. APPLICATION IS BASED
ON HEARSAY, AND CONCLUSIONS OF LAW AND FACT.

Under defendant's requests:

BLOOD TESTING, JUDGMENT OF NON-PATERNITY, DIS-
MISSAL OF ACTION WITH PREJUDICE. OTHER RELIEF
COURT DEEMS JUST AND PROPER.

"Wooo," I say, handing back the paperwork. "This sounds kinda harsh."
Camille's going to flip when she sees this. Especially that blood-test part.
"Blood testing is standard procedure, step one. We have to have deter-
mination of parentage."
"Wooo."

Driving home from Giovanni's office, I think about how I'm going to
broach this blood test to Camille. She's going to be insulted. I decide to deal
with Camille immediately before fear has a chance to settle in too deep. I
go home, page, and arrange to meet her.

She yanks open the door.

"I don't have a lot of time. Come in."

Camille's wearing white jeans, a thin black blouse, and a bad attitude.
She's having a tough day. It doesn't seem to be affecting Nicole, who's toss-
ing little blocks and balls around in her playpen. At almost nine months,
she's looking more like me all the time. I walk over and toss some of the
blocks in her direction. She throws them back. These simple gestures
bring me so much joy that I'm afraid to push my luck and try to pick her
up.

"What did you want to talk about, Michael? I've got things to do.
You're not the only one with a life to live," I hear her rattle off from behind me.

Maybe I should talk to her about this later, I think as I stand up, turn
around, and face her in the center of the living room. No, it'll only get
harder as time progresses.

"You know, Camille, I was thinking, Nicole's gonna be in my life for a
long time, and kids are sensitive, they can feel things. I don't want her

growing up feeling uncomfortable because of something I'm feeling. I'm really sure that Nicole's my daughter, but I'm not absolutely 100-percent sure and I need to be 100-percent sure, Camille. I don't need to have lingering doubts ten or fifteen years from now. That's not good for any of us, especially Nicole. I want to get a blood test just to be sure, I just need to be—"

Camille's eyes flash wildly.

"A fuckin blood test!" she screams, spittle firing out of her mouth. "You wanna get a blood test? I can't believe this. Look at her face, Michael, that's your damn blood test. How can you even say something like that? You think I don't know who the father of my child is? Huh? Is that what you think? You think I'm some type of whore? Look at her, Michael! If you can't tell that's your daughter, you're outta your mind!"

Camille's eyes are welling up with tears. She's really hurt.

"Camille, Camille. I do think she's mine, but I can't think, I've got to know for sure, I—"

"If you want to know for sure, look in a mirror. I'm not takin no blood test. This is crazy, coming up in here, bringing this outta left field. Get outta my house."

"Camille."

"Get out!"

Nicole starts to cry. Frustrated, I turn and let myself out.

My relationship with Camille changes dramatically. Suddenly, she becomes very busy and very unavailable. I begin to see Nicole less and less. When I do go by, Camille's openly hostile. This goes on for months.

The court-ordered blood test is finally set for September 11. *Image* folded back in March, and at the beginning of September I started working as a staff writer for the *Los Angeles Sentinel,* the second largest black paper in the country. I have to awkwardly ask for a day off, after a week on the job.

I'm relieved when I leave Long Beach Genetics. This all is coming to an end and it really hasn't been worth it. I'm hoping that since the test is over, Camille and I can start getting along a little better and I can see Nicole more. She turned one on August 30, and she still has never been to her own father's apartment.

Jimmy seems to think I have a pretty good chance of getting joint custody because I've been diligent with all my record-keeping. I keep holding on to the faith that things will get better once Nicole and I are able to build our own relationship. I just pray that not too much damage has been done.

As expected, no call comes from the genetics lab the next week, or the second week, or the third week. I've been to enough clinics to know they call you back only when there's unexpected news to report.

Unfortunately, I'm not right about Camille and me. Things haven't gotten better. Hurt, she's moved squarely into battle position. Nicole has become her weapon of choice. Now that it's October, Camille's bitterness, coupled with Giovanni's earlier advice not to spend as much time with Nicole until the court case is resolved (his logic: If we're claiming the child is not yours, why are you there every day?), has resulted in my seeing Nicole only a few times in the last three months. I'm feeling like a very bad father.

One benefit of being a reporter is that you're always on the phone gathering information, so it's easy to handle personal business at work without being detected. I'm looking through the file containing all the receipts and legal paperwork I've collected to strengthen the custody case. I realize I never received a copy of my blood-test results. I can imagine Camille forging her copy of the document, trying to claim Nicole wasn't even mine during the proceedings. Jimmy said the paper trail is everything.

"Long Beach Genetics."

"Hi, I need a copy of my—"

"Your case number, please."

"BYO16153"

"Please hold."

I'm hoping they'll be able to fax it over so I won't have to drive way down to Long Beach.

"Negative."

"What? No, I'm calling—"

"The results are negative, sir."

"What's negative? What are—"

"Sir, the results of the blood test are negative. Case BYO16153. You are Michael Datcher, right?"

"Yes, but—"

"Sir, is there a—"

"Hold on, what are you saying? I mean, are you saying that the results of my blood test are negative?"

She starts to laugh.

"Yes sir, negative."

"What does that mean? I mean, are you saying I'm not the father?"

She laughs again.

"Sir, if your name is Michael Datcher, I'm saying that you are not the father of Nicole Ann Datcher. The results are negative, sir."

"OhmyGod."

I hang up the phone. My mind is racing hundreds of scenes per second, my heart is in hot pursuit. I have to stand up. I rush out to the *Sentinel* parking lot and start pacing hard back and forth past the parked cars. Up five cars, down five cars, up five cars, down five cars, up five cars, down five cars.

My mind is flashing like an old-school Kodak flashcube: My pinky in Nicole's hand/Camille's white short-shorts/back-flipping off the curb/Nicole's red screaming face/Camille's arching body shuddering on top of me/Mariam's face breaking/brown nipple in my mouth/Club Flame/walking on the beach with Camille/forty-ounce at my lips/Nicole lying on my chest/state of Illinois certificate of live birth.

lakers break

The Rodney King verdicts hurt me deeply. I had taken a part-time job as a community-service officer with the campus police. I was trying to confront my intense hatred for cops. As a CSO, I studied them up-close. Asked questions. Although I found most of them to be narrow-minded control freaks with an unhealthy need to exercise power over others, some were genuinely concerned about the citizenry. These good cops softened my perspective on law-enforcement officials. "Not guilty" hardened me right back up.

King's videotaped beating gave the international community a chance to witness the savagery I'd seen police perpetrate against blacks since early childhood. The trial was supposed to be a public vindication of our decades-long police-brutality complaints ("Thank God we got it on tape" was the oft heard neighborhood refrain). Instead, the trial was confirmation of what American history had taught us but we didn't want to believe: White people don't give a fuck about black humanity. "Not guilty" broke my heart and broke me free of the Caucasion Church of Christ at the precise same moment.

In early June 1992, I returned to L.A. with a boulder on my shoulder and my first freelance assignment. Amy Rennert, the editor in chief of *San Francisco Focus* magazine, was in the studio audience during a *My Brother's*

Keeper television interview. Afterward, she approached me about writing a first-person narrative about the uprising. I agreed.

My sister, Cyndi, picked me up from the airport and let me crash at her West Hollywood apartment until I could find a crib near UCLA. Cyndi's passionate pursuit of her acting dream had always inspired me. She had recently nabbed the female lead starring opposite Wesley Snipes in *Passenger 57,* soon to be number one at the box office.

In the *San Francisco Focus* article, besides expressing my own voice, I thought it was important to explore the perspective of young black kids. At an early age, they are acutely aware of the breach in the American moral contract that supposedly governs human relations.

On June 12, forty-four days after the rebellion, I visited 99th Street Elementary School in Watts. I wasn't sure if the school was in Crip hood or Blood hood, so I dressed in the most neutral browns and tans I could find. I left my sister's West Hollywood apartment, walked up to Sunset and Crescent Heights, five minutes from Beverly Hills, and hopped on the number 2 RTD, heading southeast. As the bus rambled east, then south, I was struck by the gradual change in skin complexion of those riding the bus. By the time we passed the first burned, soot-covered remains of a former business, the only white face I saw was on a campaign poster next to the decimated building, ironically urging South Central to "Vote Lyndon LaRouche." I exited the bus in front of a large dark power plant and walked to the school.

The two-hour trip had provided me with ample time to confront my fears of returning to an environment I hadn't dealt with in six years. An environment I felt fortunate to have survived the first time through. On the evening of the day I received my acceptance letter for graduate school at UCLA, I had a haunting nightmare that upon returning to Los Angeles, my first night I was murdered.

I walked through 99th Street Elementary, visiting classes with the no-nonsense principal, Althea Woods. I met with six young black boys in an empty classroom for a closed-session, round-table discussion. Their ages ranged from Alexis, eight, to Donte, twelve.

I asked the group, "Why do you think those policemen beat up Rodney King?" Derrick, the biggest and most aggressive, talking fast with a slight stutter, jumped in with "Because he was black, and maybe they thought he was high cause he was driving fast. They [police] don't like to see blacks driving fast. They stopped him. Beat him because he was black. One time this man was walking down by the power plant. A policeman rolled up on him, and said, 'What are you doin?' Then two more police cars pulled up. The first policeman pushed his [the black man's] head against the [police] car for nothin. Then one of the other policemen came up and started hitting him with his baton."

I asked the boys, "How many of you have personally witnessed a policeman beating a black man?"

Five of the six boys raised their hands.

"Are you guys afraid of the police?"

Nine-year-old Gregg, chubby, with dimples and wearing a Jheri curl, raised his hand and slowly said, "I'm afraid of them."

"What would you all have done if you were older and the police beat someone in your family or in your community like they beat Rodney King?"

Eleven-year-old Steve, startlingly intense for his young age, responded very matter-of-factly, "I'd take the police off." He was one of the five who had witnessed police beating a black man.

There was one dissenting voice throughout the discussion: Donte, a thin, soft-spoken, but very confident twelve-year-old. He confronted Derrick and Steve's opinions with an agenda of peace. He calmly and firmly spoke of patience and love.

"Donte, what would you have done if you were old enough and the police beat someone like they beat Rodney King?"

"I would have been mad, but I wouldn't have done a Rambo like you [talking to Derrick]. I would have made sure my family was okay. Then went and passed out food [if stores were closed after looting] to people without cars because my family has a car. Ain't no need for all that killin. Ain't gonna change nothin anyway."

As Donte presented his nonviolent agenda, I felt ashamed at my anger.

Ashamed because I had given up hope that the racial hatred I had been exposed to could be overcome by love.

Moms believed. She was born in the 1940s and raised just outside Birmingham, Alabama: the heart of Dixie. She had known racism intimately; deep hatred had been her companion. Yet she raised her children to love all people regardless of race. She taught by example. She still believes. I wanted to believe too. "Not guilty" was making it hard.

I spent my days in the Westwood apartment hunting for a job, my evenings working on the article. Crossing the street in Westwood, I saw a slim brother with large eyes and a close haircut who looked familiar.

"Excuse, didn't you go to Cal?"

"Yes I did. You look familiar, too. My name is Gregory," he said, extending his hand.

"Michael."

"Are you in school here now?"

"Yeah, I start grad school in the fall. I'm looking for a summer job and a place to lay my nappy head."

"It must have been meant for us to run into each other," he said laughing. "The shoe store I work in around the corner is hiring, and I'm looking for a roommate."

"Dammn."

Snap.

Gregory and I became roommates and coworkers. It couldn't have happened at a better time. I was in a lot of pain. It wasn't just the Rodney King verdicts. It was the Church of Christ drama. Though the San Francisco Church had set me up with the Los Angeles Church, I never showed up. I just disappeared from the struggling list.

I was reeling. I had spent almost five years allowing others to dictate my life. Trying to squeeze myself into someone's definition of what my life should be. Someone else's definition of what was right and wrong and backing it up with God. I wasn't sure what I believed anymore. I accepted the fact that if somehow I were to get in an accident and die, there was a good chance I was going to hell.

Although I tried to hide it, I clung to Gregory. I needed a friend so badly.

I needed someone to affirm me, to hold my hand while I got through this period.

After a while, I stopped hiding my need because I began to see that Gregory was going through a lot, too. Late at night, we'd sit around our candle-and-incense-furnished apartment, listening to Bob Marley and Jimi Hendrix, talking shit full of male posturing and bravado. Then one phrase or story or question would open the door to where we really were at. My pain would usually stumble out of the closet first. Funking up the room with salvation doubts and a need for a new Jesus.

We balanced these soul-searching sessions with what became the second component of my bargain-basement cult deprogramming: hard-core partying. Four or five nights a week, all summer long, we spent our little Westwood paychecks in clubs all over Los Angeles. Dancing, sweating, drinking, smoking major weed, and trying to be born again inside the wombs of women we barely knew.

I was especially ravenous. I had been suffocating my strong sex drive for years in the Church. When I did slip, the intimacy was so guilt-ridden, it was difficult to enjoy. L.A.'s highly sexualized culture provided an atmosphere to express myself. I had forgotten how much I loved women. The warm flush of instant chemistry in a café, the backs of soft hands, good conversations, beautiful smiles, sly flirting, post-zinfandel hunger in eyes, the taste of arched necks, the firm terrain of inner ears, the unsolved mystery of liberated nipples taking a stand in thin blouses, how the air electrifies when she wants to undress you.

There was an odd spiritual element to my bed-hopping. In the Church, I had gotten accustomed to having my spirit touched by the constant prayer, the singing, reading psalms. When I left, I experienced an incredible vacuum. I missed the emotional intensity of tapping into that God energy. I began to find that feeling in the orgasms of women. I worked hard to make them come hard. In the moment of shuddering and arching and screaming, I wrapped my arms around them tight, pressed my face close. My spirit needed to feel all that pure energy. I held on to these shuddering women like they were epileptic messiahs.

Amy Rennert liked my uprising article. It won the Walter White Award for commentary and was a finalist for the National Magazine Awards. I became a frequent contributor to *San Francisco Focus*.

Sandy Close, the editor at Pacific News Service, got my number from Amy and offered me an opportunity to be a Los Angeles correspondent. I'd always been frustrated by the scarcity of young black male voices in the press (a significant factor in our international PR problem). I jumped at the chance. Soon I was appearing on Op-Ed pages around the country, writing about politics, race, and culture, trying to articulate our humanity.

I hated UCLA because it wasn't Berkeley. Location was everything.

Couched between Beverly Hills, Bel Air, and Westwood, the campus atmosphere reflected its surroundings: The Dollar seemed privileged above the Idea. Most students stepped onto campus right off the pages of *Gentlemen's Quarterly* and *Vogue*. I didn't see any spontaneous gathering places to debate. Political activism was not a priority. There was no poetry scene. Black students didn't even give the communal wassup nod when they passed each other. I was very disappointed. Berkeley had me spoiled.

To make matters worse, my African-American studies program didn't have department status, so all of my professors were first and foremost beholden to their specific discipline's departments (English, Poli Sci). We African-American studies grad students were like red-headed stepchildren. When it came to us, money, time, and resources were short. Several students transferred. I decided to make the best of it.

I started writing a hard-hitting sociopolitical column called "Under the Overpass" for the *Daily Bruin* (which eventually moved to the Pacific News Service). I also organized a weekly writing workshop in our apartment and a biweekly, cross-generational black men's discussion group there as well. I was trying to bring a slice of Berkeley to the fashion district.

The apartment I shared with Gregory didn't come with a refrigerator. We used one of those brown grocery bag–sized units until our place became a central gathering spot. We needed to buy a real fridge.

A new one was out of the question, so we started scouring the *Recycler* magazine for used appliances. We had $97 between us until payday. We made numerous phone calls and came across a UCLA grad student who was selling what sounded like a nice refrigerator for $125. Gregory said we'd be over in an hour. He was the professional salesman, so he figured we could talk the guy down.

We drove to the address in Gregory's early-model gray Volkswagen Jetta. Gregory parked in front of the building, pulled the emergency brake, and turned to me.

"Here's the plan. As we're checking the refrigerator out, you'll like it and be friendly with the guy. I'll be distant and find whatever I can wrong with it. Kind of that good cop/bad cop thing. Then—"

"Good cop/bad cop refrigerator negotiations!" I screamed. "You're killing me. I wanna be the bad cop. . . . 'You call this a refrigerator? You think I'm stupid? You think I was born in a pickle wagon, huh, Mr. Frigidaire?' Gregory, this is too much, three much."

Gregory didn't even smile. He was dead serious. That's what made it so funny.

"You finished?"

"Yeah, go head, man, break down the master plan," I said, barely able to suppress my laughter.

"Okay, take some of the ones out your wallet. Crumple them up, put a couple in a front pocket, a couple in your back pocket, maybe one in your sock, and I'll do the same. When we get inside, just follow my lead."

"Roger!" I shouted, doubling over.

As we strolled through the large complex, trying to find the correct apartment, I caught a bad case of the giggles. I swiveled my head, quickly looking to my left, then quickly right, then left, humming the theme from "Mission Impossible."

Gregory's face was tensed, ready. Fully in character. He *is* Greg Morris.

An Asian man in his late twenties answered the door in sweats, flip-flops, and a T-shirt.

"Hi, we called about the refrigerator," I said, extending my hand. "My name is Michael; this is my roommate, Gregory."

I made myself avoid looking at Gregory's face. I knew I would blow our cover.

As we checked out the fairly new refrigerator, which really was a great deal for $125, I talked the guy up. He was a Taiwanese national graduating with a degree in math from UCLA and returning to Taiwan.

Gregory spent the thirty minutes we were there with his arms folded across his chest. When he unfolded them, it was to run his hand slowly against the surface of the refrigerator: the door, the left side, the right, the freezer. Every time he came across a small dent, he would let out a breathy little grunt—"huummph"—then say, "Look at this, Michael."

Gregory as Greg Morris as Perry Mason must have asked the guy fifteen questions. When did you buy it? Are you the original owner? Has the Freon been changed? Has it ever been laid on its side? I had to keep my face turned away.

Finally, the guy said in broken English, "Do you want or not?"

I concentrated, then looked at Gregory.

"It's not perfect, but I think it's awright, man. But since you're putting up most of the money, you make the call."

"I don't know, man. He's not the original owner. We don't know what the original owner did to it—"

"I told you it work fine."

"How much are you asking for it again?"

"One twenty-five."

"With all the dents, I really think ninety's a fair price. What do you think, Mi—"

"No way. Ninety is too low. It work fine. Look at it, it's very nice," he said, turning to me.

"Well, it looks awright, but we're concerned about it working awright."

Noticeably perturbed, he said, "Okay, I take off fifteen dollars, charge you one hundred and ten. No lower."

"What do you think?" I said, turning excitedly to Gregory, who was standing by the refrigerator, running his hand over it again. He pulled out his wallet. I pulled out mine. I retrieved all the cash and handed it to Gregory. He put it together, arranging the bills from large denominations to small, with all the bills facing the same direction. Gregory began to count aloud: 20-40-50-60-70-75-80-85-86-87-88-89-90.

"You have any more cash on you, man?"

I patted my front right pocket. Pulled two crumpled dollars. Patted my left. One dollar bill. Patted my back. Another single. I handed the money to Gregory. He checked his pants pockets but found nothing. Checked his breast pocket and pulled out two folded ones. When he reached down to roll up his pants leg, I had to turn away. He dug inside his black socks to no avail. The last dollar had slipped deep down into the foot. When Gregory took off his brown penny loafers, I almost lost it. He added the seven wrinkled singles to the stack and recounted the whole bundle.

"Listen, man, we're students, just like you. All we got is ninety-seven dollars. I know it's less than what you deserve, but whaddayasay?" Gregory said, smiling for the first time all afternoon.

When we got the refrigerator home, Gregory and I spent two hours cleaning it with sudsy bleach and Pine Sol.

We saw the first roach about a week afterward. Both superclean cats, we figured it came from one of our neighbors. We saw three more the next day. We immediately went out and bought two insect foggers. When we returned to the house, we swept up the few roaches lying paralyzed on their backs. We cleaned the refrigerator again.

Within days, roaches reappeared. This time they were newborns. A bad sign. We bought the Raid Max bomb. We bought two Max bombs the next time. We complained to the landlord about our neighbors. She brought in the exterminator. Within a week, the newborns were back.

It seemed we were wasting money, so we stopped buying the foggers. A mistake.

Gregory usually came home from work at around 11:00 P.M., which was around the same time I would get back from the library. At times I'd walk in and find him just outside the kitchen, in the dining area, staring down at the kitchen floor. Once in a while I would get home first, come into the dark house, cut the kitchen light on, and see literally *hundreds* of different-sized roaches scurry for cover on the floor, cabinets, countertops, stove. It made my skin crawl. I never walked barefoot in the house.

In time, we began to see that there were two different strains. One was your basic flat-bodied oval cockroach of the family Blattidae. The other was a huskier cousin with a bigger head and two long, thin, almost transparent wings.

Soon both strains and their bad-ass children were everywhere: in the bathroom sink, on the living room walls, on my zebra-print bedspread, in Gregory's dirty-clothes basket, and most of all—in the kitchen. It was occupied territory. We rarely cooked anymore.

Gregory was a night owl and vegetarian. During the period we began to call "B.R.," he would watch TV into the wee hours and often make a late-night salad. A.R., I'd often hear him late-night in the kitchen screaming, cursing out roaches.

Having company over, especially at night, was nerve-racking. Afternoons were usually cool, but we never knew when day-trippers would make a surprise appearance on the wall. When they did, we'd punish them. Our favorite was spraying the husky cousins with Raid to slow them down, then pulling out a lighter and burning them to death.

By home-field study, we learned that when pregnant roaches are in the act of dying, they push out their long yellowish egg sacs to give their unborn a chance at life. I called Gregory into the kitchen when I saw the banana sac slide out for the first time. It touched him, too.

"As a species, they have an amazing survival instinct."

"Yeah, it's incredible."

Then I set the little sac on fire.

After almost a year of insect high drama, I came home from a club one night at about 3:00 A.M. to find Gregory in the kitchen with the back of the refrigerator facing outward. He had a flashlight in his hand.

"Look at this, man," he said, handing me the flashlight. "In the back above the motor."

I squatted down. There were dozens and dozens of egg sacs on a metal shelf just above the warm purring motor. Our refrigerator was a Blattidae incubator.

We should have gotten rid of it months before. We thought we could deal with the problem. Instead, the Blattidae family dealt with us.

"Motherfuckers."

"Yeah, but you know we brought this on ourselves, trying to be slick," I said, handing Gregory the flashlight.

"You right, but goddamnnn."

"Even if we did get rid of the fridge," I said to Gregory, "there's no telling where else the little beasts were laying eggs. I think we should look for a new crib, man."

"Mike, I been thinking that for a while, now. It's time to make like a breast and bounce. Speaking of . . . those things . . . how was the club?"

"It was cool."

"You come up?"

"Yeahhh, I met a *saucy* little sister named Camille."

shall set you free

After I receive the blood test results in early October 1995, I go into a cocoon for a few days. Work, then home. Turn my ringer off. I don't tell anyone. Not even Camille.

When I get in from work, I light the red candles on my coffee table, burn incense. Keep my blinds closed, lamps off. Slide in Coltrane's *Crescent*. I begin to walk slowly through my dark apartment. From the six-foot bookcase that holds my stereo to the coffee table against the wall on my right to the Victorian chair where I used to pass out drunk. Through the hallway, into the bathroom, looking at my shadow in the mirror. Listening to the saxophone filter in from the living room. Into the bedroom. I sit on the edge of my zebra-print spread, reminisce. Enter the candleless kitchen and lounge at the round wooden table. Coltrane coasts into darkness. Back to the living room, turn the tape over, start another roaming course through my life.

I slow-walk, head shaking, cursing Camille, cursing myself. I meander, wondering out loud how long she's known. From the beginning? Since the pregnancy test? Did she have a feeling when her cervix began to dilate? Maybe it was when she held Nicole in the delivery room? I don't care how scared she was, she should have told me.

She had me stretched out of my mind. Pulled from fear to joy to depression to triumph to regret, literally, from hour to hour. She fatigued my soul. Made me hate her. She took life from me. I was Nicole's daddy, now I'm not.

Nicole was my fractured dream, my guilty nightmare. Now she's not. I'm in love with my daughter who's not mine. In love with my daughter who doesn't exist.

I know I can't blame it all on Camille. I can't front and say I don't understand. I'm sure she's been dealing with brothers like me for a long time. Cats who can commit to multiple positions but not to a relationship. She's probably been piecing together a patchwork man out of a bunch of tired-ass niggas for a long time. Camille wanted a baby, she got pregnant, and when Nicole was born she probably figured I'd be the best bet as a father. She was in a bad situation so she made some bad choices. Camille was looking out for herself. I just got caught up in the mix. I should have seen the mix coming and gotten out of the blender.

Camille won't return my pages. It's been a week since I found out, three days since I've been calling. I'm sure she knows I know. She's scared. She could be telling her family anything about me, so I don't think it's safe to just show up at her crib. She's already shown me she's a convincing liar. I don't want to knock on the door and get a hole blown through my chest by some irate family member caught up in Camille's drama.

I've just been punching in my digits on her voice mail/pager. I decide to leave a message.

"Camille, I know about Nicole. . . . That was ill. I haven't forgiven you; I may never forgive you; we'll just have to see what happens over time. I'm really calling to let you know that I still want to be in Nicole's life in some way. Right now, I don't know how or what or whatever. We need to talk. You know the number."

Camille doesn't call back that night or the next. A week passes. I consider taking my chances and swinging by her crib. I decide to give it a few more days.

On Saturday, I'm on the return leg from an early morning walk up and down hilly Angeles Vista. A car speeds up the hill past me. I catch a swiveling head out of the corner of my eye. The car screeches into a hook slide.

My previous experiences with the random nature of L.A.'s violence has me in a quick semicrouch, arms flared out from my sides, eyes darting for an escape route. The door flies open. To my surprise, a twenty-something woman jumps out of the driver's side, leaving the door open.

"Michael."

Hearing my name—and seeing that it's a woman—involuntarily raises me out of my crouch. The woman strides quickly toward the sidewalk. She senses my confusion.

"It's Sasha, Camille's friend."

My mind is moving in too many directions to recognize the name, but as she steps up on the curb I recognize her face. She threw a little get-together during the Thanksgiving holidays. Camille and I stopped by, played some cards, had a few drinks, and bounced. Camille and she seemed pretty tight.

"You know Nicole's not yours, right?"

She's speaking with the kind of excitement that tells me that she and Camille have definitely fallen out.

"Yeah, I just got the blood test back a coupla weeks ago."

"You know who the father is, don't you?"

"Naw, I don't."

"The white boy she was dealin with. Nicole looks just like him. I thought you'd be suspicious when you saw her."

I can't even talk.

"She was with him, my brother, and a coupla other niggas, tryin to be a playa. She didn't know who the daddy was. She had to say it was somebody's."

"Damnnn."

"Yep, she's a scandalous ho. I told my brother he needed to stop messin with that bitch. He don't deal with her no more. So, wassup? I mean, how you doin? Have you talked to her? What is she sayin now?"

I tell Sasha that I was thinking about swinging by Camille's crib, but I was afraid of walking into a situation.

"Booy, Camille don't live there no mo. She moved. I think she's out in Moreno Valley. I think that's where the white boy lives at."

Her car horn blows.

"I gotta go, but I'm gonna give you my number in case you ever wanna talk or something. Let me just run to my car and write it down."

She comes jogging back across the street, chest thrust forward like a business card.

"Here, call me."

I never do call Camille's ex-friend. Camille never calls me. Maybe it's all for the best. I'm fooling myself if I think I can have a relationship with Nicole without dealing with Camille on some level. I need to push them all out of my mind. Pour my energy into my job. Move on. And that's just what I do—until about a week before Christmas.

Sitting at my *Sentinel* desk, I can't shake my thoughts of Nicole. Maybe it's because the Christmas season is for children and Nicole Ann Datcher was my child. She could grow up thinking I'm really her father. Wondering each year why her daddy doesn't ever bring her anything for Christmas. Wondering why her daddy deserted her. Why her daddy doesn't love her. Why her daddy had to be another tired-ass brother who ran out on his own flesh and blood.

I have a feeling that Camille hasn't even told her mother and the rest of her family about the blood test. They probably just figured I couldn't handle the pressure and stopped coming around. An easy confirmation of their Niggas Ain't Shit theory. They probably saw it coming.

I grab the copy of my blood-test results, make a photocopy, fold it into an envelope, and slip out to the parking lot. I can tell how nervous I am because the ignition slot won't stand still. I make the five-minute drive north from the *Sentinel*'s Crenshaw Boulevard offices to Camille's block. Park across the street from her building. Quick prayer.

I grab the white envelope from the passenger seat, fold it in half, and place it in my back pocket.

I cross the street, keeping my eye fixed on the front door. It's propped open with a piece of junk mail. I step quickly up the raggedy carpeted stairway. I stop at the top of the stairs. "Calm down, man." Although it's the middle of the day, the long unlit hallway resembles the dark underpasses that allow you to cross busy highways. I breathe in deeply . . . breathe out deeply. Walk quickly down the hallway straight to Camille's door and knock forcefully.

No answer.

I move in closer to the door. Listen. No one's home. I want someone to be home, but I'm relieved someone's not. I hurry back down the hallway, fly down the stairs, and jump back into my ride. As I'm moving out in traffic toward Crenshaw, I see Camille's mother walking with Camille's sister, who is pushing a blue baby stroller. They're walking southbound on Crenshaw.

I have to turn around. Crenshaw is busy, so I drive several blocks before I can make a U-turn. I race back up but I don't see them. They must have turned toward home. As I make a right, I see them passing behind the tinted, all-weather bus stop near the corner. There are no parking spaces, so I make a quick left onto Camille's street, park the car, and jump out sprinting, arms pumping, toward the covered bus stop. I'm surprised at how far they are down the street. The sight of their distant tiny bodies immediately accelerates my frantic heart rate and my pumping arms. Running southbound, I can see head after head turning toward me in the cars whizzing by. It hits me that I'm sprinting down Crenshaw Boulevard in the middle of the day—like I just stole a whole lotta money.

Although I slow to a relaxed jog, my heart doesn't seem to recognize the downshift. Camille's family is only a hundred yards ahead of me. I don't want to frighten them, don't want them to think I'm coming to bring harm. I change gears to a brisk walk. At fifty yards, they're normal-sized, real. I close in for about ten seconds, then call out, "Excuse me."

I'm only twenty yards from them but either they can't hear because of the busy Crenshaw traffic or they think I'm talking to someone else. I lunge forward, running a couple of steps. Louder.

"Excuse me!"

Startled, Camille's mother flinches into a semiturn the way kids do when they hear close-range gunfire.

Her eyes widen in genuine terror. Camille's sister turns around to face me and completely freezes up.

I stop walking ten yards from them and raise my hands, palms up, like their eyes are stickup pistols.

"It's okay; it's me, Michael. It's okay. I just want to let you know what's been going on."

I take a step forward. Camille's mother shrieks, and jumps in the opposite direction.

"It's okay, it's okay. Listen, I just wanna talk for a few seconds. I'll stand right here. It's okay. I don't know what Camille has told yall, but I'm not Nicole's father, I-am-not-Nicole's-father. I don't know if she told you this or not, but we took a blood test, it came out negative. I'm not Nicole's father."

Camille's sister is the Statue of Liberty.

"I just thought you should know, for Nicole's sake, for medical reasons, for the simple fact that she should know who her real father is. It's not me."

My mouth is a Victrola phonograph; their curious faces tilt like the RCA dog.

"I brought you a copy of the blood test. I think you should know the truth."

I watch their eyes follow my cautious hand into my back pocket. I slowly pull the folded envelope out and extend my arm toward Camille's mother. I take one step. Another. As I move the envelope down toward her palm, she snatches her hand away, body recoiling like I'm trying to give her the wrong end of a blowtorch.

"Ma'am, I just want you to know the truth."

I pivot toward the Statue of Liberty.

"You understand, it's important for Nicole to know who her father is. Take this and talk to your sister. She knows what it is. I'm sure she has a copy."

I place the envelope in her palm. I stick up my hands and start backing away from them.

Camille's mother lunges at her daughter, snatches the envelope, shrieks, and throws the folded paper with all her strength into the traffic.

"Ma'am, I just want you to know the truth," I repeat.

She lunges at me, screaming at the top of her lungs, "I know the truth! I know the truth!"

Startled by her intensity, I jump back, point to the envelope tumbling in traffic, and shout, "That is the truth, goddamit, that is the truth!"

Cars slow like we are a bloody roadside accident. Camille's mother, head swiveling, palms both her ears, closes her eyes, and starts screaming in a rhythmic maniacal voice, "I-know-the-truth-I-know-the-truth-I-know-the-truth-I-know-the-truth-I-know-the-truth-I-know-the-truth-I-know-the-truth-I-know-the-truth-I-know . . ."

I reach for the sky. Back out of Dodge to the rhythm of pain.

world stage

Sharing an apartment with roaches taught me that peace of mind begins at home. Gregory and I both felt we needed our own space.

My apartment hunt became a holy mission. I was looking for a crib that I could thrive in. On weekends, I jumped in my ride and just drove. I rolled through neighborhoods all over the city: Santa Monica, Mid-Wilshire, Hollywood, Ladera. Sometimes I'd make these treks in the day, sometimes at night. I wanted to get a feel for the places when the sun went down.

After a couple of weekends, I'd found some possibilities but none that moved me enough to say, "This is it."

One Saturday, I was driving south down Crenshaw, just past the Baldwin Hills mall. I was surprised to see people walking in and out of a series of small boutique-sized storefronts up ahead. Car culture is so dominant in L.A. that you rarely see people walking the streets. I made another left turn onto this unusually wide street. There were more boutiques, and dozens of people strolling leisurely. A particularly large crowd was gathered in front of one of the shops. When I parked a few spaces down and turned off my stereo, I could hear the music: jazz.

I hopped out of the car and rushed toward the saxophone honks. I couldn't see over the people bunched around the door. I squeezed over to the picture window. A hard-driving quintet was playing on a tiny stage. The audience was screaming back at the musicians, "Go head! Go head!" The place reminded me of some of the small blues clubs I used to go to in Oakland. I didn't know anything like this existed in L.A.

After the set, I pressed my way inside. I approached the man behind the counter.

"Excuse me, man, what is this place called?"

"The World Stage."

"What's the neighborhood called?"

"Leimert Park. This must be your first time here."

"Yes it is."

"I'm Brother Don Muhammed."

"Michael. So, what goes on here?"

"Well, as you can see, we have jazz. Billy Higgins . . . Do you know who Billy Higgins is?"

"I know the name, but . . ."

Muhammed told me that Billy Higgins is the world's most recorded drummer. He's played with everyone from Coltrane to Monk. Higgins owns the World Stage with a brother named Kamau Daáood. Kamau's a poet.

"There actually used to be a poetry workshop but they haven't had it for a while," Muhammed said.

"Is that right?"

I told him that I ran a little poetry workshop out of my apartment in the Palms but that I was about to move. I asked how I could get in contact with Mr. Daáood.

"Well, you could walk around the corner. Brother Kamau owns a record store called Finyl Vinyl right over on Forty-third Place."

I walked down Degnan, hooked a left on 43rd, and saw a bright yellow sandwich board shouting FINYL VINYL. I stepped inside the record shop. There was a salt-and-pepper–bearded brother sitting on the staircase, talking on the phone. His eyes followed me in. I browsed through the large collection of used jazz records, waiting for him to finish his call.

"How can I help you, brother?" a deep baritone inquired behind me.

"Mr. Daáood?" I said, walking toward him.

"Yes."

I told him that my name is Michael Datcher and that I was a graduate student in African-American studies at UCLA. Brother Muhammed at the World Stage had just mentioned that there used to be a writer's workshop at the venue.

"Yes, because of staffing issues it's been on hiatus for the last six months."

"Well, I currently conduct a workshop out of my apartment. I live in the Palms, but I'm considering moving here to Leimert Park. I would love the opportunity to help the workshop get up and running again."

Kamau didn't say anything. He had been studying me closely since we'd been talking.

"Michael, may I call you Michael?"

"Please."

"Michael, please don't take this the wrong way. I don't know you. I don't know the kind of person you are and how you approach business. It's a little awkward for me really because you've just walked in here off the street and asked to be involved in something that's very, very important to me and other people in this community. What I'm saying is that if things work out in such a way that you can come and lend your energy here, you have to understand that the World Stage is a sacred space and we approach the work from a sacred space."

I could respect what he was saying. In fact this sounded like the kind of place I was looking for. I told Daáood that I'd do whatever I needed to do to fit with the program.

"Okay, I'll speak to the coordinators of the workshop, Anthony Lyons and Nafis Nawbawi. Why don't you give me a call next week, and if Anthony and Nafis are interested, maybe we can arrange a meeting."

V. Kali Nurigan comes rushing through the World Stage's white wooden door. She's five-foot-none of black-woman energy in the shape of a dreadlocked poet in perpetual motion.

"Hi, Michael, is the list filled yet?" she says sliding me her three-dollar admission.

"Sister, now you know that the list gets filled by seven forty-five, seven-fifty at the latest. It's almost eight-thirty."

"I know, I know. I was trying to get here but had a little drama. I was at home working on the poem *about the drama* I wanted to read tonight."

"Why don't you workshop it? There's probably time for one more person."

One of the brothers stands, relinquishing his seat so V. can sit down.

There is no sign-up list for the workshop segment. The first person to bound onstage in front of the mic gets to read and receive feedback. After two years of being involved, I realize that the poets who workshop the most have become the best poets. As a result, the workshop section has become extremely popular. Poets who plan to receive feedback arrive early and cluster in the front-row seats. As soon as the person onstage finishes and steps one foot off the stage, the would-be-next workshoppers aggressively jump on. If it's close, the crowd determines who was first. This good-natured ritual sends the message that while others flee from constructive criticism, the World Stage poets are hungry to get better.

When the workshopping poet finishes, V. leaps onto the stage, but so does another sister. The crowd calls it a dead heat. The other sister says she's leaving town the next day. Clearly disappointed, V. takes the big role and allows the sister to read.

The featured reader finishes at 9:00 P.M. During the break, Anthony takes over the door duties and I make my way through the crowd to host the open mic.

I start pulling names out of the red-and-green Cross Colours bag. The poets rise out of their seats, squish past knees and backpacks, climb onto the stage, and kick their work.

After the first two readers, I pull a third name from the hat. The poet is not in the room.

"Now, is there someone who would like to fill this person's—"

"Michael, I have to read!" V. Kali says, jumping to her feet. The audience's laughter decides that her passion will not be challenged.

"Awwright. Please place your hands together for V. Kali."

V. makes her way to the stage.

"Wheww. Thank ya, chuch. Wheww. Let me just breathe for a second. . . . Okay."

Her eyes are moist with emotion. Usually she sits on the wooden stool when she recites, but now she stands in front of the microphone, still breathing heavily.

"Earlier today I had a very awkward conversation with Akin's father. Akin, member of the Too Live crew—also known as my children—is my six-year-old son. A few months ago I called his father and told him to come pick up his child. Akin needs to live with a man, his father, for a while, just to be able to understand what that energy is about."

V. has to stop. Has to slow herself down. She steps away from the mic, bows her head as if she's praying.

"It's awright, V.," someone in the audience intones.

"Take ya time, girl, we ain't goin nowhere."

V. steps back to the microphone.

"When I brought Akin to him, I explained exactly the kinds of things that Akin could and could not eat because of a medical condition he has. I explained to this fool that if he simply followed these basic instructions, there wouldn't be a problem, but that if he didn't, it could endanger Akin's life."

She takes a deep breath.

"Earlier today, Akin's father called to inform me that Akin was coughing up blood."

V. pauses again, but there are no shouts from the crowd this time. Watermelons are lodged in throats.

"He said he didn't know what to do. What he should have done was follow instructions. I told that fool to take our son to the hospital and do whatever is necessary to make sure my son is all right."

Tears begin to roll down V.'s face.

"I told that idiot if anything happened to Akin . . . that I would kill him. I'm serious. I told him I would do a drive-by on his ass and do my prison time. And I'm very serious. I hung up on him and wrote this poem. It's entitled, 'I'm Raising Children.' I'm reading it here tonight because if I saw him now, I'd kill him. I'm serious. I have the technology."

i'm raising children
i'm not the farmer's daughter
raising chickens
to be slaughtered
not the sharecropper's child
raising cane to be
cut down
i'm raising children

V. stops, backs away from the mic, and begins to jab her finger toward the stage as if to say, "Right here."

She begins to cry harder and jab harder.

"Take ya time, sister."

"It's awright, sister, take ya time."

She takes a deep breath and confronts the mic again.

raising
not california singing dried fruit
raisinettes
not raising strange fruit
to hang from some oppressor's tree
i'm raising precious fruits
to grow high on the vine
precious fruits reaching toward
the sunshine
raising the fruits of my womb
to multiply by fives
to stay alive
i'm raising children here.

V. pauses; her finger jabs down to the stage again. "Here."

"That's right, girlll."

"We know where ya at Wednesday nights."
"Tell it. Tell it."

                no little bo-peep
        leading her sheep to be slaughtered
            these are my daughters
            these are my sons
            i'm raising children yall
            raising them up
            above the flood waters

V.'s voice begins to rise.

            I am the crossing guard
        cross me and you'll be sorry
        cause i'm raising children here
        between rock and hard space
            betwixt slim and none
        tween fatback 'n' no slack
            i'm raising children yall
        the instructions are included
        don't fold spindle or mutilate
        the instructions been included
        do not fold spindle or mutilate
            neglect misuse or abuse
        just follow the instructions
        like you do ogun osun and the
                moon
        just follow the instructions
        cause i'm raising children here
            i'm raising children yall
            i'm raising children here.

"And don't fuck with me!" V. adds as a spontaneous addendum to the piece.

The crowd jumps to its feet.

V. steps off the stage into the hugs and kisses of the people standing for her. She begins to sob harder. The crowd keeps clapping and stomping. It takes a long time for the next poet's name to be pulled from the Cross Colours bag.

the bomb

When Peter calls and says a friend of his wants to introduce me to a great sister, I'm immediately on the defensive. It's been only a month since my holiday street scene with Camille's family. I'm determined that 1996 will be a year of discernment. Drama is waaay outta style.

"If she's all that, why's he not trying to get with her himself?"

"Michael, I don't know nothin about that," Peter says. "All I know is he asked me to see if it'd be okay to give your number out. Now, you know it ain't no pressure. I could tell him no easily as I could tell him yes, know-what-I-mean?"

"Why don't you tell him to give me a call first?"

The next day Richard leaves a message on my voice mail explaining that he's Peter's friend. Before I can get around to calling him back, he leaves a more specific message two days later.

"Hi, Michael, it's Richard again, Peter's friend. I have someone I think you'd like to meet. Her name is Jenoyne Adams. She's a good friend of mine. I just think you'd like her. Jenoyne's the Bomb. So anyway, call me back and let me know if it's okay for me to give her your number."

It's the first time a cat has ever tried to hook me up with a sister. I call Peter back.

"So, what's up with your boy Richard? This is a little different for me, bruh, it's not every day cats are tryin to play matchmaker for me."

Peter laughs.

"Well, brother, he's always in the company of attractive women, so you can take that for what it's worth. And I don't imagine that he's gonna hook you up with a mass murderer—but then again, you never know. So, my friend, you do what you think is best for you."

"Hello, may I speak to Michael?"

"Michael is speaking."

"This is Jenoyne Adams. My friend Richard May forwarded your number to me," she says, her tone precise but warm.

"Is-that-right?"

"That's right."

"Richard had some wonderful things to say about you. He mentioned something about you being . . . the Bomb. You tryin to claim that title, sister?"

"Well, I must say that particular word is not the first one that comes to mind when I describe myself—but don't let that stop you using it if it makes you feel comfortable."

"I'll keep that in mind. How's your day been?"

"It's been busy but good. I sing in my church choir. We performed at the eight o'clock service, the eleven o'clock service, and I'll be going back to perform at the six o'clock service."

"You be up in church all day, huh?"

"Nooo. If I attended church all day, I wouldn't be talking to you from my apartment right now."

"Now don't get me wrong, church is cool an all, but it just seems to me with all the pressing needs in the black community to be spending all day in church seems kinda . . . counterproductive. I mean, with all the juice Christian ministers have, why aren't they more involved in trying to organize black people to better help themselves?"

"How do you know what black ministers are doing?" Her voice is much crisper than before. "Have you visited every small storefront church? You must get around."

"I don't need to visit every church to see a trend."

"Black ministers have always been in the forefront of black leadership."

"What are they doing now?"

"What are *you* doing now?"

"I do a few things. So, what do you consider yourself?"

"I'm not sure what you're asking."

"I mean, do you consider yourself a believer in God, or do you consider yourself a Christian, or some other—"

"I'm a Christian."

"So, is Jeeeesus the only way for someone to know God?"

"Listen, I don't put God in a box. For me, God manifests Himself in the form of Jesus. That doesn't mean that God can't manifest Himself in some other form or under some other name. Jesus just happens to work for me."

"Do you share your faith?"

"Why do I feel like I'm been interrogated?"

"Sister, I'm just makin conversation."

"If this is your idea of making conversation, I'd hate to see you as a prosecutor. I . . . You know what? I'm going to let you go. I need to go spend all day, oh, excuse me, all the rest of my day in church."

We say our terse good-byes, hang up. The Bomb has just exploded, I think to myself. I won't be hearing from her again.

When Jenoyne calls a couple of weeks later, I'm surprised and strangely excited. We didn't really get along in our first conversation, and the drama with Camille has made me look at women with a tighter shutter. I'm not even trying to like her.

Our second conversation, which lasts more than two hours, goes much smoother. Jenoyne tells me that she was a tomboy growing up because she spent so much time with her father, even after her parents separated during her early childhood. When she was eleven she went to live with him full-time. God never enters our subject arena. Our first discussion showed me I still need to shake some sticky Church of Christ residue.

When Jenoyne calls the next weekend, I'm not surprised, just excited.

"What are you doing tonight, Michael?"

"I haven't made any plans. Why, you tryin to ask me out on a date?"

"No, I'm just making conversation."

"Funny."

"I was thinking maybe we could get together and do something?"

"What do you wanna do?"

"Well, I'm very open."

"There's a great jazz club called Fifth Street Dick's right near my house. You'd love it."

"I'd rather not meet on your turf; let's meet in neutral territory."

"Are we signing a peace treaty or tryin to have a date? Should I invite my Secretary of State? C'mon, now. Listen, I'll throw on my apron and hook up the pasta à la Datcher. We can have a nice dinner right here at the crib."

"I'm not coming to your house for dinner on a first date. I barely know you. You might be the boogey man."

"Be serious."

"Do I sound like I'm chuckling?"

"Boo."

"We're trying to have a date where both you and I feel comfortable. I would feel more comfortable if we could meet someplace that's in an area between your home and my home. There's a place called Applebee's in West Covina. That's about halfway between L.A. and Chino. About a half hour from both directions."

"West Covina? I don't even know where West Covina's at."

"Michael, look at it as an adventure. A search for hidden treasure."

"Riiiight."

West Covina is not a half hour from Los Angeles or anywhere else except God's back. After almost an hour heading east on the 10 freeway, I'm thinking about turning around. It's then that I see the Applebee's sign glowing in neon off the freeway.

I'm glad I make it before Jenoyne so I can chill and relax before she walks in. I'm working my black slacks, black turtleneck, black Italian dress shoes, and oversized black leather jacket.

I order a Guinness, position my stool toward the front door, and chat with the fresh-scrubbed, talkative bartender. I'm the only black person in the entire place.

Jenoyne comes through the door with the focused urgency of someone arriving twenty minutes late for a first date. Striding in three-inch black leather pumps and mid-thigh-length black dress, zipper down the front (which make her slender five-foot-nine body six-foot), she takes three giant steps into the Applebee's. Jenoyne scans the bar like a triage officer surveying the damage: The domino effect of twisting necks has hit both men and women.

"Wooooo" opens my mouth and closes it just in time for her not to catch me so obviously impressed. As she pivots in my direction, I raise off the stool. We meet at the corner of the bar.

"JenoyneMichael?" we say almost simultaneously, extending our palms into a handshake she makes firm.

Her light-brown gaze is direct and intense. Hair pulled up and back into a French roll, sly part slanting left.

"I'm sorry I'm late."

I've heard only her telephone voice, never seen her mouth move. "I'm-sorry-I'm-late" has me fixated on her quick parting and closing lips.

"It's cool," I manage to say, recovering.

We walk over to the bar, and I pull out the stool next to mine. She sits; her long crossing legs give me pause. We're facing each other.

I pick up my beer for security.

The concentration it's taking to appear calm *and* not glance down at Jenoyne's legs *and* not worry about stuttering doesn't leave me much energy to think of anything clever to say. Instead, I grip the Guinness tightly, raising it from my lap in ten-second intervals. Between sips, I say things like

"Nice place. . . . It's kinda cold in here. . . . This brew's hittin the spot. . . . How's your cranberry juice?"

Since I keep jumping in nervously with these snippets that can elicit only one-word answers or none at all, the conversation sputters for the first fifteen minutes. Jenoyne rescues me by excusing herself to the bathroom. Grateful for the reprieve, I quickly lie down on the mental dating couch.

C'mon, cat. What are you doin? Relax and pull yourself together. You're blowin it. Have fun. She likes you, she likes you, she likes you.

When Jenoyne returns, I chill out enough to rest my beer on the bar. I remember that she's been working on a freelance article about drug treatment programs, so I ask her about it.

"I finished it this week, but my editor wants to make all these crazy cuts. I can't believe it," she says, her voice rising. "I put so much work into this article. I really worked hard to craft the story so each paragraph flowed into the next. If he makes even some of the changes he's discussed with me, he'll change not only the content but the whole rhythm of the article."

We spend an hour talking about editors and the publishing industry. Jenoyne tells me that *Resurrecting Mingus,* the novel she's been working on, has received some encouraging interest.

"A few months ago, I sent query letters out just to see what would happen. Four agents requested that I send the whole novel. It was weird. Their interest completely freaked me. It made everything so real. I started feeling insecure about the quality of the writing and I just stopped working on it. What if they all rejected it? The whole thing's gotten so big in my mind now that I can't even sit down in front of my computer. I know it sounds crazy, but it's just so big now."

"No, it doesn't sound crazy. Writing is such a complicated mental exercise. It can make you do strange things. Whatever goes down, you can't just give up on a novel. How far have you gotten?"

"Well, I'm definitely not going to give up on it, I'm just stuck. I've got about two-hundred pages."

"Sister, you betta sit down with that book."

"I know, I've gotten so far."

Jenoyne and I spend the next few hours talking and laughing until we are the last customers in Applebee's. They finally kick us out.

As we approach the door, I stop at the gum-ball machine by the exit. The clear body of the base allows you to see the spiraling, plastic gum-ball track inside.

"Wait, Jenoyne, I want you to have a memento."

I put a quarter in the slot, turn the knob, and a red golf-ball gum-ball rolls its way down and around.

"Don't say I never gave you nothin."

"I'll cherish it."

I walk Jenoyne to the parking lot, where we talk fifteen minutes more. She finally gets into her bright sun-yellow Geo Storm. I watch the Bomb drive off. She forgets to take her heat.

the dating game

I call Jenoyne the morning after and tell her how much I enjoyed myself. I don't tell her I'm keeping my weekend schedule free, hoping we can go out again.

On Saturday, we go dancing at Kingston 12, a Santa Monica reggae club with a smoking roots band. Since Jenoyne seemed somewhat conservative at Applebee's, I'm pleasantly surprised when she immediately starts swaying and skanking so freely.

The following week, Jenoyne relents and agrees to come down to my territory after I explain that it's Malcolm X Festival weekend. Every February near the twenty-first (the day of Malcolm's assassination), Leimert Park hosts a two-day festival celebrating his life. It's the most inspiring event of the numerous annual festivals.

Malcolm had a major impact during the black-arts movement of the 1960s. He especially influenced the poets and the jazz avant garde, many of whom were from Los Angeles. The World Stage's Billy Higgins and trumpeter Don Cherry had rehearsed in Watts with Ornette Coleman (who was married to seminal black-arts poet Jayne Cortez) since they were teenagers in the mid-fifties. In the sixties, along with Watts resident Eric Dolphy and John Coltrane, they became the fiery musical counterparts to Malcolm's fierce activism. The World Stage/Leimert Park scene is their legacy. The Malcolm X Festival is the reminder. The whole neighborhood comes out to bear witness. I want to share this experience with Jenoyne.

When she arrives at noon, we head straight to the festival. My new apartment has great views. It's in the hills just above Leimert Park. When you drive down Angeles Vista (a curving, mile-long, palm tree–lined avenue that connects Windsor Hills to Leimert Park), you can see Los Angeles stretching beyond the downtown skyline to the Santa Monica mountains. Across the sprawling urban landscape, thousands upon thousands of palms lean in rows like a platoon of slender brothers with bushy afros.

Angeles Vista's last quarter mile is a steep decline that heads right into Leimert Park Village. From the hill, the Mediterranean-style village looks like an *Exodus* movie set. Degnan Boulevard is the floor of the Red Sea; the picture-glass boutiques, theaters, and jazz clubs have split and moved to opposite sides. The masses are crossing through the middle toward the stage on the far south end. Just seeing all the people gets me excited.

"Man, look at the crowd down there. It's massive."

"You're not going to see all your friends and leave me sitting somewhere, are you?"

"C'mon, now. You know that's not gonna happen—unless you bump my arm and make me drop my red beans and rice."

We find a parking spot a few blocks down Degnan in the residential area. The sun and a saxophone screeching through the late February breeze greet us when we exit the ride.

"I wonder, who's that playing?"

"Look at you, you look all happy. Is it your good company or the music?"

"Both."

As we're walking up Degnan, doors are constantly swinging open in the 1930s-style apartment buildings. Twenty-something women in bright-colored head wraps, crews of pimp-limping brothers, mothers filing out with their children—all make their way to the sidewalk and head in the same direction. Greetings fly among strangers every twenty yards.

"Mornin, sister . . . Wassup, bruh . . . How you doin, ma'am . . . Peace and blessings . . . As-Salaam Alaikum."

Festival season brings out the home training that many tuck away when they move to the Big City.

We reach 43rd Street. In front of the Leimert Park Fine Art Galley, we can see throngs of people coming from east and west. When we cross 43rd and walk through the traffic barricades, I grab Jenoyne's hand and navigate us through the crowd and the senses.

We squeeze past leather purses, loaded Cross Colours backpacks, and kente cloth. The Phillips BarBeeQ sauce mixes in the seasoned air with jerk spice and fried catfish. The strong lemon scent of Senegalese yassa sauce mingles with the sweet smell of plantains. Depending upon which direction we go, we run into curry crab or garlic chicken. The food booths and grills lining the perimeter of Degnan are to blame.

I get in the jerk chicken line; Jenoyne moves toward the catfish. We take our food and find an empty spot to sit about thirty yards from the bandstand.

It was Phil Vieux, from the Dr. Art Davis Quartet, we heard three blocks ago. He's the screaming young tenor saxophonist in the group of veterans. Art Davis, Coltrane's longtime collaborator, is on bass; Billy Higgins is swinging and smiling on drums; and Horace Tapscott is sitting in on piano.

It's like an outdoor church revival.

When Vieux screams, the crowd screams back. When Higgins erupts polyrhythmic into the cymbals, the crowd yells, "Go!" A Tapscott right-hand piano run: "Thasright!" I had been concerned that the curbside vibe might be a little too spartan for Jenoyne, but her head's bobbing and her hands are moving catfish and greasy fries to her mouth; she's totally caught up in the scene. It makes me look at her differently. She seems softer. Her casual attire also helps: jeans, a white cotton blouse, tennis shoes, and big hoop earrings hanging in the shadow of her long wavy hair—pulled back into galactic afro puffs. She catches me staring.

"Can I help you?"

Her eyeballs cut to the corner, looking up at me, fingers full of catfish suspended midair.

"The question is, do you wanna help yourself?"

"I wasn't aware that I needed help."

"Sister, that's why God brought me into your life," I say, squeezing her wrist, grinning like the good Reverend Dr. Feelgood.

Jenoyne and I go out the next weekend and the next and the next and the next. We're hitting everything from poetry readings to black nationalist conferences to reggae festivals to political rallies. We're hitting everything but the sheets, and it ain't because I'm not trying. Jenoyne is a sexy sister with a cool fashion sense. Every time we have a date, she's in some clever attire. Yet whenever I push up on her, she slips me the lukewarm shoulder. The lukewarm shoulder is not the cold shoulder, but as horny as she gets me, it feels frigid.

Early every Saturday and Sunday morning, I go to the beach to pray and meditate. After leaving the Church of Christ, the Pacific Ocean became my shrink's office. The Church left me confused and very insecure about my relationship to the spirit realm. It complicated God for me. Sitting alone on a sand dune at 7:00 A.M. before a living body of water makes God simple.

This peace pulls me back to the ocean, rain or shine. I always wear shorts and flip-flops because at times I just need to go stand in the water. I need to feel the waves crashing against my knees as I pray. A cleansing. A baptism I never felt in the Church of Christ.

After one of our dates, I ask Jenoyne if she would like to go to the beach with me. She recently had found an apartment in L.A., so I said I would come by and pick her up.

"What time?"

"Seven."

"In the morning?"

"Yep. You down?"

"Okaaay. I'm down."

I knock Sunday morning at 7:00 A.M. sharp. Jenoyne is not a morning person. She opens the door in jeans and a big coat, looking aggravated. My apartment is only fifteen minutes from the beach, but from Jenoyne's crib in the Palms, it takes a half hour to get to my special spot in Playa Del Rey. Jenoyne's quiet the whole drive. She's tired.

We park, and start walking toward the water. As we approach, our view of the ocean is obstructed by the large sand dunes. We climb over them.

"Wowww," Jenoyne says.

I feel warm inside, seeing her moved by the ocean.

"In San Bernadino, not many people go to the ocean because we're so far removed from it. When I was eleven, I went to live with my father. He used to take me fishing all the time, but then the water was like a backdrop. Maybe it seems different now because it's so early in the morning and no one's really here."

We talk about the healing power of the ocean. I tell her that a friend who's a high school teacher told me that she has students who've lived in L.A. all their lives and have never been to the beach.

"That's so sad," she says. "I think kids, especially kids in L.A., could really benefit from being out here."

"No doubt. Well, let's pray together for a while and then separate and spend some time meditating and praying by ourselves. Is that cool?"

I instinctively grab Jenoyne's hand and get very nervous. My times at the beach have been so personal and intimate. I've felt so unrestricted. Now that Jenoyne is next to me, I feel myself tightening up. I'm concerned about letting my shield down. Showing the pain that spills out during these mornings when I lay my struggles before God. Usually I keep my eyes open to take in the view, but with Jenoyne next to me, I close them to concentrate.

When I finish, Jenoyne starts. Listening to someone pray gives you a clear access to that person's heart. Jenoyne touches me. She seems to have such an intimate relationship with God. I feel as though I'm eavesdropping on private dealings.

There is a Hitchcockian quality to love. Things are not what they seem until the surprise ending. You've been snuck up on. Suddenly your heart is in danger. There's a reflex urge to flee for safety, but curiosity has you stuck. You've just go to know what's behind that door. You enter, and find yourself looking at a mirror. You look the same but the air seems thinner. Your lungs work harder to catch up, but you're always a half breath short.

After our time praying together, I find myself slightly winded in Jenoyne's presence. The air between us has become insufficient.

In late May, after one of our dates, we're lying on my bed, talking. I take her hand and look into her eyes.

"Jenoyne, if you were my lady, I would try to make you feel as special as you make me feel. If you were my lady, I would try to make smiles seek you for their permanent home. If you were my lady, I'd never cheat on you. I've never met anyone who's made me feel as much joy as you have these last few months. It's a feeling I can kinda get used to. I'd be honored if you'd be my girl."

Jenoyne just stares at me. Doesn't speak.

"Helllloooooo?"

"I'd love to be your girl, Michael."

In the World Stage poetry crew, there are lots of Geminis, including me. Every June, my partner Paul Calderon and I throw a major party called the Gemini Suga Shack. It's a volatile mix: sexy people, live music, spicy barbeque, erotic poetry, dirty dancing, strong drinks, and a lot of funny cigarettes.

My apartment is really a loft built on top of a garage behind a Windsor Hills home. Since no one lives in the house up front, I feel like I have the whole crib to myself. There's a wooden deck attached to the back of the main house, and a nice-sized backyard, which serves as my front yard. The perimeter of my yard is surrounded by yellow and red roses. I like to have breakfast and read my folded and redoubled *L.A. Times* on the porch hanging over the flowers below.

Paul and I front all the money for the food, drinks, and the official Suga Shack DJ—G-Rock. My brother, Elgin, and his partner Julian volunteer to work the grill. Jenoyne helps me clean and decorate the crib. Everything is set.

People start arriving soon after 8:00 P.M.; by 9:30 P.M., G-Rock has the wooden-deck dance floor packed with bouncing bodies. The crowded backyard is buzzing with high-energy macking. The Suga Shack's official drink, Cosmic Fade Juice, is flowing freely. A thick mist of marijuana smoke hovers above the backyard like a private storm cloud.

By midnight, Cosmic Fade has taken over the party. Dancing has become dirty, macking has become coupling, smoking has become munchies, and the barbeque is gone. It's time to kick some poetry.

During my post-Camille mourning period, I wrote a poem called "i am open," about the kind of woman I would like to have in my life. I had always imagined myself getting married in my late teens or early twenties. Hungry to start building a fence around my life. Many of the women I dated were wonderful, but I had so much tied up in my dream, the fit was never quite right. I was looking for balance. A woman of deep spirituality who is not afraid to get free behind closed doors. A woman with book sense but still able to hang on the block with everyday folk. A woman committed to helping improve the quality of life for black people. A woman with some home training. I felt picky, but I knew if I settled, I'd never be happy.

I wrote the poem out of frustration. I was open but couldn't find the sister I was looking for. There's a belief in the African cosmological system that you can literally speak things into existence. That's what I feel has happened with Jenoyne. She seems to represent so many of the qualities I was asking for in the poem.

After a few poets read, I walk to the microphone and call for Jenoyne. She steps out from the apartment onto the balcony overlooking the backyard.

"This poem is dedicated to you, baby."

crawling backwards along shore
foraging for woman answers.
surveying where i have been
where i may return.
Cross-examining scattered cowrie shells

remains of receding waves.
they woman spirit
compressed into sea stone by osun
for whispering sweet water secrets.

gather seven shells to ear
they afraid to speak.
pounce on nosy seagull
try to pry insight from beak
with long wisdom prayers.
she breaks silence
only after i promise to go down.
she comes mystic shaman tongues
pausing finally to moan:
what comes around goes around
what comes around goes around.
death chant of progressive macks
urbane snakes who wear goatees
heavy hearts on sleeves.
i am open.

come woman
come woman.

I briefly pause and glance up at Jenoyne. I love the way she looks at me when I'm reading poetry. There is such a warmth in her eyes.

woman whose root doctor breasts
will strengthen spines of my warrior sons
whose seraphic light spirit
will show them god.
woman see me weep waterfall tears
when i cannot write.
see me electric stutter, skipping cd

not glance away.
woman whose third eye exposes my cowardice
whose assata courage inspires my change.

woman who be truth.

come woman
come woman.

woman who love to fuck on stove top
like crisco smoking, popping, in a black skillet
who make love like morning mist
caressing african violet.
who know my scorching sunstar heart is sincere
even when salt in peanut gallery doubts me.
woman know i'm afraid of my dreams
call me "punk"
when I cave to fear.
woman big lip, french kiss my mind
get sticky wet reading fanon
carry secret ankh shaped vibrator
inside bulging metu neter.

come woman
come woman.

woman say "muthafucka"
with gospel conviction, seven languages
then conjugate.

The men and women burst out laughing. No doubt some of them have
been in relationships when this word has made its way into heated conversation. I glance up, happy to see Jenoyne laughing too.

woman make me smile.

come woman
come woman.

woman know god a black woman
woman sense enough to worship herself.
who keep my nose open
like fifth street dick's
on south central, summer solstice nights.
who perry masons my nigga/nationalist contradictions.
woman let me lick her
like never ending roll, jelly roll morton, 32 cent stamps.
woman serious bout her people.
woman with low hanging
speed bump ass, no speed limit.
woman who can suck some dick.
woman know love oxygen of soul, water of spirit.

come woman
come woman.

woman black love her momma monk deep
got down home, home training.
woman fullmoon, barefoot, damballah dance
to crackling vinyl coltrane.

woman know god.

come woman
come woman.

nigrescent sherlock holmes
sandals, egyptian musk
mystery solving along shore.
searching for soul mate clues
praying waves wash up
cowries in hieroglyphic formation
ocean divination
prophesying my love story.

negotiations

Going out with someone is very different from going steady. The jump in commitment level creates changes.

Going steady with Jenoyne begins a negotiation process involving what, how, and when changes will occur. Of course, neither of us owns up to this. We're just making conversation.

The weekend following the Suga Shack, Jenoyne and I are talking on our way to the Saab dealership to buy me a new fuel line.

"Often black women lose themselves when they get into relationships," she starts, her free hand talking like a young attorney giving her opening statement. "Their lives begin to revolve around the lives of their men, and what begins to happen is the very independence and spark that attracted the man in the first place gets lost in trying to meet the man's needs without making sure that their own needs get met. I believe in loving my man, but I'm not going out like that."

"I think you're right. Brothers are drawn to these sisters with mad flava, then once they get them, they try to tone their program down. A sister with a lot of flava can attract a lot of male energy, which can attract a lot of trouble. So trying to keep the peace, many sisters allow themselves to be toned down, and before they know it, it's like they're a different per-

212 | MICHAEL DATCHER

son. Now the brother's got the wandering eye, looking for a sister with more flava. It's a cold-wash cycle."

"Is that a concern of yours, me attracting male energy?"

"Well, not really. You don't have as much flava as some of my past girl-friends."

As soon as I say this, I want to strike it from the record. But it's way too late.

"What?" she snaps, her neck jerking from the road ahead to me. "What are you trying to say, that I don't have flavor?"

"Naw, baby, that's not what I'm saying. I mean, it's that I'm naturally attracted to women with a little more urban vibe. I know you spent your early years in the black part of San Bernadino, but I think that little Orange County stint—"

"That's bullshit, Michael. I'm so sick of you throwing Orange County up in my face. Ever since I've met you, you've been cracking on me about how I talk. People were saying I talk too proper even when I was living in the projects as a kid. I don't need my man teasing me, too. What, I'm not black enough because I enunciate my nouns and conjugate my verbs? And if you don't like it, why are you with me?"

"Wooooo, baby, slow your roll," I say, throwing my hands up. "Baby, you're making more of this than there is. Listen, I'm with you cause you're wonderful and special."

"But not because I have flavor?"

"I never said you didn't have flava. I just said that, umm, you know, that some of my other ladies had more of a street thang going on."

"I'm not one of your other ladies. Fuck those punk-ass bitches! Now, is that enough *flava* for you?"

The tears start to flow. I can't think of a way to clean up the situation, so I just sit in the car, keeping my eyes straight ahead like I'm the one driving.

"I hate it when you compare me to your past girlfriends. I'm never being viewed on my own merit. It's never just about me and you. You're always putting me in a position where I have to measure up or jump through some additional hoop. First I'm not dark enough, then I'm too tall, then I'm not black enough. You probably still want a petite little dark-brown sister since you're always saying that's what you've always preferred. Well, that's not who I am. I'm me, and I want to be loved for me."

I know I'm in trouble now, because Jenoyne's digging back into past heated conversations. One day we were talking about how the American idea of beauty is based on a white European aesthetic system. Rejecting this system, I said if we could somehow gather the fifty finest women from all over the world, the finest would be a dark-brown sister from somewhere. Which segued into an ill-fated conversation about my historical preference for petite dark-skinned women. A preference that may have been influenced by being a light-skinned brother who was constantly having to defend his toughness.

I told her that I've dated sisters of all hues and sizes but petite dark-brown sisters have moved me in a special way. She probably sensed I was reminiscing a little too hard. We had a big fight over that one. Now she pulls that argument again from the bottom of the deck.

"Do you ever wish I was darker?"

"Jenoyne, c'mon, now. I'm with you because I want to be with you. Period. You're taking this too far. I can't help what I'm attracted to. If in the past that happened to be darker-skinned sisters, so be it. It may even be cool because a lotta brothers will only talk to light-skinned sisters. A lotta those dark-skinned sisters catch hell."

"Like light-skinned women don't catch hell?" She starts tearing up again. "The brothers think we're stuck up, and the dark sisters give us attitude. They think that we think we're all that. That's why I don't have that many girlfriends. I'm just tired of people judging me because of the way I look. And it really hurts my feelings that my own man is judging me, too. Ever since we started dating, you've been making little out-the-box comments to me, making me feel that I'm not black enough. It's like you don't even know me. I'm sick of your shit. You-know-what? Get out of my car."

She screeches to a stop along the side of the curb.

I cut her a look, grab my old fuel line, and snatch open the door. Jenoyne grabs my arm.

"I'm sorry, Michael. You just really hurt my feelings. All these things have been building up. I don't want you to get out of my car. I just want you to accept me for who I am. Love me for who I am."

I just look at her. I'm steaming.

"I'm trying to be cool cause I hurt your feelings, but you're pissing me off. Don't-you-ever-come-at-me-like-that-again."

Stiff words run and break into silence. We toss glances back and forth over fences.

"I'm sorry, Michael. . . . I think we should pray."

We awkwardly reach out and hold hands. Jenoyne prays.

Listening to her sincere, heartfelt words always touches me. There is a real magic in prayer. It's hard to hold a grudge when someone genuinely says she's sorry. We open our eyes into postdrama syndrome.

"Can I have a hug?" she says.

"If you promise to let me kick you out my car once we get it fixed."

This argument brings us closer. Speaking frankly gets the issues quickly laid on the table, where they can be discussed more deeply. In our young relationship, these arguments happen on a weekly basis. Jenoyne and I are hyperopinionated. The arguments are intense, but if we can just calm down enough to pray together, the entire process seems to strengthen our bond.

A few weeks after Jenoyne tried to boost me from her ride, we're talking over a postbeach breakfast.

"You ever think about having kids?" Jenoyne says with a coy smile.

Conversations about children between unmarried, unengaged couples lead to uneasiness, especially if marriage and engagement haven't yet entered the dialogue. To intensify matters, Jenoyne really values family. She was born three months premature, and as a result, she had series of preemie-related problems that often landed her in the hospital as a child. It helped Jenoyne develop a great appreciation for spending time with her close-knit clan of mostly women, and especially with her younger sister, Jolena. Often they all gather over at her mother, Bertha's, house.

"Yeah, I've thought about it a little bit."

"Say God calls you on the phone and says, 'M.D., because I know you're going to be a wonderful father, I'm going to let you choose how many kids you get to have.' What would you say?"

I want to tell Jenoyne about Nicole and Camille, but I feel ashamed. Ashamed to tell her about my ugly side. Ashamed at how I treated Camille when I found out she was pregnant. Ashamed I thought about running away, a checkbook father. Ashamed that I wanted to abort my own child.

"I don't really know. I guess I would kinda like to have a big family. I wouldn't mind having five kids. It'd be cool to have my own basketball team."

I don't want Jenoyne to think badly of me. Our relationship is still so young. I'm not sure if I should be exposing it to my R-rated drama.

"Five kids? You talk like a man who's never been around children. And you've got two nieces, too? You must not baby-sit very often."

"I haven't baby-sat Ashton and Torin that much, but I've spent enough time with them to know if you provide a firm but loving hand and communicate with children like they're human beings, five kids can definitely be handled."

Maybe I could tell her just some of the story. This sister tried to hem me up. The child wasn't mine. That would even be the truth.

"Oftentimes in relationships, the women have most of the child-rearing responsibilities, even when both parents have careers. That just doesn't seem right to me."

What if Jenoyne had gotten pregnant? What would I have done? If I tell her the whole story, I know she'll be contemplating the same question.

"I had a daughter once."

I begin my story at Club Flame. In a slow, deliberate voice, I tell Jenoyne everything.

When I finish, I'm embarrassed. Jenoyne's silent. She has a way of looking into you the way a child does. Emotions appear in her irises like slides in a little girl's View-Master. There is no judgment, only compassion, rotating, repeating itself.

Jenoyne reaches across the kitchen table and grabs my hand.

"Thank you for sharing all of that with me, Michael. I don't like Camille. Scandalous ho. I better not run into her."

a decent proposal

Telling Jenoyne about Camille and Nicole is a turning point in our relationship. The mutual honesty makes us extremely close. We spend one of those California summers together that inspires passions. Driving up and down the coast; setting up residence at the Museum of Contemporary Art's free weekly jazz series on Thursdays and the Los Angeles County Museum of Art's jazz series on Fridays; salsa dancing on the Santa Monica pier; skanking at UCLA's annual outdoor reggae festival; making spontaneous love during Sunday-afternoon backyard picnics; Poncho Sanchez at the House of Blues; the National Ballet of Spain at the Universal Amphitheater; erotic poetry readings at the Stage; naked candlelit dinners at the crib. The summer of 1996. I didn't have a choice but to fall in love with Jenoyne Adams.

By Christmas, everyone in my immediate family has met Jenoyne. Cyndi takes an especially strong liking to her. As the only girl among three siblings, she likes the idea of Jenoyne joining the family. They both are well-read women deeply involved in the arts, and their conversations sizzle with the chemistry that comes when two people have similar passions. Cyndi always wanted a little sister to share her life with; Jenoyne may become just that.

Jenoyne was raised by her father, a construction-worker foreman, so she loves to build things and is a freak for gadgets. My brother also is an Inspector Gadget disciple and has a great knack for building things. Jenoyne and Elgin's rapport easily could be found on a cable home-improvement show.

Sitting in my grandparents-in-law's living room, watching Jenoyne and my mother have a lengthy conversation, I think, OhmyGod . . . I'm dating my mother. They're both so opinionated, and equally fierce when defending their perspectives. My mother's got to have the last word. I have the same problem. So does Jenoyne.

After the holidays, I call Moms in Alabama. She had returned to her Southern roots several years before, buying a home and reconnecting with old friends and family.

"Moms, I think Jenoyne's the One."

"Michael, you've been saying some girl's the One since you got out of high school."

"Right, right, but I was wrong those other times. I really think Jenoyne's the One. What do you think?"

"Well, baby, she's seems to be a very nice girl. And you're not going to find a girl prettier than her."

"I'm thinking about asking her to marry me."

"Well, I'd love to have her as a daughter-in-law, but I'll tell you, if I was her, I wouldn't have you."

"Mama-what-kind-of-thing-is-that-to-say?" I blurt out, hurt and offended.

"You quit a good job at the newspaper. Talking about you freelancing. I don't know why you don't use your master's degree. Seem like you worked hard enough to get it. I wouldn't have you because you aren't in a position to take care of a wife. And I don't care how progressive or modern or whatever you call it yall supposed to be, but a man's supposed to be able to take care of his wife. It just doesn't seem like you're able to do that. Seem like to me you just want to struggle all your life."

"What a terrible thing to say—"

"I don't mean to hurt your feelings. That's just the way I feel about the matter."

"Mama, Jenoyne's her own woman. She doesn't want a man to take care of her."

"Have you asked her?"

"No, but—"

"But nothing. A man's supposed to be able to take care of his wife. Now, if she decides to work, that's fine. But if she wants to be at home, she should have that option. The husband is supposed to provide for the wife. Don't you want to provide for your wife?"

"Anyway, Mama, I didn't—"

"Don't you?"

"I didn't call you to talk about this, I called you to talk about Jenoyne."

"Sound like we are talking about Jenoyne."

"Awright, Mama. I love you. Imma let you go."

"Okay, baby. I think Jenoyne's a lovely girl. I love you too."

I had quit my job as a reporter at the *Los Angeles Sentinel* in October to spend more time on my own writing. As only Moms can, she tapped into one of my biggest fears: living the struggling-artist life with someone else to be responsible for. Throughout my writing career, I haven't minded dining on Top Ramen or wearing sweaters in lieu of having the heat on. I viewed the spartan lifestyle as a necessary evil to allow me the time to work on my craft. Having a wife adds another dimension. I've always heard that finances are the leading cause of marital problems. Maybe Jenoyne will not want the struggle that being married to a writer can be. Maybe Moms is right.

The conversation with Moms sticks in my head for the next couple of days. I don't want to bring up the matter directly with Jenoyne, and I can't really think of a way to approach it. She should understand, though. She's been struggling to work on her novel before and after work. I decide to let the situation slide. Cross that bridge when we get to it.

I call my sister and brother to get their feedback. They obviously like her, but I just want to hear them verbalize those feelings. I also conduct an informal, nonscientific Homie Poll. I call Jimmy, one of my oldest friends.

"Man, I'm thinking about asking Jenoyne to marry me. I think she's the One, cat."

"You know what this'll mean, don't you?"

"What's that?"

"No more new booty. You gotta be sure here, man."

He says it with such sincerity, I can't laugh. He knows of my deep convictions about the sacredness of marriage and my commitment to being monogamous. He knows I'd never cheat on Jenoyne and that I'd break up with her before I'd ever creep. He also knows of my wild past. When I was single, I was very single, supersingle. In his own way, Jimmy is asking me a very practical question: Are you sure this is the person you want to commit to having a monogamous relationship with for the rest of your life?

After the long pause: "I'm sure."

"Then why are you calling me? Handle your business."

"Yeah, no doubt. Thanks. Peace."

I call the homies who are part of the World Stage poetry crew: Paul, Kamau, Wendy, Derrick, Sequoia, and A.K. They're very encouraging and seem genuinely excited. I'm not sure why I'm even making these phone calls. I guess I want and need some affirmation beyond my own. Now that my picket-fence dream is coming into focus, it's a scary sight. Like going to see an action thriller at the movies, looking up, and seeing your face filling the screen.

In some ways, the dream was more exciting when it was just an abstraction. I didn't have to make any decisions. Didn't have to listen to my mother lecture me on what a "real husband" is supposed to do. Didn't have to consider whether I have what it takes to be a good husband and eventually a good father. Can I even provide for a wife? For children? Can I handle the pressure? And my God, what if she just says no? I try to push that possibility far from my mind. I know Jenoyne's the kind of woman who will utter that word if she's not completely feeling me. I need to go to the beach.

It's January, just after the new year. I make a special nighttime trek to the prayer spot. I spend a good hour reassuring myself that God will help me be the man I imagine myself to be.

When I get back to the crib that night, I'm still a little shaky, but I'm committed. And I know that I want to propose to Jenoyne in some way that makes her feel as special as she is to me. I think about doing it on the beach or on a dance floor somewhere or over a private dinner. I go through a number of ideas. Finally I decide to make a public proclamation of my love for her.

I decide to write a poem and then read it at the World Stage. It will be in two parts. Part one will be the poem I wrote when I imagined the kind of woman I'd like to have—the poem I dedicated to Jenoyne at the Suga Shack. Part two will be about me and Jenoyne and our relationship.

I pull out the World Stage master calendar and look at the slots for the half-hour featured reader. I want to choose a day near Valentine's Day, which is, incidentally, close to the one-year anniversary of our first date: Wednesday, February 12, 1997. There is no featured reader scheduled. I take this as a sign that God has ordained the plan.

In the next couple of weeks, I'll casually tell Jenoyne that the featured reader canceled so I'm going to read on February 12 as an emergency stand-in. I'll have about a month to write the poem. I also want some of our poet friends to read after I propose.

While making the plan, I keep telling myself that she absolutely, without a doubt, will say yes. I get on the phone and call my friend and fellow poet Peter J. Harris to host the night and read.

"Sounds like a great plan to me. I'd be honored to be a part of it. Honored that you want me to host it," he tells me. He even offers to host a private dinner for Jenoyne and me afterward at his place.

Peter's got an amazing crib in Mt. Washington, on the side of a tree-dotted hillside in Los Angeles county.

It occurs to me that after I propose, I could actually blindfold Jenoyne and then drive to Peter's, which would give the evening another element of surprise.

"I'm sure V. would love to be involved," Peter says. "If you'll pay for the food, I bet she would jump at the opportunity to prepare it for such a special evening."

When I get off the phone with Peter, I call V. She's excited and very eager to help. I also call the other poets I want to read: Sequoia, A.K., Paul, Ruth.

Last, I put in a very nervous, late-night call to Jenoyne's father, Virgil. I have such respect for the job he did in raising his daughter, for how close they are. I often think about the poem she wrote for her father because one day I would want my daughter to write a poem like it for me.

Daddy
how you get so beautiful?
planting collard green
and hotwater cornbread love
Between my plaits
turning ash trays into candy bowls
and scraped knees
into orange soda kisses

I see you in the sun rays
feel you when I step my feet
into the ocean

You are the current that brings me home
to chat and watch history channel for hours

You are my first friend
and best magic

You are the spirit in me
that catches my rainbows

You are my hopscotch
and jump rope memories

You are the hope I will give my children
And who I want to become

Daddy
You are black sunshine
radiating

Virgil is surprised to hear from me.

"I'm sorry to call so late, but, umm, I'm going to ask Jenoyne to marry me and I guess I kind of want your blessing."

"I don't know quite what to say. You know, Jenoyne's my baby and I know she really loves you. You two seem to make each other happy. I'd be happy to have you be my son-in-law."

"Thank you, Virgil. That means a lot to me. God is my witness, I'll try my best to do right by your daughter."

All that's left is the ring.

Usually, I spend my 5:30 to 8:30 A.M. writing time working on long-term projects, but I decide that from now until February 12 I will dedicate this time to working on the poem. The last thing I need is February 12 arriving, all my elaborate plans hooked up, and no poem.

During the first week, the process goes very slowly. There is so much to say and I don't know how to say it. I'm putting too much pressure on myself. I have to relax, commit to the truth, and just let the poem come to me. The second week, it starts to flow. I spend a lot of time reminiscing about all the special moments: the beach, writing poetry together, our two-person book club, the dancing, the dinners, the passionate lovemaking. But also the hard times. The difficult arguments. The screaming, the mistakes, the professional disappointments, the fears. I want to write a poem that encompasses the fullness of our relationship.

During the first week of February, I really start to get nervous. As hard as I try, I can't get "no" out of my mind. Furthermore, I haven't finished the piece. I've got some good ideas down, but the poem hasn't come together. I want to finish so I can practice reading it. I'm going to be nervous. I don't want to be on the stage bumbling and stuttering on my big day.

Then there's the issue of the ring. I found one, but I'm broke as the Ten Commandments.

I'm waiting for a freelance check so I can make the last payment. All kinds of truly nightmarish scenarios are constantly running through my mind in heavy rotation: I don't get my check, can't buy the ring, so I have to get a little fake replacement to act as a stand-in on February 12. Then, as I'm proposing, I whisper in Jenoyne's ear, "The real ring's coming."

Or I get to the packed Stage and don't feel confident reading a poem that's not finished and say something corny like "I had this piece prepared, but I'm just going to speak from my heart."

Or the ultimate in proposal terror: I get to the packed Stage. Poem's ready. I'm ready. I kick the piece, pull my ring out, and ask this amazing woman to share her life with me. And then there's a very, very long, un-comfortable, black hole–like silence. Finally Jenoyne says, "Michael, can I speak with you outside, please?"

A week to go, and I'm a wreck. I have no control over the scenes sprint-ing through my mind.

I'm so preoccupied, I almost forget to remind Jenoyne I'm the featured reader on the twelfth. I wanted to remind her early to make sure there are no schedule conflicts. I tell her over the phone.

"You'll be there, right?"

"I need to check my schedule. My dad's birthday is coming up. I told him I was coming to San Bernadino to see him. I'll get back to you."

Great. I'm going to propose to a woman who's not there. After I hang up, I immediately call Jenoyne's dad. As it turns out, his birthday is on Feb-ruary 13. I ask him to call Jenoyne and tell her he's coming down to see her Wednesday, the twelfth, so they can have dinner after the workshop. He agrees. That fire's put out.

By Monday the tenth, the food is set. The poets who are going to read have finished their poems. Jenoyne's father is confirmed, along with my brother, Elgin, my favorite cousin, William, and a slew of my long-time homies. Furthermore, word has spread quietly throughout Leimert Park Village that I'm going to propose to my lady.

All month, musicians, shop owners, artists, the neighborhood folk have been stopping me and whispering some version of "I heard; I'll be there." Given black people's well-deserved reputation for being the worst secret keepers on the planet, it's a minor miracle Jenoyne hasn't found out. Or if she does know, she hasn't tipped her hand. In fact, everything's straight except for two minor problems: I haven't finished my poem and the check hasn't arrived.

There's a hilarious scene in the Steve Martin comedy classic *The Jerk*. The mailman delivers the new phone book to Martin's "residence." Martin goes wild with excitement, jumping, and screaming, "The new phone book's here! The new phone book's here!"

When I go to my mailbox Tuesday morning the eleventh and see that check, I break into a spontaneous version of the Phone Book Dance. I immediately get dressed and roll down to the jeweler. He even hooks me up with a super-nice black velvety flip-open ring box. I come straight back home and start working on my poem.

Wednesday, February 12. It's here. I've been lying in bed awake since 4:00 A.M., waiting for my alarm to go off, thinking about my life. Adopted. No father. Survived the ghetto. Put myself through college and graduate school. Camille. Now, I'm preparing to take the biggest step of my life.

My God, I've been dreaming about this for so long. God has kept Her promise to me. I'm going to break the cycle. I'm going to step up.

I work on my poem most of the day. Jenoyne comes over at 6:00 P.M. to wait for her father. I usually stop working when she comes over in the evenings. This time I keep typing when she walks through the door. Putting the very last finishing touches on the piece two hours before showtime. A last-minute brother to the end. She asks me what I'm working on.

"It's a piece for A.K."

The workshop has a group of extremely charismatic writers. Often, poets will honor each other with poems. I'm hoping Jenoyne will accept this explanation and not get up to look over my shoulder.

"When are you gonna write a poem for me?"

"In time, baby."

She pops open a book and starts reading on the couch.

It's 7:15 P.M. when I start printing my poem out. Seven-fifteen on the day of the proposal, fifteen minutes before the workshop begins. No time even to rehearse it. The poem has ballooned to seven single-spaced pages.

Jenoyne's father hasn't arrived by 7:30 P.M.

"We need to go, baby. Let's leave him a note."

I'm in my black denim, black boots, and black leather jacket. I fold my poem in my poetry book and sling my backpack on. As we are about to get in my car, Jenoyne's father pulls up. I'm thinking, God's gonna work this out.

It's only a two-minute drive down to the World Stage, but somehow, that fast, my newfound confidence slips away. I'm so nervous that I don't even attempt to make small talk with Jenoyne's father.

When we get to the Stage, it takes us a while to find a parking spot. I can see the place is packed. I tell Jenoyne and Virgil I'll be inside shortly. I've got to get myself together. I take a walk away from the Stage, say a prayer, and head back toward the entrance.

When I walk in, seventy-five people are squeezed into the small store-front built for fifty-five. A whole row of people are standing in the back. Heads turn when I cross the portal. Huge knowing smiles abound. People whispering. Giggling. Shifting and fanning in their seats. The place is electric. I see Peter and Paul. Sequoia and A.K. Ruth and Derrick. Kamau and V. My brother and my cousin. The owner of the Comedy Act Theater. The whole neighborhood is out. I sit, trying to calm myself, as Peter conducts the preliminary workshop. Eight-thirty P.M. Peter introduces A.K., who begins his introduction.

"Tonight's featured reader is one of our own here at the World Stage and he's also my good friend. Please put your hands together for Michael Datcher."

The place erupts. Hoots, hollers, whistles, shouts. All their love makes me more nervous. I pop up but take special care in walking toward the stage. I'm trembling. I grab the mic stand to steady myself. I glance at Jenoyne sitting against the wall, next to the seat I just left.

"Thank yall for coming out. This first piece is dedicated to my lady, Jenoyne. This is for you, baby."

> walking backwards along shore
> foraging for woman answers.
> surveying where i have been
> where i may return . . .

Jenoyne has heard this part of the poem before. When I get to part two, she leans in toward me.

> we stand meditating on this beach
> where i used to meditate alone.
> sun at my back, casting cosby family fantasies
> across the sea like a martinique fisherman
> hurling his heavy net
> starboard into a salty wind.
> i called to the ocean.
> you appeared hightide, a sunday morning.
> pacific seashells rushing across my naked toes.
> it was the matterhorn-shaped one
> pearl and orange colored.
> you were curled inside, fetal position
> like an early term black butterfly diva
> waiting impatiently for her wings.
> when you flew out
> my heart was slow to recognize your beauty
> like picasso with down's syndrome.
> i had you all wrong.
> didn't see virgil adams chanting
> on the front porch of your mind
> *girl make your daddy proud*
> *girl make your daddy proud.*

i prayed for you in a picket-fence poem
come woman be my wife, come woman be my wife.

When I say the refrain, I look up from the page to glance at Jenoyne.
She has a quizzical look on her face. I've never mentioned *wife* in a
poem.

you are gazelle graceful.
handle struggle like george gervin finger roll.
pay the car note, gas bill, rent
one arm tied behind your back
the other testifying to god.
you are warrior
lionheart will accompany your name.
i see you on my mental canvas.
gardenia in your hair from billi's casket.
her gift to you:
a reminder that love does see color.
sometimes it is blue
like the man you have chosen.
i pick sunflowers from the sky.
your name and other mysteries
stenciled on the stems:
hieroglyphic ebonics for black lovers.
we are red hibiscus liberated from
oakland's jack london square
by a poor poet
who cannot afford the florist.
at sunbreak you open yourself to me
like the purple morning glories in my yard.
you let me be the sun
even when i bring the weight of
my heavy shadows across your face.

i prayed for you in a picket-fence poem
come woman be my wife, come woman be my wife.

we have been through so much so soon.
we are the premature child born in winter
cold winds hitting our hearts
before the protection of spring.
bills trail us like home invasion robbers.
they know where we live.
you know all my fears.
i share them as if you're my bathroom mirror
my former closest confidant.
even when my sky is a blue note album cover
your smile streaks across it
like a dc 10 zooming above inglewood palmtrees.
you are the bruised blue jay cautious of bad weather
leaping from your nest into my storm
chancing being wounded in the house of a friend.
i walk among wolves for a living
selling ideas to the other world stage
that does not love me.
religiously i fall on my knees in desperate prayer
to barter myself, highest bidder
to people who'd slit my throat
if the light was right.
i lay on a bed of sharpened uni-ball pens
trying to sleep as my dream hangs by its ankles
out a 12th floor manhattan highrise window.
sometimes the wine color of my glasses
leaves my vision stumbling.
i'm so busy looking for god in people
i miss the bright yellow
diamond shaped street signs
hanging from their necks that caution

devil straight ahead.
you recognize beelzebub when you see him.
you got my front and my back.

i prayed for you in a picket-fence poem
come woman be my wife, come woman be my wife.

I can feel and hear the audience rocking and swaying with the poem.
"Go head, bruh! That's right."
I glance up from the page again. Jenoyne is leaning in, listening hard.
Her eyes are moist. My eyes are moist too.

i sit in cafés meditating
my palms up, searching for truth between breaths
seeing the future, no crystal ball.
even the seer needs someone to see for him
when his eyes are clouded by doubt.
i need you to believe in me.

watching you sleep
is like sneaking up on the sun
napping behind kilimanjaro.
your body is a raw pine music box.
i open and wind you up.
a siren song keeps me from straying
like the cat i am.
you smile at me in the morning
breasts still sensitive
from the intensity of my late night touch.
i smell your melody in my goatee.

At the end of each line, the crowd urges me on, "Yeahhh. Yeahhh." I
glance at Jenoyne, her eyes are red. I start to pick up the pace, reading with
more force.

you have become a romare bearden collage:
you're the faded photo of ella and diz
in front of birdland
torn from an old downbeat magazine.
you're a piece of chewed, tattered licorice root
found in the back seat
of a 1977 red and white cadillac
gangsta white walls.
you're the salt in betty's tears
the day before malcolm fell.
you're the cotton balls stuffed
in the point of ballerina toe shoes
you never wore.
you're the crashing waves in a bathtub
filled with every storm
you couldn't stop with a prayer.
you're a page torn from the book of psalms.

The intensity in the room has skyrocketed. People are cosigning almost every image, "Go! Go! Yeahhh!" Tears are rolling down Jenoyne's face. I have to finish before I break down. I start reading faster.

you join my gemini i and i and i
with your aries hoodoo.
alone i am an out of key sextet.
together we are the duke ellington orchestra
live at the 1955 monterey jazz festival
blowing through "caravan."
for our screaming encore
we appear as ourselves, naked before thousands
making love
dripping the sweaty bassline of coltrane's "olé"
from our vibrating bodies onto the wooden stage.
we levitate above jagged cliffs, no net, no parachute

we are holding on to each other's prayers.
wind in our face like the peppermint breath of god
blowing kisses clothed in jet streams pushing us east.

some say i'm hard to please
say i don't know what i want.
they are wrong.
i know exactly what i want.
everything.
i have found that in you.
i see us standing naked on the beach
our dreams sandwiched in our embrace.
we are our own holy trinity
praying the horizon glows
in the crevice of our first son's smile.
i look into your eyes
see my grandchildren sitting around your skirt, asking
nana read us a poem.

I begin to fumble in my pocket. My hands are shaking so violently I can't get the ring out. I finally snatch out the black velvety box. On sight, Jenoyne bursts out screaming, crying, and stomping her feet over and over again, beating her fist against her thighs, shaking her head from side to side, screaming again. As if her background singers, individual sisters spontaneously start screaming and crying, creating a kind of collective wail. Brothers start standing, clapping, and shouting, "Yeahhh! Yeahhh!" I open the box. Extend my arm and finish.

i prayed for you in a picket-fence poem
come woman be my wife, come woman be my wife.

Jenoyne is hysterical. She's crying so hard that I burst out crying, too. I can tell she's not going to be able to make it up to the stage. I step off, walk over to her, and fall to one knee. I'm crying so hard, I can't even ask

Jenoyne to marry me. I look at her. She gives me her hand. Jenoyne's extended ring finger signals the sweetest sign language: Yes.

Earlier I arranged for A.K. to slip on a tape with Stevie Wonder's classic "You and I." As the room fills with Stevie's imagination, Jenoyne and I pull each other to our feet. We kiss and embrace into a gentle swaying slow dance in the company of poets. Peter, eloquent as always, later tells me that he skipped our planned break because "You don't break joy."

We caress tears from each other's damp cheeks. After Stevie's last notes, we finally sit down and people come up to offer their congratulations. I'm moved by the room's emotional intensity. I have never seen so many black men crying in the same room, at the same time. Stereotypes slip, lose their footing.

Person after person greets us with such a sincere appreciation for sharing our special moment with them that we're both extremely touched. One woman approaches. She tells me it's her first time coming to the World Stage.

"You have restored my faith in love."

My partner Frank, a stone-cold player in recovery, walks up to me and says, "You get props for this, kid. This was some beautiful shit. Niggas was mad touched by this here." Jenoyne's father walks up to me but doesn't say anything. He just hugs me and excuses himself outside.

Peter presides over the next part of the evening, introducing the eight poets who are to read poems about Jenoyne and me. We sit back, hand-in-hand, listening, luxuriating in the love of our friends. When the poetry is finished, I escort Jenoyne to my car and blindfold her. I make the drive up to Peter's, where he and V. are awaiting us. *Le Peter* is in full effect. V.'s hooked up a five-course meal full of stuff I can't pronounce. I take Jenoyne's blindfold off at the elegantly set table for two. We talk for hours, holding one hand, eating with the other, dreaming with our eyes open.

Chapter Twenty-five

VOWS

When I began to bring Jenoyne to Leimert Park, we both noticed people staring at us. Mad-doggin volley stares and "Whachu lookin at, man?" became a part of our public discourse. It was when we began to notice the stares of the grandmothers, the Audubon seventh-graders, their teachers, that we realized it wasn't about simply tittie-watching or rudeness. There are so few young black couples walking through the neighborhood, so little black love on public display. We were an oddity.

People tend to stare at what they find unusual. The attention we get goes from aggravating to sobering.

Jenoyne and I want our wedding to be a village celebration. We want to involve the friends and artists who have touched our spirits. Abalaye, one of the West Coast's leading West African dance troupes, agrees to open the wedding. Jazz vocalist Dwight Trible makes himself available to sing. Poets Kamau Daáood and Wendy James agree to perform. Former Wolfgang Puck chef Michael is willing to handle all the food preparations. Taumbu International Ensemble, the critically acclaimed Afro-Cuban jazz band, agrees to play the reception. Photojournalist Venus Bernardo, whose photos have appeared in *Time* and *Newsweek,* agrees to shoot the wedding. At every level, we try to involve the members of our talented close-knit circle of friends.

Our May 17 wedding date doesn't give us a lot of time. We want a location that represents our mutual love and respect for the ocean. Our beach times have been the foundation of our relationship. We want to lay our wedding vows before the ocean the way we have laid so many of our prayers. We finally find a place near Palos Verdes, on a cliff overlooking the ocean: Angel's Gate Park.

As the wedding date approaches, a few of my old school friends start calling to inquire about the bachelor party. They're expecting decadence. They're wrong: I'm not feeling the titties-and-ass cliché. My friends don't want to hear it.

"Come on, man, I can hook up the strippers myself," Jimmy says.

The best man usually makes the bachelor party arrangements. I'm on the phone, trying to tell Elgin what I'm looking for. He interrupts, "Oh, don't worry, man, I talked to cousin Will. We're working on the strippers." It becomes very clear that I need to plan my own bachelor party.

After the Wednesday-night poetry workshop, fifteen of the homies caravan over to poet D-Knowledge's crib. The first hour we sit around sipping wine, chugging brews, and talking shit. Then Kamau arrives.

Kamau Daáood has been married to Baadia for more than twenty years. He raised and educated five children living as an artist. Kamau and Baadia have been getting stares for a long time.

Earlier in the week, I had asked Kamau to jump-start a dialogue about men and women, marriage and community. Soon the other brothers join in. The few married brothers offer me their experiences as advice. Several of the brothers in the group are divorced. Very painfully, they share their wrong turns. I listen hard.

At the end of the night, I get my chance to speak. I stand.

"I feel so blessed to know you cats. You can't imagine how much your lives have touched me. You never know who's watching you. You don't really understand the impact you have had just by living your life. Well, I've been watching all you cats. Watching you closely. Watching how you deal with people. How you love. Your integrity. Your strength. Watching and trying to follow your examples has made me a better human being."

▌ ▌ ▌ ▌

After the bachelor party, it's crunch time. Three days to go. Even with the help of Leslie Cagnolatti, a friend and professional event planner, we still are overwhelmed with the arrangements. Jenoyne wants to make her own bouquets for the wedding party. We go to downtown L.A.'s flower mart to haggle over rose prices with merchants.

We have to find a piano—and then get it on the edge of a Palos Verdes cliff. We get word on Thursday that instead of a $2,000 check being in the mail from *Emerge Magazine,* they killed the article. The check was the honeymoon money. We're starting to sweat. The good thing is that our outdoor wedding is in May, we've had great weather all week, and the forecasts in the paper have been predicting that sunshine will continue through the weekend.

On Friday, the day before the wedding, Jenoyne and I decide not see each other until the ceremony. She's at her apartment placing the finishing touches on the elaborate handmade fruit baskets (with kiwis, mangoes, grapes) to be used as table centerpieces. I'm completing an article an editor advanced me the payment on. I finish just after midnight, then start writing out my wedding vows.

Soon after I proposed, we decided to compose our own vows. We chose a structure and an opening and closing refrain. Besides these elements, we want to keep the vows secret from each other until our wedding day. I had spent many evenings thinking specifically about what being married means to me and what vows I wanted to make to my wife. After so much thought, actually writing the vows is a very moving experience. I'm about to be married. These vows are going to be the standard by which I live as a married man.

For as long as God continues to raise the morning sun, I will hold these vows
sacred.
I vow to love you as I love myself.
I vow to tell you the truth, even when it hurts.
I vow to embrace humility; to admit when I'm wrong; pride will not keep

"I'm sorry" from my lips.

I vow never to lay with another woman.

I vow to aggressively pursue our dreams until our dreams become our lives.

I vow to have your back in good times and bad, sickness and health.

I vow to cherish you like an unending gift from God.

*For as long as God continues to raise the morning sun, I will hold these vows
sacred.*

I'm up until 4:00 A.M. I sleep until 6:00 A.M., print out a copy of my vows,
and drive to the beach. I stand in the shallow water, meditate, pray, then
read my vows before God. When I finish, I lay the words on an outgoing
wave, watch them turn and fold out into the ocean.

I drive back home to pick up my tuxedo. I realize that the normal early
morning clouds are not dispersing. As a matter of fact, it's starting to
sprinkle—in L.A., in May, on my wedding day. I'm stunned. It's only 8:30
A.M., so I'm hoping this is just *extreme* early morning cloudiness. I check
the newspaper again, even though I know it's all suns on the five-day fore-
cast. The wedding is scheduled for 11:00 A.M. There's still time for the
sun to break through. I hop in the car and head toward the wedding site.
The closer I get to the ocean, the worse the weather gets. When I get to
Angel's Gate, it's sprinkling harder—as if it's trying to actually rain on
my wedding. The musicians and wedding party members start to
arrive—carrying umbrellas. I just sit in the car and start laughing. It's
three much.

As kick-off time approaches, it stops raining, but it's still completely
gray. I'm not going to worry about things I can't control. Leslie gives me
the signal. A long saxophone call starts the ceremony. Elgin and I emerge
from behind the ornate fifteen-foot iron bell that was bequeathed to the
city by the Republic of Korea. Wearing our Italian-cut, four-button tuxe-
dos, we take our positions. When the saxophone fades out, the five African
drummers in traditional attire with loincloths, cowrie shells, and feathers
start playing. The five dancers wearing flowing white-and-purple robes
start swaying to the rhythm up the 300-foot-long, 50-foot-wide procession
way. It's an epic scene.

Heads turn to face them. They dance all the way up to the wedding altar in front of Elgin and me. Another saxophone call.

A different drumming rhythm begins, which provides the music for the wedding party. We look back down the long procession way. The women are in elegant, form-fitting, royal-purple dresses that match Angel's Gate's purple landscaped flowers. They meet their respective groomsmen in the center, and two-by-two, arm-in-arm, they glide toward the altar to the drum rhythms. Another saxophone call. A different drumming rhythm announces the three flower girls (my nieces Ashton and Torin, and friend Sishay), wearing matching long white lace dresses, spreading rose petals. They carry the kind of smiles on their faces that explain why children always steal the show.

I look back down and see Jenoyne appearing from behind a tree like a sudden breeze. She's wearing a form-fitting, sleeveless white satin dress, with embroidered, pearl-colored beads curling designs all the way down to her waist: the Bomb. As her father escorts her up the procession way, Jenoyne's thirty-foot white lace train blows in the salty ocean wind. Braids run up her head, then sprout into a fountain of hair over the top of the white tiara resting on her braids. She looks like a sea angel making her first pilgrimage on land. We meet at the altar. As we face each other, Dwight Trible sings an emotion-filled version of our favorite song, "A Song for You," by Donny Hathaway. Reverend June Gatlin presides over the ceremony. Our first time hearing each other's vows.

For as long as God continues to raise the morning sun, I will hold these vows sacred.

I vow to love you with my mind, body, and spirit. To be a caretaker of your inner man, to keep your name in God's ear.

I vow to be a fertile clearing for your dreams to help you bring them into reality. To challenge you, as I challenge myself, to become a better person daily.

I vow to be a nurturer of our children, to endow them with love, knowledge, and understanding to become whole beings and high spirits.

I vow to behold you as my dearest friend, to be a pillar of truth
and faithfulness.

I vow to accept you as my lifetime mate, to believe in you and
work with you in hard times so that we can become
stronger in adversity.

I vow to cherish your smiles and to appreciate the time we share.

I vow to serve you, as well as accept being served, to respect your
thoughts, to approach our goals as a child, believing all
things are possible.

For as long as God continues to raise the morning sun, I will hold these
vows sacred.

happily ever after

Just before our wedding, Tyrone Tillman offers Jenoyne and me a chance to share one of his homes for a few months. My place is being sold, and we've decided to move to New York in September. We wanted to save a few thousand dollars before we left, so Tyrone gave us a great deal on a room in his large Inglewood home.

Tyrone's a twenty-seven-year-old wunderkind. A high school dropout from Watts who became a successful realtor and chess master; I had seen him playing for years in the competitive Leimert Park chess scene that runs seven nights a week at the long row of tables in front of 5th Street Dick's jazz café. He was very moved by the bachelor party.

Tyrone's background as a professional boxer adds mystique to his well-known success story. His thick-necked, stocky frame and pugilistic surname are counterbalanced by his quick smile, gentle manner, and gold Mercedes convertible.

Tyrone's offer is made sweeter by my close friend Paul Calderon's presence as a resident in the guest house. I had wanted to spend time with Paul before we moved east; I couldn't ask for a better situation.

After Jenoyne and I return from our honeymoon in Rosarito Beach, Mexico (Tyrone's wedding gift to us), we settle into our new digs. Swimming pool, pool table, two big-screen TVs, and terrace are amenities we quickly get used to in our first week of marriage.

Our temporary household is a spirited environment. Tyrone met his girlfriend Tasha when she was newly pregnant. She recently gave birth and is living with him. Paul's strong-willed lady Juanita is over often. At nights we all converge in the living room to talk politics, argue black man/black woman issues, share dreams, start impromptu poetry readings, and watch the NBA playoffs.

On our second Friday night married, Jenoyne and I are talking in the kitchen. Paul and Juanita are downstairs. Tyrone and Tasha are in their bedroom.

"What are we doing tonight?"

"I was thinking about a romantic evening together experiencing the subtle charms of the NBA."

"I know you're trying to spoil me, but you don't want to give me too much romance too early in our marriage. I think we should go dancing."

"Baby, we can dance vicariously through Jordan and Malone. See it, baby, see it: jumping, twisting, spi—"

"Did you hear that?"

"What?"

"Sounded like some bumping."

"I didn't—"

"There it is again. Did you hear it? I think Tyrone and Tasha are fighting."

"Arguing, or fistfighting? I—"

"Fighting. I think we should we should see what's going on."

"I didn't hear anything, but I'll go check."

Jenoyne and I walk toward the back of the house. She stops in the hallway; I approach the door. It's cracked just enough for me to hear Tasha whimpering. My heart starts pumping. Since I was a kid on Long Beach basketball courts, I've been hearing men chant, "Don't come between a man and his woman." When Tyrone and I were discussing my move into the house, we both agreed to stay out of each other's bedrooms—literally and figuratively. I freeze. Listening. Through the sliver of light between door and frame, I see movement. One body. Then another. The whimpering is louder. I hear Tyrone's voice, low and harsh. I can't make out the words, but the tone is threatening.

"Tyrone, you guys okay in there?" I say firmly.

No response.

"Tyrone! Bruh, are you guys okay in there?"

Nothing.

"What's going on?" I hear Paul say behind me.

"I'm not sure. I think they were fighting."

"Yeah, I heard some bumping on our ceiling. I thought they were moving furn—"

"Do you wanna see what the iron feels like?"

"Tyrone! Tyrone!!" we both scream at the door.

"We're gonna have to go in and handle this, man," Paul says quickly, looking me in the eye.

Tyrone snatches the door open and steps out hard toward me.

"What, man?"

"We were concerned about yall, that's all—"

Tasha brushes past him, infant in arm. Her black-and-purple right eye is puffed out like a blowfish. Almost swollen shut. I look back at Tyrone.

"You gotta beef wit me, nigga?!" he says, lunging toward me.

I jump back, shocked and scared. I'm stuck between peacekeeper and self-protector against a man who'd been nothing but cool to me.

"Tyrone!" Paul screams, trying to shake him out of his trance.

Tyrone stops advancing.

"You gotta beef, huh, nigga?!"

I can't talk. I'm slow to adjust when situations come from far left.

"Tyrone!" Paul screams again. "No one's trying to judge you, man. We're just concerned about both of yall. Tyrone, it's cool, man, it's cool. No one's trying to judge you, brother, we're just trying to help. It's cool, man."

Tyrone turns and storms away.

"Bruh, you okay?" Paul says, placing both hands on my shoulders.

"Come on, let's go check on Tasha."

Juanita has joined Jenoyne in the hallway. Walking past them, I feel a deep shame. I have to discern situations and respond to them more quickly. I shouldn't have let Tyrone get in my face in such a threatening manner without defending myself more aggressively. My hesitation and fear make me feel like a coward.

We find Tasha outside leaning against her car, holding the baby. She's crying. Paul and I walk up and embrace her.

"Nothing like this has ever happened to me before. No man has ever hit me. I can't believe he would do this, I can't believe it," she says, shaking her head. "He hit me with his fist. When I fell, he kicked me in the stomach, he kicked me in the face. I can't believe it. How could he do that? How could he treat me like this? Look at my eye, look at my eye."

Paul and I look at each other, shaking our heads too.

"Juanita, will you hold him for me? I'm getting my stuff and getting out of here."

Juanita takes the baby. Jenoyne stands by her side. Paul and I accompany Tasha back into the house. She gets two large brown grocery bags out of the kitchen and starts piling in shirts, dresses, diapers, bottles. Jenoyne walks in and starts helping her. Paul and I stand by the door, looking bewildered.

"Can we help you, Tasha?" I say awkwardly.

"No, thank you. I'm just going to get a few things and get out of here."

Tyrone walks in and sits on the bed. I ball my fists tight. Tasha's near the far wall, pulling things out of the baby's crib and placing them in one of the bags. Tyrone turns to her.

"Tasha, can I help you with anything?" Tyrone says gently, looking at her feet.

"No, that's okay. I can get it."

"Do you need some money?"

"No, I'm fine."

Tyrone's very embarrassed. He can't make eye contact with anyone in the room. He leaves.

Paul, Jenoyne, and I walk Tasha out to the car. Juanita's still holding the baby. Tasha places the bags in the trunk.

"Do you have a place to stay?" I ask.

"I'm going to my mom's apartment. Thank you guys so much. I don't know what would have happened if you weren't there."

Tasha gets in the car and drives away. Paul, Juanita, Jenoyne, and I stand in the middle of the street, watching the car disappear down the curving well-maintained street. We look at one another. We all shake our heads.

"Michael, we should stay somewhere else tonight. Maybe get a hotel. Tomorrow, get the rest of our stuff. We can't keep Juanita and Jenoyne around this dude."

I agree that we should leave. We all start walking toward the house again. When we get to the door, it's locked. We knock. No answer. Knock again. No answer.

"Anyone have their keys?" Paul says.

Juanita hands her keys to Paul, who begins to unlock the door. As we're stepping in, Tyrone runs from the back to greet us.

"What's going on here?"

"What?" Paul says.

"This is my house; you can't come in."

"My property is in there!" Juanita screams at Tyrone over Paul's shoulder. "The rent money we've paid your ass makes this our house too!"

"If you try to come in again, I'll look at it like you're breaking in. I have the right to protect my home. I will protect my home."

"I'm getting my stuff!" Jenoyne screams, trying to walk past Tyrone. I grab her arm and pull her back.

Tyrone slams the door.

We step away and walk back to the curb. Jenoyne sees the light go on in our bedroom window. There's a crashing noise.

"Michael, he's going through our stuff! We've got to call the police."

"Dammn!" Juanita says. "I left my cell phone inside. Paul, you've gotta get my cell phone. He might run up some charges."

Jenoyne walks to our car. Juanita walks after her.

"He's got a gun in there," Paul says. "When I first moved in, I found it in my closet downstairs. I guess he forgot to get it before I moved in. It's a nine-millimeter, but it's been customized or altered. Maybe we can sneak in through the back. Go through the sliding glass door."

I just look at Paul. I don't think that's a good idea. Tyrone has a gun and his anger has been directed at me. But I'm so ashamed of my fearful reaction earlier in the house, I don't want to sound like a punk and say no. The truth is, I'm afraid of getting shot.

"What do you think, Mike?"

"I don't know, man, I don't know. Hold on, let me go check on Jenoyne."

I need some time to think. When I get to the car, Juanita and Jenoyne are talking, comforting each other. I lean in through the driver's-side window and kiss Jenoyne on the cheek. I hear Paul calling. I meet him at the curb.

"I'm going in through the back," he says, looking for support in my eyes. There is none coming.

He walks toward the house, disappearing into the side. An incredible wave of guilt consumes me. I'm letting my friend go in there alone. I don't have his back. Just like I didn't have that white kid Bobby's back. I start to pace hard up and down the sidewalk near the gate. God, please protect him. Every ten seconds, midstride, I shoot a glance at the closed gate. A minute passes. Another. Another. Then five. I hear movement at the side of the house. I run to the gate. It's Paul. Smiling. Cell phone in one hand. A leash attached to his red Rottweiler Pharoah in the other hand. I jump, and hug Paul with so much force that Pharoah begins to growl.

When the police arrive, they escort us in to get our clothes and valuables. After a lifetime of hating the police, I'm struck by the irony of their presence: I'm glad they're here.

It's a tense situation. We're yelling at Tyrone. Tyrone's yelling at us and the police. The police have their hands resting on their guns.

Before the cops leave, I call Kamau. He says Jenoyne and I can crash at his crib. Paul and Juanita are going to Juanita's sister's place. We exchange numbers, hug, and head out.

When Kamau answers the door, I struggle to control my emotions. In

my moment of shame, his eyes do not judge me. They carry concern and
kindness. Gift offerings from a man whose opinion I value. Gifts that help
me begin to forgive myself.

Few words are exchanged as we bring in our belongings. Jenoyne lies
down in the office. Kamau and I sit on the couch. Sometimes being a friend
means sharing the burden of silence. I begin to write a poem in this still-
ness.

WITNESS

two poets stand before door
number one
like indecisive let's make a deal
contestants.

the grotesque prize is a weeping
epilogue, vicious soundtrack
to our house mate
beating his woman. this urban dirge
r^{e}v^{e}r^{b}e^{r}a^{t}es
through wood fibers
echoing the memories of 9,000,227
                              wailingwomen
abused behind eyewitness walls.
a choir that includes my own mother.

disbelief and fear
make me hesitate. i need to be pushed
into action by intuition
of my wife. childhood ghetto chants
                              reincarnated
like imposter messiahs
walking on water

in medulla
oblongata.

don't come between a man and his woman
don't come between a man and his woman

i pick up
the refrain
screaming tyrone's
name hoping
my voice will intervene
          for me.

pleading for him to open the door
praying his conscience
will step into the line of fire
so i will not have to.

a view through a cracked door.
front row seat to an insecure boxer
          seeking security
inside
          the swollen eye
of his girlfriend.

he is hiding
          just behind
thin film of concave mucus
covering her pupil.

this is where he is safest.
where beauty is in the black eye
of the beholder.

manhood is easy here.

welcome to ringside.
the ring is roped
with short-term broken
                promises
connected end to end
with elastic truth. it stretches, straining
to reach the batter's corner.
truth
        snaps and disappears into his mouth.
lies
        emerge
carried on warm spittle
of his nervous twitching speech.

                                he is the champion
of sleight of hand: you never
even see the punch.

finally comes out firing
denials in dazzling
sugar ray combinations.

all his bobbing and weaving cannot
slip
        the straight jab
of tasha walking past him
faced puffed
like a pimpled blowfish
        breathing
to keep her head up
                and away
from the crying

eight week old

witness

she carries in her arms.

history stutters:
black men
searching for manhood
in obsidian facial bones.

don't

come

between

a man

and

his woman

Kamau has a ten-by-ten home office. He makes a pallet on the floor for us. It's 2:00 A.M. Emotionally exhausted, Jenoyne falls asleep lying on my chest. For the first time in our relationship, she begins to snore. I can't sleep. I lie on my back, listening to the heavy breathing of my wife. What kind of life am I providing for her? What is her father going to think when she tells him tomorrow? I'm not even going to be able to look him in the eye. He didn't give his baby girl away for some cat to have her living like this.

After the wedding, we don't have $100 to our name. I wonder what Jenoyne thinks about me now. I come from a family of fighters, stand-up people, winners. I've always prided myself on coming through in the clutch, but in this situation, fear has clutched me. We haven't been married two weeks and I have my wife sleeping on the hard floor of my friend's office. Homeless. My mother would be ashamed. I'm a horrible husband.

work

The day after the attack, Tasha files a police report. The Inglewood police come and take Tyrone to jail. Tasha calls Paul and me; we rent a huge moving truck and pack all of our things.

We move half of Tasha's belongings into a storage facility, the other half to her mother's apartment. Paul and Juanita and Jenoyne and I decide to leave our things in the truck until we both can find apartments. Paul and Juanita find theirs within a couple of days. We call a few of the poets and move them in.

Jenoyne and I spend five days on Kamau's floor before we find a place. We have to borrow money from D-Knowledge and other friends to make the move. It's humiliating.

Paul and a group of our poet friends help Jenoyne and me move in. Our place is one of the few apartments in Windsor Hills. We own our clothes, a bed, a chair, two desks, five book cases, and twenty boxes of books. When the last mover leaves, the first thing we do is put up our huge California king-sized bed and get in it. Both our bodies are aching from Kamau's hardwood and moving three separate households. We have a new appreciation for the art form known as the mattress.

We lie together, holding on tight. The ordeal has made us incredibly close. Jenoyne falls asleep on my chest. I lie on my back, thinking in the dark about one of her wedding vows.

"I vow to accept you as my lifetime mate, to believe in you and work with you in hard times so that we can become stronger in adversity."

My wedding gift to Jenoyne is to allow her to stop working for a year so she can finish her novel. I increase my freelance load with current clients and start aggressively seeking new publications to write for.

The financial pressure is intense. To help finance the wedding, several of my long-term clients gave me advances against articles that had yet to be written. I'm writing pieces for money that's already spent. Our rent is more expensive than I've ever paid. We owe friends a great deal of money. My response is more discipline and harder work. My Day-Timer organizer becomes essential. My schedule is tight.

On weekdays:

4:45 A.M.	Wake up
4:45–5:25 A.M.	Meditate
5:30–8:25 A.M.	Long-term book projects
8:30–8:50 A.M.	Read Quran/Bible
9:00–10:30 A.M.	Run hills
11:00–11:25 A.M.	Pray and read Bible w/Jay
11:30–11:55 A.M.	Lunch
12:00–6 P.M.	Freelance assignments
6:15–7:15 P.M.	Gym
7:30–9:00 P.M.	Dinner/except Wednesday: World Stage
9:00–11:25 P.M.	Chill w/Jay, write poetry or extra freelance
11:30–11:50 P.M.	Write in journal
Midnight	Bed

After a few months of this schedule, I'm exhausted and extremely frustrated. I can rarely get all of my freelance work done in my six-hour block, which means that increasingly my late evenings are spent working as well. This begins to perturb Jenoyne.

"Michael, let's go to the Novel Café and hang out," she says, approaching me at my desk.

"I can't, baby, I didn't get my work done today. I've got to knock it out tonight."

"It's ten o'clock! We haven't spent any time together all week."

"I know, baby, but you know I've got to get this done. We'll chill this weekend."

"You always say that, then when the weekend comes, you've got to catch up on work you didn't get done during the week. It's like I'm the last thing to do in your damn Day-Timer. I hate that thing."

She storms away into the bathroom. I hear the door lock. She's sobbing. I get up and talk through the door. She finally opens it. Jenoyne's sitting on the floor, back against the tub. I sit on top of the toilet.

"Baby, once we get on better financial footing, we'll be able to spend more time together. For now, I've gotta make this money."

"I know, but the money's not more important than our marriage. We can't keep living like this. I don't feel connected to you. You're always working and you don't like me to bother you when you're working, which is all the time. Where do I fit into this equation? I feel like I'm living in this apartment alone."

She begins to cry again. I give her a long hug and go back to my desk. I hear the bathroom door close and lock. Kirk Franklin echoes through the house.

I hate hearing Jenoyne cry. I can't write. I sit at my desk, stewing. I'm working like a slave, and we're still barely eeking by. Jenoyne wants more of my time, which I don't have. I want some more of my time. I'm working for her. Does she think I want to be living this crazy schedule? I wish she'd hurry up and get that book done so I can pull back some. I don't know how much longer I can maintain this routine.

As the months pass, Jenoyne's having a hard time finishing *Resurrecting Mingus*. She's frustrated. I'm frustrated. We're arguing constantly. We're literally living check to check. Paying bills late. Parking the car around the corner in case the repo man makes his move. Getting the phone cut off for a day. The gas off for three. The lights off for one. All this just to get out of debt.

By our first anniversary, I'm completely burned out. Jenoyne's book's not finished, and we're still broker than the Ten Commandments. Marriage is hard.

I start talking to Kamau. I need some help. Often he initiates with a baritoned "How's the family?" He can see it in my face. We go to the beach or to a café or to his living room, or sometimes we just sit in my car outside the crib. I ask lots of questions about schedules, money, sex, commitment. He listens, then gives me advice in the form of his real-life stories. I come home feeling like I can do this.

Kamau says the first year of marriage is the most difficult because you're trying to merge two lives into one and, "As the old folks say, 'That's more than a notion.' "

The experience with Tyrone makes me a lot more cautious about the kind of people I bring into my life. Jenoyne's a more diligent judge of character. Her beauty and charisma constantly create opportunities to test her deft people skills. She has the ability to discern the good-intentioned from the many men who try to speak to her on the street. That's how she met Dee Black. Shopping for curtains, she invited him down to the World Stage, and now he's one of our best friends. History has shown that my instincts are not as good.

The Tyrone Show also makes me start working harder at seeing myself and Jenoyne as One. Every Thursday night we begin to have Family Time. Over dinner we discuss how each of us is doing individually and what we can do to make our marriage stronger. We always spend part of this time imagining how we want our lives to look. Jenoyne and I both love kids, so we fantasize about how we're going to raise them. What it's going to be like to have little people who look like us running around the house. After imagining a world, we get dressed up and go out on a date. This mixture of relationship-building and fun becomes a major stabilizer in our marriage.

The time away from a nine-to-five has given Jenoyne a chance to blossom personally and artistically. Even with all the drama, it's been amazing to sit back and watch her.

Jenoyne's thrown herself fully into the Leimert Park art world. Through constant rewriting, she's crafting compelling characters in *Resurrecting Mingus* who jump off the page. Her writing is so strong now. Although the year I promised her is up, I tell her I'll support us until she finishes.

Jenoyne has been accepted into Abalaye and quickly has become one of the West African dance troupe's principal dancers. The money she brings in helps. She's emerged as one of the most respected poets in the World Stage crew. The daughter of a construction foreman, she does woodwork to relax. She paints on the back porch and makes Cuban instruments known as *shakeres* from scratch on the living-room floor. On the same hardwood, she relentlessly practices her West African dance steps. Her wavy hair has grown out. She wears it long and wild or in braids. She sports a nose ring, African-print wraparound skirts, and colorful *geles* around her head. It's not hip cultural assessorizing; it's a woman naturally evolving into her true self.

the spinners

Dee Black opens the door in green pajama bottoms and a white T-shirt. He wears his tough day in his wassup. His bald head is perspiring, the last remnants of the flu. Courtesy of the 12:00 to 10:00 P.M. shift he works at a Pasadena residential home for troubled boys. The boys have suffered the kind of abuse, with the kind of sick regularity, that makes heavy medication a philosophy rarely challenged. Dee says they tell him stories. Stories hard to hear from the mouths of children. Stories that follow him home.

"How were the kids tonight?"

A.K. and I walk through the door as we have so many times since Dee Black moved to the neighborhood a year before. A child recipient of the Black Panther Party Breakfast program in the sixties, he grew up around brothers who were willing to fight racism with education and violence. Dee's a complicated black man in a world that draws us as stick figures. An eloquent former boxer. A retired Crip from a family of ministers. An ex–Nation of Islam soldier teaching white children poetry. A jazz connoisseur in a blue baseball cap. A single father raising a straight-A fourteen-year-old daughter. A black man looking for a black woman to commit to.

"They were awright, but when I first walked in, wild little Shakespeare Jr. was like, 'Man, where you been? I ain't been doing good since you been gone. They ain't been treating me right.' The other staff started telling me how bad the kids were when I was out sick. I'm back, so it's cool. Shakespeare Jr.'s a trip, man, he's so smart, he's got hundreds of pages of Shakespeare memorized, but that little fool is bad as hell too. That's my homie, though. We called you. You get our message?"

He was staggering out of a difficult marriage when he landed on Degnan Boulevard. He brought the World Stage his confessions. That's why we embraced him so. He stood before us and let us share in his suffering. In the months that followed, A.K. and I spent many late nights and early mornings sharing our own battle wounds and listening to Lee Morgan at Dee's crib.

"No, I haven't checked my voice mail."

I tell Dee that I'm teaching a course at UCLA Extension called "The Poet as Activist and Healer" and A.K. and I have just driven back from campus together.

It was Dee's second marriage and the second wife to cheat. Bitter gall to swallow after a single player turns monogamous in marriage. Two wedding rings to squeeze through. We're helping to pull him through the second one. Urging him to write that hurt; to retch that truth up from his gut and spit it past his lips. A.K. and I snatch our poems from our backpacks and lay ourselves down first. Dee Black leaps in, spinning.

"Yeah, Shakespeare wrote this cold new piece. It's about how his parents' abuse affected his life, man. How it makes his relationships go bad as a twelve-year-old. It's deeeep. He wanted to read it to you. He left the poem on your answering machine."

This collective effort to make art from pain makes for vulnerable friendships between, A.K., Dee, and me. It's liberating and dangerous to have other men so close to you. The mysticism of being known. If a problem arises, we'll run it by one another. When Dee's job was trying to stop him from teaching the children poetry, we huddled up. The kids love to write; it's one of the few things they sit down and do together. Dee Black had to take the poetry underground. Secret hand signals were created. He became aware of a child's newly finished poem by the sly twisting of fingers. Folded and creased words were slid to him in stacks of Pokémon cards.

"Yeah, it sounds deep. I'll listen to Shakespeare's poem when I get home tonight."

We have shared the kind of memories that I've always fantasized about sharing with my father as an adult. The 7:00 A.M. Saturday-morning drives to the beach with Bob Marley's "Get Up, Stand Up" blasting from my woofers. Kicking late-night guerrilla poetry on South Central street corners to crowds of hustlers and homeless. Midnight phone calls from A.K. with a poem in progress. Dee dropping a freestyle verse on my voice mail. Arguing with white boys who said we were playing our Coltrane too loud on their basketball court. Sitting in Magic Johnson's Starbuck's, trying to get a handle on our relationships with sisters.

I ask Dee if he's still going to meet with Shannon, his ex-flame, to see if they can rekindle the passion.

"Yeah, we're supposed to meet at Starbuck's at two. We had planned to meet a couple of times before, but Shannon didn't show up. I can't blame her. I know she's still hurt. Everything was going cool. I was starting to feel her strong. I just got scared. Straight tripped on her. Stopped calling, stopped going by to see her. She was getting close, and a nigga started thinking about his ex-wives."

I have found my wife; I'm getting tired of holding out for a father. Still learning not to look for him, not to want him. It's difficult when I see in my friends what I wish he was. Sometimes I find myself spinning in A.K.'s and Dee's gaze, as if the disappearing men in my life hide in their eyes.

"Dee, I feel the same way about Caula," A.K. says. "She was so good to me. A poet, too. I thought she could be for me what Jenoyne is for Michael. I was trippin, though. I told her I wanted to get myself more together. I let her get away. I'd love to get her back now."

At first, Jenoyne was upset by how much energy I invested in these friendships. They were siphoning off some of the little free time that I could have been spent with her. She quickly began to realize that these men were helping me become a better man. A better husband.

"I figure tomorrow at two is my last chance," Dee Black says. "She said she was really gonna show up this time. I went to Congo Square and bought this phat candle with roses made into it. When it burns, the rose fragrance is tight. I also wrote her a poem to go inside the card I bought. The poem came to me at three this morning. I jumped out of bed and started writing it down. I'm not gonna read the poem to her, though. I'm gonna just talk straight. Sometimes when you talk too much you get yourself in trouble. I'll apologize and hand her the candle, the card, and the poem. But I did want to run the poem by yall. Shannon is Louisiana Creole, and we met at the Louisiana to L.A. festival. Anyway, it's called 'A Second Calling for a Catholic Girl.'"

> Woke up sweat back rolling me out of dream.
> Crooning like a timeless Jackson 5 in key of
> I want you back.

> When spilled moments dry up
> In wet stain memories.

> Fondling the paper, I ball up notes to be canned,
> with truth riding on a second page.

> You were passion flower and rosemary in body wash.
> A dream care, witch hazel lending a touch of aloe vera
> and vitamin E.

> La La Festival and Cajun dances
> with the sweet taste of JuJu Beads
> wrapped around my neck.

> Matching me of black pants, and gray shirts
> Leaving a De Coud of flirtation arousing the air.

Voo Doo and Déjà Vu on location in an empty park,
where all drummers have gone home
and Wednesday nights are no longer a part of this week.

I keep my eyes closed so that I may see your face.
I keep my eyes closed so that I may see your face.

I have come to believe that I need help in my marriage, in my own personal development, with my own issues. The struggle is to be up front about where I'm really at. To fight the temptation to hide behind an image of manhood I created. Manufactured because no real father was coming to show me how. In his place, others have arrived, carrying pens behind their ears. Writing their scriptures on my memory. This could be better than a real father.

"Heh, Mike, it's me, Shakespeare Jr. The title of my new poem is 'Daddy's in the Dark, Mama's Asleep, A Poet Awakes.' Okay, here it goes."

When I picture your vague silhouette of what I dreamt
you looked like, I wonder, did you care for me?
Or were you trapped in a dark cloud of marijuana and stuck
in confusion not knowin what your own name was?

Mother, you led me into severe hostility and a childhood
of solid anguish, leaving me to display hatred on you and that
crack-headed bastard that was my father who severed my face,
cracked my bones just for letting tears of hope and sorrow spill
down my split-masked facial features.

You knew I was growin into a human inside you,
a person who would have to deal with consequences,
beatings and broken relationships,
but still you forced tobacco into your lungs and swallowed alcohol
not knowin it would mix with my blood,

bringin me almost to death at one week in '87.
I hate you!, but my heart loves you, somewhere . . .

I find words of poetry stuck in a once forgotten child
standing in his windowsill every night after ten
praying for discharge while concealed
in a dreamless orphanage.

tao of fences

The seasons have been wronged; July Santa Ana winds railroaded into January. The warm swaggering air. Saturday night is heated by the bracing force that causes trees to stagger. Leafy bushes gangsta-lean and stand eight-count straight again. Pinecones and twigs street-race down Degnan. The block is hot. A baritone whir presses against room-temperature windows, whispers under panes. It's the theme that calls couples from the bedroom to the center of hardwood floors. Many lights are low when the Santa Anas hit town.

Seven A.M. Sunday morning comes quickly, not quietly. I jump out of bed and pounce on the clock radio blaring jazz on 88.1 KLON from across the room. Jenoyne is still knocked out. She has grown used to this gymnastic ritual needed to draw me from the warmth of her bed. I stand near the hushed clock and watch her sleep.

She sleeps with the peace of a woman who stands up for herself. A woman who keeps REM regret at bay by making the most of opportunities during waking hours. There is no twisting and turning. No flip-flopping. Her spirit is calm.

Peter J. Harris has a poem that starts, "I want a grown woman in my bed." That's what I have in mine. I look at her baby face and I'm amazed by the things she's witnessed. Lived through. Most of which happened before she met me. Now she has jumped into my storm. So little shelter. So many I'm sorrys.

I tiptoe to the side of the bed and sit down. I like to study her when she's asleep. Learn the microlines on her eyelids. The curve of her cheek. Slope of her nose. The slight parting of her lips. I lean down and kiss them softly. She mumbles, "Thank you."

I walk into the living room, stepping over blankets and pillows tangled across the hardwood floor. We keep our wedding vows framed on the west wall. I stop to read them, as I do every morning. I need to be reminded of what I have promised.

I grab my keys from the desk, unlock the French doors, and step onto our back balcony. The Santa Anas have left and taken all shades of brown from the Los Angeles sky. The sun has nothing to break through but crisp air. It yellow-tints the downtown highrises visible in the distance. The Santa Monica mountains seem only a long touchdown throw away. Clarity has a way of making things seem closer, possible. I breathe in deeply.

I come back inside and dress in a sweatshirt, shorts, and sandals. Load my backpack with Bible, Quran, and Metu Neter. On Saturday mornings, A.K., Dee, Wyll—a young poet we're reaching out to—and I go to the beach to meditate and pray. Sunday mornings I go alone.

I jump in my ride and make the fifteen-minute trip to Playa Del Rey. I park, and head for the sand. My body is never prepared for the first glimpse of the Pacific in the morning. Involuntarily, I stop in my sand tracks to take in this beauty. The ocean's clever choreography makes me want to be still.

It's high tide. I pull my sandals off and walk until I reach the edge of wet sand. Sit down semilotus position. Dozens of sea gulls swoosh above my head and glide over the water. No one else is out. The ocean is ours. Waves are breaking, hissing into white foam, and rushing up the sandy slope, stopping just a few yards from my crossed legs. I open my mouth to sample the cool breeze. I taste the salt of the many spittle-filled prayers I have shouted into this sea.

I taste the tears that jumped from Nicole's eyes onto my cheek, cutting a trail down into my mouth. A trail my own tears followed. The tears my tongue missed, I caught in my open palm and laid in the ocean.

I taste the salty sweat from spinning hard for would-be fathers. A dervish of want and need. But no father is coming to show me how. No father is coming. I am done spinning. It is time to be still. I close my mouth. Close my eyes. I breathe in deeply.